C0-BEF-130

On Architecture, the City, and Technology

On Architecture, the City, and Technology

Edited by
MARC M. ANGELIL

ASSOCIATION OF COLLEGIATE SCHOOLS OF ARCHITECTURE

BUTTERWORTH ARCHITECTURE

In memoriam
Giuseppe Zambonini

Butterworth Architecture is an imprint of Butterworth-Heinemann.

∞ Recognizing the importance of preserving what has been written, it is the policy of Butterworth-Heinemann to have the books it publishes printed on acid-free paper.

Photograph (page 1): Bestor/Silverman, 1989.
Editing, Design and Composition: Karen L. Eldridge

Library of Congress Cataloging-in-Publication Data
On architecture, the city, and technology / edited by Marc M. Angelil.
p. cm.
Proceedings of the 8th Annual ACSA Technology Conference, held in Feb. 1990 at the University of Southern California.
Includes bibliographical references.
ISBN 0-7506-9149-2 (casebound)
1. Architecture--Technological innovations--Congresses.
I. Angelil, Marc M. II. Association of Collegiate Schools of Architecture. III. ACSA Technology Conference (8th : 1990 : University of Southern California)
NA2543.T4305 1990 90-2242
720'.1'05--dc20 CIP

British Library Cataloguing in Publication Data
On architecture, the city, and technology.
1. Architecture
I. Angelil, Marc M. II. Association of Collegiate Schools of Architecture
720
ISBN 0-7506-9149-2

Association of Collegiate Schools of Architecture
1735 New York Avenue NW
Washington, DC 20006

Butterworth-Heinemann
80 Montvale Avenue
Stoneham, MA 02180

10 9 8 7 6 5 4 3 2 1

Printed in the United States of America

Contents

Acknowledgements

The 8th Annual ACSA Technology Conference, held at the University of Southern California in February of 1990, and this publication, were the result of the efforts of a large number of people.

The Association of Collegiate Schools of Architecture, under the direction of Executive Director Richard E. McCommons, provided the opportunity for the meeting, while Karen Eldridge was crucial to the conference organization and publication production.

USC's School of Architecture provided the location for the conference, with the support of Dean Robert S. Harris, as well as provided staff support from Julia Galici, Laura Koepke and Dana Smith.

The sponsors of the conference are also gratefully acknowledged: the Carpenters/Contractors Cooperation Committee, Inc., the USC/Maguire Thomas Partners Architect-in-Residence Program, the American Institute of Steel Construction, and the Structural Steel Education Council.

Special thanks are extended to the keynote speakers: Fritz Neumeyer, Frei Otto, Peter Rice, Martin Spühler, and John Whiteman.

I would also like to thank the plenary debate session panelists for their contribution: Michael Davis, Diane Ghirardo, Michael Hays, Craig Hodgetts, Jeff Kipnis, Diane Lewis, Ben Nicholson, Dagmar Richter, Bahram Shirdel, and Mark Wigley. I am also grateful to the session moderators for their effort and support in the organization of the conference: Susan Stevens, Max Underwood, Ralph Knowles, Dana Cuff, Paul Sorum, Sheila Kennedy, Judith Sheine, Marc Schiler, Barton Phelps, Jeff Chusid, Goetz Schierle, John Whiteman, Douglas Suisman, Marco Frascari, Edward Allen, Shane O'Neil, Margaret Crawford, Giuseppe Zambonini, James Ambrose, Stefanos Polyzoides, Ken Nakaba, Mark Cigolle, Tom Peters, and Peter McCleary.

Marc M. Angélil, Dr.sc.techn.
Chair, ACSA Technology Conference
Associate Professor, USC

Introduction

MARC M. ANGELIL
University of Southern California

" ... that architects who have aimed at acquiring manual skill without scholarship have never been able to reach a position of authority to correspond to their pains, while those who relied only upon theories and scholarship were obviously hunting the shadow, not the substance. But those who have a thorough knowledge of both, like men armed at all points, have the sooner attained their object and carried authority with them."
Vitruvius, *The Ten Books on Architecture*[1]

Investigations in the nature of architectural technology commonly attempt to formulate a definition of technology and to delimit that definition to the particular case of architecture. Definitions, in general, allow the systematic exploration of a subject matter as developed from the structure of specific concepts.[2] Since such a point of departure is marked by the position from which definitions are determined, it is important to develop understandings of their underlying historical and theoretical contexts. Consequently, technology is addressed in view of ideas and considerations pertaining to the domain of knowledge. Definitions of technology, in other words, must be considered in view of theoretical and philosophical propositions, not in order to advocate a specific theory of architectural technology, but rather with the intention to identify different approaches to the field, which are to be seen as essential for understanding attitudes for the production of architecture.

Such an approach suggests that the physical, material reality of architecture can be seen in relation to the formulation of thought. This duality between mental constructs on the one hand and physical construction on the other offers the grounds for understanding definitions of technology. The word *technology*, binomial expression formed by the terms *techne* and *logos*, implies a twofold reference to the realm of human activity. *Techne* pertains to the work of the maker in the creation of artifacts and recognizes the predominantly operative quality of his processes of production.[3] *Logos* addresses the realm of thought and recalls the reflective nature of human activity. In this sense, while belonging to both domains of man's system of thought and action, the field of *technology* reveals itself to be mutually concerned with questions of theory and practice.[4]

Martin Heidegger asserts in his essay "The Question Concerning Technology" that the relationship between thought processes and technical production implied by the term *technology* raises a number of questions which must be addressed within a philosophical framework.[5] To explore the sources and meaning of technology is to consider the pragmatics, the basic rules and principles, as well as the methods of technical undertaking. Simultaneously, an analysis of the phenomenon *technology* must be founded, according to Heidegger, on a critical approach which offers the possibility for searching, revealing, and questioning in a very general sense. This duality within analysis allows on the one hand considerations purely within a technical framework, that is, dealing with technological problems which require technical solutions. Analysis, on the other hand, also suggests an investigation of technology's essential meaning and purpose, that of exposing the realm of technical considerations to philosophical inquiry. In this sense, Heidegger's differentiation of "technical technological" problems versus "technical philosophical" questions offers a framework for understanding technology as being inherently connected to the realms of theoretical and practical considerations.

A similar distinction between instrumental aspects of technology and theoretical implications is made by Carl Mitcham and Robert Mackey in their introduction to a compilation of essays entitled *Philosophy and Technology, Readings in the Philosophical Problems of Technology.*[6] It is necessary, according to the authors, to recognize technology as a philosophical problem. A philosophical approach to the question of technology, like philosophy itself, they write," is concerned with what have been called second-order questions," as opposed to "first-order questions."[7]

The current and prevailing understanding of technology as a means of problem solving is primarily conceived in view of "first order questions," implying an inherently instrumental definition of technology. It is this definition which is commonly applied to architectural technology. The manufacture and utilization of equipment, tools, machines, as well as materials and industrialized products for the building process, and the manufactured and used objects themselves all belong to what technology is in instrumental terms. In architectural technology, "first-order questions" are determined by the directness of operational concerns. Typical questions are such as: What are the most appropriate materials with which to construct an architectural artifact? What are the specific qualities and properties of building products? What are the methods and techniques to be applied for achieving most efficient construction procedures?

In contrast, an approach to technology in view of philosophical considerations is concerned with "second-order questions" which raise fundamental issues about the nature and meaning of technology. Within such an inquiry, technology is addressed in reference to established frameworks of knowledge. In this sense, conceptions of technology are to be understood in connection to specific models of thought as they are formed within given cultural and social contexts. Architectural technology considered as a "technical philosophical" problem can thus be exposed to "second order questions" allowing, for example, concerns of the following nature to be raised: Is architectural technology merely of the applied sciences; does it involve theories of the material sciences or theories of architecture as fine art? What are the metaphysical justifications underlying formal intentions and how do they relate to technical exigencies? What is the meaning of progress, how can it be understood in reference to technical development, and how does it inform the form of building?

The interrelationship between "first-order questions," which primarily relate to factual and empirical phenomena, and "second-order questions," which depend on reason and understanding, constitutes an essential point of concern within analyses of technology. The search for definitions of technology allow, in this sense, philosophical understandings of technical undertaking. Only from addressing the philosophical as well as the technical realms can a meaningful approach result to an understanding of technology.

The integration of thought processes in the making of artifacts therefore constitutes a primary point of analysis within the field of architectural technology. In that, attempts are to be made for identifying frameworks of thought involved in the production of architecture. Theoretical propositions, within this context, offer a body of intellectual constructs invested in technical means. For establishing an understanding of the relation between theories of technology and the processes of making, it is important to describe and analyze the way in which man has perceived of his ability to create artifacts throughout history and thus to expose technology to the history of ideas.

History, rather than considered as being, *a priori* given, can be understood as an intellectual conception; similarly, technical achievements as well as understandings of technology as a discipline result from conscious activity. In these terms, history in general and the history of technology specifically can be considered constructs of the mind. Giambattista Vico (1668-1744) and Georg Wilhelm Friedrich Hegel (1770-1831) both made history the object of their sciences, their philosophical positions being guided by an understanding of history as a primary factor of knowledge. A parallel interest can be observed in the propositions of Francis Bacon (1561-1626) and Denis Diderot (1713-84)). Their works suggested the necessity for establishing a historical awareness of technical development. They offered an understanding of technology as a discipline inherently connected within the whole system of human knowledge. Bacon advocated at the beginning of the seventeenth century that a history of the mechanical arts must be written, for the future progress of civilization would require an understanding of the technical developments of the past.[8] This idea found its realization with the publication of the *Great Encyclopedia*, compiled by Diderot and his collaborators during the mid eighteenth century. Their interest was directed towards the arts and crafts; the *Encyclopedie*, while offering descriptions of the specific instruments and methods of production, disclosed the prevailing efforts within society to order the knowledge of the advancement of technique.[9]

Such emphasis on the idea of history *per se* reflects man's attempt to assert his state of being. Technology similarly affirms man's self-consciousness in providing him with the means to overcome his natural condition. Both history and technology have assumed a liberating role for the development of the human mind in its ability to reflect upon itself. In this, the conceptions of history and technology as autonomous disciplines were given significant emphasis within the modern era. In an essay entitled "Philosophy and the History of Technology" Carl Mitcham emphasizes the very idea of the autonomy of such fields; he asserts that the concepts of history and technology, while affirming the human condition, are essentially expressions of the modern era.[10] He writes:

> *..., history and technology are both somehow characteristic of modernity. The modern period has been called the 'age of technology'; it has also been called the 'age of historical consciousness'. These views are both grounded in modern man's affirmation of himself.*[11]

As the concepts of history and technology are both indicative of modernity, Mitcham concludes, then an approach to the history of technology unites the historical awareness of the modern era with its emphasis on technological development.[12] Technology, like other disciplines, stands in relation to its past; it is in this reference to its history that technology's changing conditions can be understood. Analyses of technology must consequently address how it has been perceived within history. Different methods of historical analyses can be identified; these reveal certain attitudes towards history as given by underlying models of thought disclosing views, although sometimes contradictory, of history.

In accordance with Mitcham, an attempt to define a typology for histories of technology offers the following three categories for consideration.[13]

The first is a *technological history*, that is, the history of man-made products, objects, tools, and artifacts. This view includes also the processes of manufacturing, how artifacts are made and produced.

The second approach to the history of technology is directed towards the implications of technological development on man and his social organizations. This approach has been called the *social history* of technology.

The third category addresses the way in which man conceives of technology and is part of the history of ideas. This type of history is concerned with the changing perceptions and understandings of man's activity in the making of artifacts. An evaluation of ideas about technology as defined within different periods is the initial point of concern for this third approach.

The most common understanding of the history of technology is largely preoccupied with the enumeration of historical facts. As defined by the first category; *technological history* commonly traces a chronology as marked by technical progress and achievements. The second approach to the history of technology, which focuses on the relation of technical evolution to social conditions, has been widely addressed in the recent historiography of the subject. The third approach, however, the history of ideas of technology, has not been sufficiently studied and still requires thorough investigation. Similarly, the fields of architectural technology and building construction must be exposed to theoretical studies. Since architecture depends both on the ideological context of cultural conditions as well as on the *de facto* context of technical matters, a unique position is assumed in which thought and action converge. Technology, and architectural technology specifically, can thus be understood as fields addressing the *thinking* about *making*.

An investigation into the theoretical foundations of technology cannot be considered independent of its *technological* and *social histories* as previously defined. An approach to the theories of technology suggests that a historical understanding of technical development and its influence on social organizations should not be exclusively perceived in terms of "first order questions," the latter of which allows the various histories of technology to be addressed within the framework of philosophical questions.

The meaning of the term *technology*, as its etymological roots indicate, pertains to the theories of practice. A full understanding of technology can therefore only be derived from the history of ideas, the analysis of models of thought, and historically proposed attitudes about technology. In similar terms, the development of architectural technology proceeds within intellectual frameworks. The production of architecture is not the result of some precise accumulation of technical knowledge; the processes of making are conditions not only by social needs and values but also, and perhaps more significantly, by systems of thought.

The making of artifacts, the manufacturing of tools and machines, the production of architecture, and, in general, man's ability to create, are to be considered within the context of epistemological interpretations. Only from such a vantage point can definitions of technology reveal possible readings of essential conditions underlying technical activity. The search for definitions must include the facts of an analytical history of technology. The search must integrate in its analysis the cultural implications of social history. But most importantly, the approach must be considered in relation to systems of thought. Inherent within the exposition of definitions is the quest to reveal the essence of technology, as proposed by Aristotle:

> *The essence of each thing is that which it is said to be* per se. ... *Hence essence belongs to all things the account of which is a definition.*[14]

NOTES

1. Vitruvius, "The Education of the Architect," *The Ten Books on Architecture,* translated by Morris H. Morgan, Dover Publications Inc. (New York), 1960, p. 5.
2. The question concerning definitions of technology in general and their specific application to the field of architecture is raised by Peter McCleary in an essay entitled "History of Technology." McCleary emphasizes the necessity for definitions, for they reveal the conceptual structures underlying any systematic exploration of a given subject. P. McCleary, "History of Technology," *Architectural Research,* edited by James C. Snyder, Hutchinson Ross Pub. Co. (New York), 1982, pp. 81-91.
3. The Greek *techne*, commonly translated as "art," "craft," or skill," is rooted in the Indo' European *tekn-*, approximately meaning "woodwork" or "carpentry." It is similar to the Greek *tekton* and Sanskrit *taksan*, meaning "carpenter" or "builder" as well as the Sanskrit *taksati*, "he forms," "constructs," or "builds."
4. For Plato the word *techne* not only pertains to particular activities but also addresses knowledge, In his writings, the terms *techne* and *episteme*, art and systematic knowledge, are closely associated. In the *Gorgias*, for example, Socrates argues that every *techne* is involved with *logoi* (words, speech) bearing upon the specific subject matter of the arts (450b). Plato, however, did not join the two terms, *techne* and *logos*, to form one expression. It was Aristotle who probably used the work *technologia* for the first time in his writing on rhetoric. Aristotle's' use of the term addresses the role of "speech concerning art" or "words about *techne*" (*Rhetoric* I, I; 1354b17, 1354b27, 1355a19, and 1, 2; 1356a11). Yet, the meaning of the word does not directly correspond to contemporary definitions of the term *technology*; Aristotle understands the art of rhetoric as a *techne* or 'means' of speech. In this sense, *technology* is understood as the science addressing the techniques of a particular art. For a detailed analysis of the etymology of the work *technology* and its various applications see, Carl Mitcham, Philosophy and the History of Technology", in *The History and Philosophy of Technology,*

edited by George Bugliarello and Dean B. Doner, University of Illinois press (Chicago), 1973, pp 171-189.

5. Martin Heidegger, "The Question Concerning Technology," in *Basic Writings*, edited by David Farrell Krell, Harper & Row (New York), 1976. The essay was published in German under the title "Die Technik und die Kehre," in *Vortrage und Aufsatze*, Gunther Neske Verlag (Pfullingen), 1954. "The Question Concerning Technology" was presented for the first time as a lecture to the Bremen Club in 1949 under the title "The Enframing."
6. Carl Mitcham & Robert Mackey, "Introduction: Technology as a Philosophical Problem," in *Philosophy and Technology, Readings in the Philosophical Problems of Technology*, edited with an introduction by C. Mitcham & R. Mackey, The Free Press (New York), 1972, pp. 1-30.
7. Ibid., p. 1.
8. The writing of a "history mechanical" was strongly advocated by Francis Bacon in *The Advancement of Learning*, 1605: in *Francis Bacon, The Advancement of Learning and New Atlantis*, edited by Arthur Johnson, Clarendon Press (Oxford), 1974.
9. The significant role of technical development within the system of human knowledge was stated in Denis Diderot's "Prospectus de "Encyclopedie" as well as in Jean Le Rond D'Alembert's "Preliminary Discourse." "Prospectus de "Encyclopedie," in *Diderot Oeuvres Completes*, Hermann (Paris), 1976, vol. V, pp. 84-130. "Preliminary Discourse," in *Denis Diderot's Encyclopedia*, edited and translated by Stephen J. Gendzier, Harper & Row (New York), 1967.
10. Carl Mitcham, "Philosophy and the History of Technology," op. cit., pp. 163-201.
11. Ibid., p. 166.
12. "*Technology is designed to give ... modern man his rightful power of nature; history is the study of ... man's life independent of nature. The history of technology unites these two aspects of modernity in a paradigmatic fashion.*"
    Ibid., p. 167.
13. Ibid.
14. Aristotle, *Metaphysics*, Book VII; translated by Hugh Tredennick, The Loeb Classical Library, William Heinemann (London), 1933, pp. 320-323.
    Peter McCleary uses the same quote from another translation of Aristotle's *Metaphysics* in the conclusion of his article "History of Technology": "In the quest for an agreement on an explicit formal logic for technology, the recommendation here is to search again (re-search) for an exposition derived from the knowledge that 'the essence of a thing is what it is said to be in its very self ... so essence is composed of those things, the enumeration of which makes a definition'." Peter McCleary, op. cit., p. 90.

The New Plurality in Architecture

FREI OTTO
Institute of Lightweight Structures at Stuttgart University

What times are we living in? We have had forty-four years of peace in Europe and in many other parts of the world--the longest period of peace for a long time--and yet, there is discord between ourselves and the world we live in.

Architects have been building against nature for 5000 years. It has been their duty to protect mankind against enemies, and especially against its greatest enemy--nature. Houses have been their weapons and their symbols of victory.

We, the architects of today, still build against nature. We have destroyed nature, and we continue to destroy nature instead of conserving it.

Our duty is not to destroy but to conserve!

But have we recognized this new task? We prefer to talk about forms and styles. Highly developed construction techniques mean that we can build everything we want to build. The technical and financial possibilities have never been so great before. Feasibility is not the problem today, but rather the enormous range of options available to us.

As all buildings--since they should not collapse--are subject to the natural laws of physics, certain constructions and building designs are more appropriate for certain purposes than others. However, this fact does not reduce the number of possibilities open to the architect. Even the search for the minimal house, that is, a house which has nothing unnecessary, has led to more than one solution.

Regardless of the means and concepts used for building--the number of possible solutions defies comprehension. It is so vast that every last person on earth could have his own distinctive individual place and could live in peace with himself and with nature, if he so desired.

Against this background, the question arises: Why are so many buildings as alike as two peas in a pod if symmetry and uniformity are no longer determined by function, construction and economy, as may have been the case in the past?

It is the will to be artificial, to be deliberately unnatural and abnormal which encourages uniformity and symmetry. Man himself has invented the artificiality of uniformity by restrictions based on social conventions, doctrines, design regulations and aesthetics.

But there are no formulas for the acquisition of beauty and the creation of architecture which, when adhered to, guarantee beauty and when ignored result in ugliness.

Despite this fact, design rules, doctrines, regulations and even laws are invented over and over again. They are often born in the heyday of a style. They make the process of designing simpler. But they are an obstacle to a free search for form and formation. In our times, they are totally out of place.

At present, an army of theorists among architects and critics are concerned with trends, fashions, styles, forms and form languages. At the same time, many hypotheses and architectural philosophies, as well as the trends they promote, are thriving as never before in the history of building. Sometimes they are stronger, sometimes weaker. New ones are continually being added.

A new awareness of building history has developed as a reaction to the insipid building of the Sixties. In the wake of a new historicism, older buildings are being restored. Art Nouveau with its particular sensitivity is once again popular, especially with young people. The Modern Movement of the Twenties is experiencing a new vogue after being unpopular for some time. We are now even beginning to realize that the decade of Sixties was a period in which truly valuable ideas were conceived without ever being recognized.

The sterility of building in the Seventies led to a change, bringing the opposition to power. Now, post-modernity dominates the schools. But its stylish forms are already producing buildings that again are as alike as two peas. For all its youth, post-modernity is already aging.

In the cities of the industrialized countries, high-tech fanatics celebrate in earnest the forms they have invented for their vision of the future. The most recent movement to arise as a reaction to this is the new deconstructivism. As a true mannerism, it pursues both the high-tech style and post-modernity ad absurdum, without ever having a fundamentally new concept of its own.

Gradually, adaptable building has developed since about the end of World War II. Buildings are no longer conceived and built as unchangeable entities, but can be adapted to changing tasks. The potential for rejuvenation is built into them.

The idea of adaptable building has led many people to again build their individual homes for themselves. A new, unconventional do-it-yourself building culture, borne out by amateurs, has developed and should be taken very seriously.

Man is increasingly becoming aware of ecological problems and the detrimental effects of buildings. Already, an increasing number of architects is promoting a new ecological approach to architecture.

None of the above trends, tendencies and styles of today, from historicism to deconstructivism, dominates alone. None of these movements is weak. Each one cultivates its own techniques and forms.

The growing variety of possible approaches to architecture offers the chance to make use of a new freedom. Architects and users are still inexperienced in this freedom through plurality, in this new and open world of unlimited possibilities. They feel safer when they can follow where a few others have led.

This hesitant attitude is understandable. An architect is well integrated into society. As a servant to his fellow men, he cannot follow his inspiration like a painter, musician or sculptor. He must, above all, be aware of and observe human rights and obligations. On the one hand, his own rights are more restricted by external conditions that the rights of any other artist, but on the other hand, he has great possibilities, since he often has to administer large amounts of money, thus exercising power involuntarily. He has a great deal of responsibility.

The changing tasks with which the architect is confronted make it essential to reconsider both the profession of the architect and his ethics.

After the Second World War, the ethics of architects were linked with the term ''humanity''. This term ''humanity'' was an often used and abused formula when plans were to be put into practice. But what does humanity mean in the field of building?

It goes without saying that buildings should do no physical harm to anyone. But we need only consider in what ways buildings can do psychological harm to people to recognize the problems faced here. It is even more difficult to answer the question of whether buildings can help people to be humane in the ethical sense. But there are certainly many buildings which, although considered beautiful, influence people negatively and can sometimes even make them cruel.

In the architecture of the Fifties, humanity meant creating vast amounts of living space; in the architecture of the Sixties in meant emphasizing simple forms; in the Seventies it meant reviving past aesthetics. The term of humanity was alienated, because it was increasingly equated with beauty and finally replaced by it.

But the doctrine of beauty in architecture is not yet a doctrine for humanity in building. Humanity has no building form.

At the beginning of the Sixties the term ''humanity'', which had increasingly been overused and thus was losing much of its meaning, was also being related to the many varieties of the term ''nature'' or ''naturalness''. Some architects finally started to realize that their aims, working methods and the resulting products were, in principle, unnatural.

This minority no longer aims to serve the clients or users of a specific project alone, nor to build for man or for humanity alone, but to attain a new, all-embracing naturalness. The buildings and the people who live in them are seen as an integral part of a greater whole. It is imperative to help people, but man is no longer at the center of nature.

This new view of nature leads to a new understanding of nature, not only by architects. The most recent findings of natural science and an awakened society force us to reconsider. The awareness that vast ecological systems are ailing has a mobilizing effect on us.

The youngest ecological system within evolution is the big human city which has probably never been genuinely healthy since it came into existence. Not blind conservation of nature, but integration of the natural individual into his environment, into the world in which he lives, is our new task. And this means achieving greater knowledge of the natural processes which lead to the forms of objects which, in turn, form the overall picture of nature.

Just as architects of Twenties never found the entirely simple and inexpensive ''house per se'', so the form of the ''natural house' has still to be found today; not surprisingly, since only few architects are searching for it anyhow. Most are content to celebrate those forms which they think are ecological or biological.

Some architects think that they will find a greater nearness to nature by imitating living natural forms and structures. Most of the time this is bound to fail. Technical objects such as a house do not become natural by imitating forms found in living nature or by using so called biological building materials.

About twenty-five years ago, the idea of plurality in architecture emerged. Many architects wanted to be able to follow many different paths to new architectural styles. It was the longing for a new variety of styles which was to put an end to the thoughtless uniformity of the misunderstood simplicity of the late Modern Movement.

This longing was focused in particular on those fields of architecture which had been underrepresented until then. It was defined by the new term pluralism which unfortunately was also abused as an excuse for words of uncontrolled fashionable extravagance. The new age of plurality was initially unbalanced with a one-sided approach.

Today the idea of many roads leading to new architectures is highly topical. It is seen in the sense of a genuine plurality in architecture. The term ''plurality'' -- as opposed to pluralism--indicates that this is no idealizing or manneristic trend which allows anyone to do anything without thinking about it, but indicates an openness for new approaches under a newly formulated commitment to obligations and rights by all human beings who build or have something built.

The new plurality also makes it possible to focus on aspects that have been somewhat neglected previously, for example:

1. a new understanding of the terms humanity and nature as an inseparable whole;
2. a striving for natural security for every human being in a society which, through tolerance, encourages individuality;
3. consideration of natural self-forming processes when designing buildings;
4. avoiding unnecessary buildings and building masses, and conserving the energy needed for construction and maintenance;
5. conservation of nature, in particular of the biological macro systems and their components;
6. adaptable building through the use of adjustable structures;
7. do-it-yourself building which may lead to the development of a creative amateur architecture, at least in residential buildings, but with architects contributing their knowledge as consultants;
8. a new sensitization of the faculty of perception for quality in architecture, by reviving lost components of the senses;
9. integration contemporary painting, sculpture and music;
10. incorporation of the findings of all sciences, including behavioral research and medicine.

The new plurality is not an excuse for selfishness, harmlessness and thoughtlessness. Every human being who builds, be he owner, architect, engineer or contractor, is tied into a framework of duties and rights towards nature and all his fellow men.

It is his duty to help promote the development of nature and the observation and defense of the human rights of each individual, to create a safe habitat for people, to practice charity, and to please and appease people with buildings.

He must help people as they tackle their new role of conscious integration into the new overall naturalness of cohabitation with flora and fauna and with the immense inanimate nature.

The profession of the architect remains as important as ever. It is his duty to search out every possible means of fulfilling his global mission and to lead by example. He is responsible for a cluttered environment and for houses which destroy nature instead of conserving and promoting it. He cannot pass the buck; neither to his clients nor to assistants, advisers or authorities. An architect who cannot say "no" has no right to be an architect.

All roads are open to the architect as he sets out to fulfill these duties while making full use of the possibilities at his disposal. He should and he must make use of existing knowledge and techniques and apply them to every new task in a new manner. He must not only search for new solutions, but also invent new techniques and details himself.

Obligations and rights lie side by side. It is an architect's right to find his very own solution, to stand by it and to put it into practice. This leaves him a wide scope. Despite his limitations and parameters, his artistic freedom can be compared with that of other artists and is quite considerable.

Consider for a moment that every building is created in a particular place, at a particular time, using different means and intended for different individuals. Modern building techniques allow that no building need to be identical with another, because identical buildings have no identity of their own.

Art and the artificial are still regarded as the opposite of nature and the natural. But these opposites are outdated. However, we architects still lack the philosophical basis which could help us develop a new understanding of nature. Under these circumstances, it is no wonder that the first products of this new age of new plurality are often misunderstood and sometimes even look chaotic.

The new plurality leads to the unique building. It does not result in chaos, but leads to a strengthening of those trends which will bring about a higher level of integration and adaptation of buildings to nature and mankind.

The ability to build naturally has yet to be developed. There is still no natural architecture. But I hope that there will be peace between the man, the builder and the ever-changing nature. It is our duty today to make the many new roads to natural and humane architecture passable.

We will only make use of the irretrievable chance of our age if we set to work now; if we do what has to be done--simply naturally, and happily, with a will to peace and an awareness of what is good and right.

The Second-Hand City: Modern Technology and Changing Urban Identity

FRITZ NEUMEYER
University of Dortmund

1. Adolph Menzel, Berlin landscape, 1848.

2. Hans Baluschek, Railroad within Cityscape, 1890.

MODERN TECHNOLOGY INVADES THE CITY

I would like to begin with two key images (figs. 1, 2) that capture the essence of my lecture, in that they represent two moments in the development of the urban phenomenon of the nineteenth century. Both images illustrate the impact of modern technology on the urban environment. In the first, a painting by Adolf Menzel of 1848 entitled *Berlin Landscape*, we find the city in the distance and the rural landscape in fore- and middleground virtually unchanged in their idyllic nature. Only the track of iron rails carrying a steaming locomotive gives evidence of the fact that modern times have arrived. But the train, a dark, horizontal object, appears quite well integrated into the picturesque landscape surrounding the city of Berlin. Menzel has depicted no unsettling overtones to disturb the peaceful ambient. The city, visible in the background of the painting, seems to live its life as ever, and the train crossing in the foreground looks no more threatening than any other carriage we might expect to find in a setting such as this one. In this case, however, it is not a horse-powered carriage, but instead one propelled by a black metallic creature, the machine.

In a painting by Hans Baluschek entitled *Railroad in the Cityscape* painted almost fifty years after Menzel's, the scenery has undergone dramatic change: the black metallic object has left the urban periphery behind and has finally arrived downtown, now having gained a strange and shocking presence as the locomotive appears right in the middle of the city street. In Baluschek's painting from the last decade of the nineteenth century, the industrial era has already reached an advanced stage of development, bringing changes that drastically affect the urban environment. And, the way this painting makes its visual argument, modern reality stands in opposition to Menzel's view, and is figured in a moment of unexpected violation that seems to leave open no alternative or escape. The dynamic forces behind the process of modernization are no longer in harmony with the landscape of the city, and, in a foreboding way, their dramatic appearance at once suggests their inevitability and irreversibility. There is no doubt about what has happened. The train and the machine age have advanced toward the heart of the city, cutting through the urban space and, arriving at the front door of the city dweller, ambushing him the moment he steps out.

By the end of the nineteenth century, modern technology had deeply penetrated the cityscape, leaving in its wake the footprints of the modernist invasion. Wide-span girders and other modern construction work, no longer camouflaged or hidden behind architectural screens in historical style, irrupted into the traditional city, clashing with the space of monuments. Ironwork designed by engineers confronted the architecture of stone and the dignified language of classical forms spoken by architects. Like blades, the engineers' iron structures chopped up the body of the city, fragmenting the urban tissue and assaulting its 'beauty' by dissecting the homogeneous composition of blocks and squares. Bridges, elevated railroad structures, gasometers, and other modern objects of unfamiliar shape became significant new elements in the traditional cityscape, taking on a disturbingly powerful and threatening presence. Modernity was on the verge of erecting its own 'unpleasant' monuments and *points de vue*, which would disrupt the urban identity and ravage the urban scenery.

Artists, sensing these moments of provocative action and violation, visualized the radical changes taking place in the landscape or the city as the beginning of something new. Baluschek painted a compelling image of what his contemporaries decried as the 'brutish appearance' of iron within the city. Captured in a low-angle view of the locomotive roaring down the middle of the street is the shocking presence of modernity. The painting insistently portrays a dramatic juxtaposition that would give an appropriate compositional form to the collision between the functional and the symbolic. A new reality had sprung up, irreversible, frightening, powerful, but nevertheless imbued with its own immanent beauty, a kind of beauty whose inherent laws were only waiting to be discovered. The rupture between modern reality and historical context--which would eventually occur on all levels of society--was irreconcilable. Modern reality would take over the urban space as its own theatrical platform, instigating changes of far-reaching social and aesthetic dimensions. As Baluschek's painting predicted, within the city, both the familiar urban space that once belonged to the world of the *flaneur* and the space of monuments that had belonged to the realm of classical art would have to surrender to the modernist invasion.

CHANGING THE URBAN IDENTITY: ASPECTS OF THE EMERGENCE OF A NEW URBAN REALITY

Like the millipedes of this modernist invasion, the iron construction of the elevated railroad (fig. 3) marched into the heart of the city, introducing a new rhythm to its peaceful setting and creating the unexpected encounter. In Berlin, the train would cut right through a museum complex and run next to a wall covered on the other side with Greek and Egyptian sculptures. The Berlin Elevated offers a rich example of the potent visual effect of the iron girders. Like knives they fragmented the classical architectural composition by isolating forms and disassembling the hierarchical canon with its progressive horizontal layers of *rustica, piano nobile*, etc. This interruption of the classical logic of load

3. Berlin Elevated, c. 1900.
4. Berlin Elevated , c. 1900: 'Drive through Building'.
5. Gustave Callebotte, Point L'Europe, 1878.
6. Andre Kertez, Meudon, 1928.

and support caused portions of the structure to appear suspended, hanging in the air, their girders blocked from view. Floating pediments, disconnected from their bases, underscored the fact that modern construction work was cutting architecture's legs off: In the urban realm, it not only spoiled frontal views but also ruptured the traditional concept centrality. Furthermore, trains running on the level of the *bel-etage* violated the privacy of residential occupants. For a split second, passengers could peer into a stranger's apartment, suddenly exposing him to the surprise of having a train pass in front of the window. Not only could the train pass by close to one's window: it could even drive right through it, as one example of a train penetrating a Berlin apartment building and disappearing into the *bel-etage* shows. (fig. 4)

Other, equally strange images resulting from new urban constellations that belonged to a modern twentieth-century urban reality are to be found in painting in photography of this period: The eye of the artist seemed to be trained on the effect these new elements had on the imagery and identity of the traditional city. The urban realism of the Impressionists took early account of this change. In these paintings, modern bridges transformed into arcades or urban roofs that transformed streets and squares into steel-covered spaces, platforms of modern life, challenged the notion of inside and outside, adding excitement to the space of the *flaneuer*. (fig. 5) Some decades later, in the twentieth-century city, the situation would look quite different: As Andre Kertez' photo of 1928 entitled *Meudon* (fig. 6) seems to suggest, in a time when trains fly through the sky, the familiar imagery can only belong to the past. It survives only as a picture for the living-room wall, to be wrapped up, carried under one's arm, and taken home. Modern reality produced a city that could not be understood as a tableau.

7. Berlin 1900: Bridges climbing on top of bridges.
8. Fritz Lang, Metropolis, 1926.
9. Berlin 1900: Railroad cutting through cityscape.
10. Berlin railroad and urban backyard, 1951.

Around 1900, crisscrossed by iron trajectories, the once-static body of the city began to move in a kind of mechanical ballet. Like Oskar Schlemmer's human figure with mechanical extensions, the modern metropolis, equipped with new iron extensions, all at once began to dance. In Berlin, the elevated railroad ran straight into the walls of buildings or collided with a museum of ancient sculpture as if in a Dadaist collage, or, trains would mysteriously disappear into the *bel-etage* of an apartment building through an opening in the facade. It would not be long before another moment of initiation would take place, when bridges would climb on top of one another like copulating animals, intermingling in their excitement to form clusters of steel-webs, which, as multilevel viewing platforms, promised the pleasures of ever-greater visual experience of--and insight into--urban space. In the joints of this mechanical system, where subway and streetcar, ships on the canal, interurban railroad, and long-distance trains intersected and met for a split second on their independent routes, the model for the city of the future was born. (fig. 7) The image of a metropolis was laid bare in the multilayered movement and omnipresent bridges that were a response to the need for connections between the isolated objects of the cut-open city. Modern reality, already further advanced than traditional modes of perception, was only waiting to be kissed awake by a futurist imagination so that it could come to life in the icon of the modern city. (fig. 8)

The modern city manifested itself as a new urban type: a city of fragmented space and isolated objects that assembled themselves to form an urbanized corridor, one that would be experienced from multiple *points de vue* rather than with traditional *Perspektivität*, or single point perspective. The space of this city would no longer be determined by the continuity of walls and facades, but would instead consist of a vast array of isolated objects gathered as a society of autonomous volumes. In opposition to the homogenizing and perspectival effects of the Serlian conception of the cityscape, the modern urban space would have no dominant centrality: It would instead engender a panoramic conception and perception as building came to be understood as object and fabric at once. This intrusion of modern technology into the city of monuments conjured up unfamiliar notions of space and urbanity. Railroad trajectories, slicing through the homogenous block system of the city, left behind the incoherence of fragments and voids. Modern construction work had deconstructed classical hierarchies and discounted monumental perspectivity, but furthermore, it confronted the eye with the previously unseen view of the 'backyard' of the city.

Writing on the subject of urbanism in 1890, Josef Stübben throws light on this peculiar late nineteenth-century urban condition from the point of view of an academic architect:

> "In most cases, in older parts of the city, the urban railroad cannot assume a place in the middle of the street, but must instead cut right across the perimeter block system, and therefore has to bridge streets and intersections. Unfortunately, this type of construction has the disadvantage of causing great unpleasantness both for the pedestrian walking on the street, to whom the unadorned sidewalls due to the opened thoroughfare become visible in their bare crudity, and for the passenger on the train, who, on his journey through the city, already has tasted a sequence of disgusting images composed of backyards and rear views of buildings, and has thus gained obnoxious insights into the miseries of metropolitan life before ever having set foot onto the magnificent boulevards. In these terms, the Berlin urban railroad offers us an exemplary deterrent."
> ("Der Städtebau," in the *Handbuch der Architektur*, Darmstadt, 1890, 217).

Cutting through the nineteenth-century city, the train paved the way for yet another urban phenomenon: the modern 'drive-through city'. As Stübbens' observations make clear, with the train cutting through the urban block system, the disorderly character of the periphery is brought into the center, whose interior is all the while becoming exteriorized. Once the eye was directed away from articulated spaces and facades, this 'other' city exposed the unpleasant, dark side of the well-built urban world, of the 'ugliness' of its interior, of things once shielded from view. Instead of a world governed by classical order, one would encounter a hitherto invisible urban desert of backyards and voids and fire-walls. This other, or 'second' city, crowded with absence, became apparent only as a collection of leftovers and fragments, of unadorned, impoverished buildings, masses of brick and windowless walls. (figs. 9, 10)

Lined up in unfamiliar spatial and rhythmical sequences, the urban corridors of the postarchitectural landscape, with its zero-degree-architecture zone stretching out alongside traffic lanes, no longer had anything in common with the classical notion of the 'city as house' handed down to us from Plato and Alberti. Modern reality at work had left behind a violated urban context that no longer corresponded to the terms of classical urban topology. Perception of this city no longer depended upon the distinction between front and back; nor was it anchored by monuments or places for art. The modern urban reality of the drive-through city, with its cut-open and fragmented space and continuous boulevards, demanded a new urban optimism and new aesthetic terms to replace the classical ones.

With the cut-open space of this second-city-within-the-city, the margins invaded the urban center, and the very structure and character of the buildings there caused its peripheralization. For this second city, the urban metaphor of the 'theatre'--the perspectival box of classical Serlian space (fig. 11)--was no longer adequate. Neither was the traditional metaphor of the 'city as house', of the city as a sequence of *indoor* spaces, able to express this type of urban structure. Instead, it demanded an *outdoor* model as its new metaphor, one that would help us to understand the laws of a transformed visual world, because the clear distinction between actor and spectator, between inside and outside, are effaced as these spheres overlapped in the unpredictable movements of the city's mechanical ballet.

Like an embryo, this second city existed first as a drive-through city-within-the-city of the nineteenth century. Only in our century did this second-hand city begin to assume its autonomous urban life. (fig. 12) Its fabric is characterized by the metropolitan fever of circulation, which causes the fragmentation of space and the isolation of objects and transforms the city into a composite of heterogeneous elements. Cross-programmed, juxtaposed, and in permanent flux, this vibrant metropolitan plankton demands a dynamic perception instead of a static point of view in order to connect its piece-meal of parts into a sequence. The eye, moving through this modern landscape, is asked to construe an essentially new visual order, based on time, matter, space, and light in flux--driven by the perpetual activity of the modern city that forces us to reconsider our assumptions about what is urban.

Together with the necessity for another type of perception, that of the moving eye, goes a new notion of the urban object and its relation to architecture, even of its very identity as 'architecture' and as something 'urban'. The modern building does not belong to a precisely defined wall system anymore--for example, Hausmann Boulevard in Berlin--but has asserted its autonomy as one element in a rhythmic succession of space and matter, voids and solids. As 'lone' objects in the urban landscape, these solids 'without architecture' are not governed by the principle of frontality nor by the terms of the classical facade. The primacy of the facade is cancelled as one drives by, around, or through these objects. Caught in an involuntary rotation, they now play a role in a larger kinetic composition that is

11. Sebastiano Serlio, Scena Tragedia; from: Tutte l'opere d'architecttura et perspettiva, Venice, 1584.
12. Drive-through city: Wim Wenders, Houston.

the urban landscape.

The organization of space also depends upon a different sense of perspective. In the traditional city, the *point de vue* has been the perspectival organizer, but in the city-without-center, there is no fixed point of view. The absence of a focus in perspectival space allows--even demands--panoramic vision because no vanishing point arrests the movement of the eye. In the modern city, a new mode of establishing relations and connections is required to connect the kaleidoscopic impressions of independent objects and surfaces. There is a shift in the visual order that displaces the *object* from a now-centerless space, and situates the *subject* at the center of spatial as well as social experience. The fixed object, which demands to be looked at and visually determined from a single point of view, surrenders to the moving eye zooming through the urban plankton. The connecting view becomes the organizer of perception, replacing a built homogeneity imposed from above.

It seems to me that the train and the moving eye, or better a cinematic perception, obviously share a common tradition. Describing the train as a "steam-camera on train tracks," Japanese film director Ozu suggested this very relationship. There is also evidence of the mutual relationship between the train and the modern city, on the one hand, and the technology of film on the other hand which underlines the symbiotic nature of both faculties: In the process of shooting movies, the camera is mounted on a track of rails. The perception of the fragmented space of the modern city requires a mental construction that differs from traditional ones. The city caused by motion can virtually only be

13. Paul Citroen, Metropolis, photocollage, 1923.

understood in motion, in terms of a sequence of singular images that, when connected in the mind of the viewer, reveals its sense and meaning.

Herman Sörgel, an early twentieth-century German architectural theorist, sensed the fundamental change in perception that the modern city required by its very nature. In a short but notable text concerning New York written in 1926, Sörgel, contradicting fellow critics and architects who sharply attacked the appearance of neo-Gothic or other historical forms in Manhattan skyscrapers, developed a generosity of argument that indicated a deeper understanding. In the face of the grand rhythm of the metropolis, Sorgel argued, the question of the vocabulary of styles and forms has became totally irrelevant and obsolete. The grand rhythm of the metropolis is altogether indifferent to whether a building is Gothic or Renaissance or any other style.

> ''The individual form disappears in the large scale; *building-mass, continuity of change, life are what count.* In terms of architecture, New York can no longer be perceived in terms of isolated individual images, but only in terms of a continuously running film.''

When we consider the impact that modern technology had on the changing identity--and visual perception--of the city, the consequences (implications) for modern urban architecture immediately beg discussion. The demise of the Serlian section view in favor of directionless, continuous space, of panoramic vision devoid of aim and hierarchy, has liberated the architectural object and its surfaces from traditional restrictions to a substantial degree, allowing the body and its planes to be independent of one another. It is only when forms are distinguished from their parts that the skin of the building can be partially peeled away. This is not only true with respect to ornament stripped off of the traditional facade, but also, in a more general way, for the dissolution of the wall itself. It transmutes--or deconstructs--into a system of rhetorical layers wrapped around the architectural object that tend to live their individual lives--a fashion of treating the wall highly favored in today's architecture!

Historically, we may sense the beginning of this process at that moment when the clash between functional and symbolic eroded the consistency of architectural form: when modern technology first appeared in the public and aesthetic sphere of the city. This process results in architecture coming under attack by the sign, and losing its predominance as a constituent visual component of the cityscape. The fragmentation into systems of layers permits the billboard--not unlike the severed pediment of a classical building whose facade has been sliced through by elevated railroad tracks--to gain an existence independent of the rest of the building. In this sense, the billboard indeed becomes a new type of urban architecture. It is this process that turns the cityscape into the ''ocean of signs'' that make up the 'postarchitectural urban landscape of the modern metropolis' (Roland Barthes). Its chaotic quality, demanding a different sense of urbanity and a sensitivity for difference rather than order, had already been captured by Bauhaus student Paul Citroen in his famous photocollage entitled *Metropolis* of 1923, an image that elevates the urban 'piece-meal' into the icon of the city of fragmentation. (fig. 13)

ISLANDS OF URBAN ORDER

Challenging the modern condition to urban fragmentation, the architect was confronted with the question of how to structure and make visible in built form, the order of the modern urban world. At the turn of the century, Otto Wagner and Karl Scheffler--to mention only two important protagonists for a modern urban architecture, or *Groszstadt Architektur*--demanded a 'New Objectivity', a *Nutzstil*, taking account of both modern aesthetics and functional purposes at once. With the particular urban language of a ''functional prose'' (Scheffler), the structuring of the architectural organism would be consciously connected to modern technology and the modern metropolis, both of which as totalities demanded form and character. The nineteenth-century Berlin architect Karl Friedrich Schinkel appears as a prominent precurser of this peculiar notion of modern urban architecture. His 'urbanism of the individual architectural object' emphasized isolation as well as departure from Baroque concatenation with its spatial uniformity and monotony of endless walls. And, with a building like his Bauakademie, Schinkel produced a prototype that assimilated modern technology at the same time as transforming it into urban architecture.

The Bauakademie appears as a massive cube of red bricks virtually plunged into the midst of the old city. In both its materials and construction techniques, the cube embodies Schinkel's encounter with the advanced industrial reality of the anonymous functional building he had the opportunity to see on his travels through England in 1826. Schinkel had remarked with surprise about the industrial landscape of Manchester, with its ''thousand smoking obelisks'' and its ''enormous masses of red brick...erected without any thought of architecture.'' (figs. 14, 15) This dark side of the industrial urban reality announced a future architecture not based on the laws of art, but rather intended to serve as a point of departure in the face of the challenge to arrive at new aesthetic virtues. Schinkel's functional classicism, embodied in the Bauakademie, assimilated this modern reality by utilizing the fireproof building construction of industrial mills and the soberness of purely functional building, and further, by bringing together art and commerce, as it provided shops for rent on the ground floor. It is not difficult to imagine the complaints of Schinkel's contemporaries about this building. It was criticized for its cubical shape, for the flatness of its facades, which lacked any plastic value, and for the uniformity of its appearance, with neither center of gravity nor central axis. In a contemporary slogan, the Bauakademie was ridiculed as ''*Kasten dieser Stadt, Ringsum glatt und platt*'' ('Box of the town, flat and smooth all around'). Few were able--or willing--to appreciate Schinkel's building as a ''cornerstone of the urban space'' (Friedrich Adler, 1869). A painting by Friedrich Klose from 1836 (fig. 16) captures the essentially confrontational nature of this installation of a free-standing cube of red bricks in a neighborhood crowded with traditional stucco buildings. Like a horizontal divider, the 'mast of the ship' bisects both Klose's picture and the city. Two different types of cities are juxtaposed on the banks of the River Spree: On the left is the traditional city with its space enclosed by the 'old wall' whose failure would be ridiculed almost a century later; on the right bank of the river, we look into the modern cubical city composed as an association of free-standing cubes--typified by the Bauakademie as the modern solid 'without architecture'--in the opened-up, panoramic urban space.

It is not surprising that we find Schinkel's architecture of urban intervention and his vision of a cubical city echoed almost a century later in the urban projects of Mies van der Rohe and Ludwig Hilberseimer. Hilberseimer's sketch for the Alexander Platz competition of 1928 seems to propose the completion of Schinkel's view from the Schlonßbrücke. (figs. 17, 18) Standing on this bridge, the viewer would be surrounded by regular cubical buildings in a full panoramic scope of more than 180 degrees. It was not a traditional concatenation of buildings, but instead a disposition of rather peculiarly dislocated structures that would become the guiding principle of modern architects who followed Schinkel. The view into the depth of urban space was no longer directed by the guiding lines of the wall, but--as Schinkel illustrates--by the corners of public buildings stepping forth in cubic relief. Hilberseimer's remark, ''better from Schinkel to Schinkel,'' found in an unpublished manuscript on the ''Architektur der Großstadt'' of 1914, is illuminated from this point of view. If we recollect the unpleasant facts of the modernist invasion of the city--as exemplified in phenomena like windowless, unadorned walls, isolated objects without architecture, an almost aggressive presence of modern building materials and technology, the exteriorization of the interior space, cut-open block structures, and their patterns

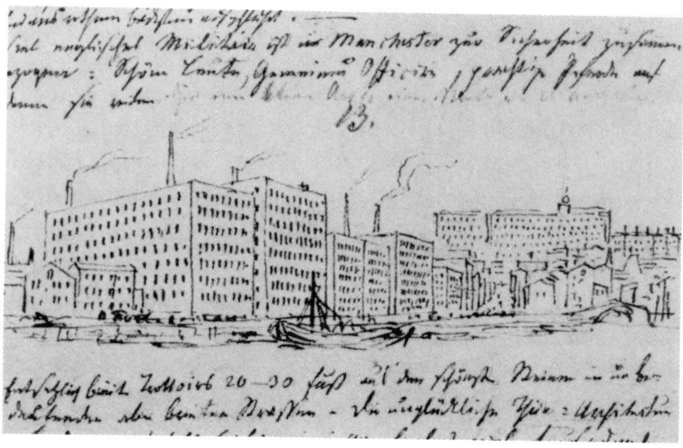

14. The landscape of the industrial city; solids without architecture: Karl Friedrich Schinkel, Sketch of Manchester, 1826.
15. Karl Friedrich Schinkel, Bauakademie, 1832.

16. Friedrich Wilhelm Klose, Schinkel's Bauakademie, 1836.

of dislocation allowing panoramic vision--there is, in particular, one project in the history of modern urban architecture that like a parasite absorbs all these 'negative' aspects in order to transform them into a completely new architectural language, one that would survive the twentieth century. Of course, I am thinking of the Miesian design for a glass skyscraper on the Friedrichstrasse in Berlin of 1922, one of the most radical projects for urban architecture the modern movement offered, and one which left its imprint on the architectural mind of this century. (fig. 19)

This prismatic design exposing modern technology--represented in the modern building material of glass as well as in the image of the steel skeleton--in an almost exhibitionistic manner towered over the city on a piece of land that, as

17. The cubical city: Karl Friedrich Schinkel, View from Schloßbrücke, (with Schinkel's Neues Museum at the right).
18. The cubical city: Ludwig Hilberseimer, Sketch for the competition Alexander Platz 1928 (with Schinkel'sNeues Museum at the left).

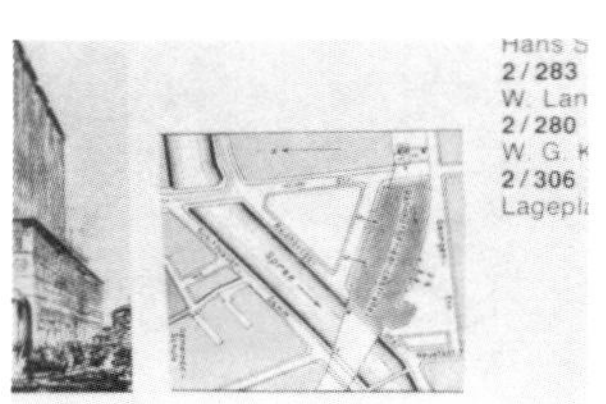

19. Mies van der Rohe, Skyscraper at Friedrichstrasse Station, 1921-2.
20. Site plan at Friedrichstrasse Station.

the site plan shows (fig. 20), had been bisected by the railroad some decades before and had been left a useless empty lot. Mies's tower summed up the windowless solid object without architecture, as it abolished all architectural decoration of the facade in order to transform the window into a wall. The window onto the city became the essential element of the wall, and the equilibrium of its former material and rhetorical qualities were now expressed in sheer transparency. The layers of architectural argumentation with which the old wall was composed were stripped away and replaced with new perceptual effects--including the reflection of light--to establish a new quality for the dialogue between the building and its surroundings. Elevated on a floating plane, one was lifted above ground and invited to enjoy a broader vista. Like twenty-two viewing platforms stacked one on top of another to provide the spectator with new panoramic sensations, the building became a viewing machine that stretched its corners out into three directions to embrace the urban spectacle. The transparency of the curtain wall allowed the passerby, struck by the visual punch of this dramatic object, to catch a glimpse of what existed behind the surface. In the same way as Schinkel's painting *View onto the Flowering of Greece* elevated the observer onto the level of the scaffolding in order to let him celebrate the sensation of being suspended above ground and participate *as viewer* in the making of civilization, the view out into the landscape of the modern city was made real. As the light reflected in the glass surface and the viewing angle suddenly made the building's skin transparent, private and public realms touched one another. Even if only for a moment, the division between inside and outside, surface and depth, was overcome: the auditorium and the stage of the urban theater became one, and viewer and actor met on the same set.

Mies's vision of a skyscraper gave an edge to Schinkel's architecture of urban intervention. Schinkel's self-conscious urban architecture was raised to the level of dramatic key object, indeed acting as urban cornerstone, distancing modern civilization from the past. Towering over the cityscape, commanding the power to transform both space and context, the glass prism cut like a razorblade into the old Wilhelminian city, which was only waiting to be violated. But even if Mies let the urban surroundings sink into obscurity to become a kind of anonymous podium for his free-standing object, which appeared as a mere fragment of the future, it nevertheless complemented the composition of the city by echoing its fragmented urban condition.

Rem Koolhaas of OMA has taught us to relate the triangular shape of the urban site to a sequencing of spaces, which, like a string of pearls adorned the city of Berlin: the roundel of the Baroque Friedrichstadt to the south, followed by the octagon of Leipziger Platz and the square of the Pariser Platz in front of the Brandenburg Gate. Other contextual references in the Miesian glass skyscraper--a project that has become notorious for its reputed disregard for its urban surroundings--can be found even in the choice of materials. The glass curtain wall of the tower picked up a theme introduced by its next-door neighbor, the Friedrichstrasse Station, built in the late nineteenth century. Mies's curtain wall takes up a certain part of the station building, which, in Schinkel's terms, could also qualify as building "without any thought of architecture," since it was the product of the engineer. It was the backside of the station that inspired those glass dreams of an architecture consisting of nothing more than the freely-suspended glass curtain. (fig. 21) Mies certainly had good reasons for not including the glass wall of the station building in any of his drawings or photomontages for the Friedrichstrasse project. Had he done so, the aura of originality of the avant-garde artist might have been compromised.

Mies's tower was the manifesto for a modern urban architecture that took into account both technological progress in building methods and the impact modern technology had already had on the identity of the city. The glass tower in a sense tested the traditional city as a backdrop for the insertions of modern presence, in the way that the gasometer and other functional and technological installations had already established themselves as new points of view within the fragmented urban tissue. In the 1920s, the cubical city took over the voids and remnants left behind by the urban desert of the nineteenth century. The voided corners of the grid structure, when cut open, provided ideal backdrops for striking implants. Like parasites on this context, modern urban architecture conquered these strategic urban positions by employing a 'cornerstone' strategy of its own: either dramatic new structures would be added, or already existing corner buildings would be remodeled in such a way that as individual objects they would express their disagreement and disgust at the notion of integration or harmony with the given context. (fig. 22)

The modernist decontectualization, dehistoricization, and intentional fragmentation made the process of urban transformation that had begun with the intrusion of modern technology into the cityscape a conscious one. Like the autonomous and absolute architectural objects of Brunelleschi, modern urban architecture was bound to penetrate the structure of the traditional city, upsetting and altering its significance. The symbolic and constructive self-sufficiency of the new three-dimensional spatiality of the modern architectural object radiated into the urban space a rational order as the absolute emblem of a strict ethical will of transformation. Just as Brunelleschi's Humanism suggested a new conception of the preexisting town as an expiring entity available for transformation--ready to exchange its significance as soon as the introduction of compact architectural objects altered the balance of the Romanesque-Gothic 'continuous narrative'--modern urban architecture of the twentieth century claimed to visually display the reverberation between rationality and the stratified urban texture.

Erich Mendelsohn's extension of the Mosse Building of 1922, stepping forth in bold relief, gave effective expression to the 'heroic caesura' of historical time by transmitting to architecture the velocity of modern machinery. Mendelsohn's staff jokingly declared that the addition represented "the docking of the Mauretania in Berlin." Their reference to one of the most famous oceanliners of the day captured both the building's intrusiveness and the flavor of machine-age speed it imparted. Indeed, Mendelsohn's almost Dadaist insertion of new fabric made the old building look as if it had been run over by an oceanliner steaming downtown, crashing into the block from behind, its prow raised up, and parts of its decks floating atop the facade of the street. The transformation of space and context, captured thirty years earlier in images like the train speeding down the middle of the street or the elevated railroad system clashing into the *bel-etage* of an apartment building, found its proper architectural counterpart. (fig. 23) In this kind of modern design, the violent intrusion of modernity was aesthetically balanced and smoothed into elegantly, emphatic curves that would become the trademark for much continental modern architecture of the 1920s and 1930s. The cubical city, without distinguishable front and back, was shaped by machine-age aesthetics into a dynamics of movement, described by

21. Glass curtain wall at Station Friedrichstrasse, 1889.
22. Leipziger Platz: Remodelled facade.

23. Erich Mendelsohn, Mosse Building, 1923.
24. Ludwig Hilberseimer, Highrise City, 1925.

the architect as the effect he had sought:

> "An attempt had been made here to express the fact that the house is not an indifferent spectator of the careening motorcars and the tides of traffic in the streets, but that...it strives to be a *living, cooperating factor of the movement*. Just as it visibly expresses the swift tempo of the street, and takes up the accelerated tendency toward speed at the corners, so at the same time it subdues the nervousness of the street and of the passerby by the balance of its power." (*Berliner Tageblatt*, 1924)

The engineered beauty found in modern machinery and objects like locomotives, bicycles, automobiles, airplanes, and steamships became typical for the modern age, as van de Velde, Scheffler, J.A Lux, and others had observed at the turn of the century. The 'engineered' construction had been raised to the status of art. The modern architect, attempting to transform the urban space and the architectural object into a "cooperating factor" of the modern movement, finally turned the city into a gigantic machine. Modern machinery became the symbol for both the aesthetic and functional concepts of the architecture of the metropolis in the era of Fordism. The dreams of a new architectural and urban order were inspired by the much admired form and efficiency of modern machinery.

Hilberseimer's project for a Highrise City provided a frightening stereotypical vision of the metropolis of Fordism in the way it was inserted into the historic center of the city, a crude urban brain-transplant which transformed Berlin into a metropolitan Frankenstein. (fig. 24) With this implantation of a scheme for 'operational units', each about the size of a small town, the exhausted metropolis could be given a

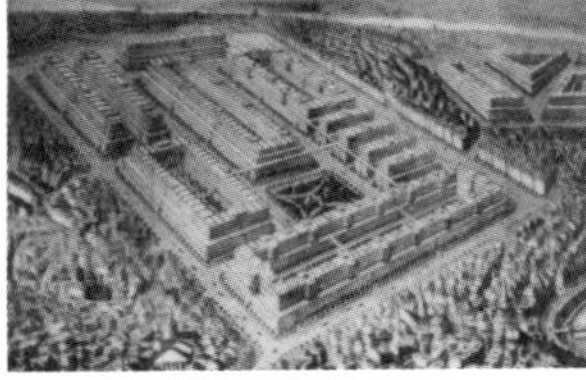

25. Henri-Jules Borie, Aérodômes, Paris 1867.
26. OMA, Exodus, 1972.
27. Mies van der Rohe, Federal Center, Chicago 1959 Model.
28. Mies van der Rohe, Seagram Building, New York 1954-58.

new, economically and socially effective center in order to resuscitate the old city with light, air, and commerce.

As a second city, a city-within-a-city, the modernist downtown could be equated with a giant oceanliner anchored at Friedrichstrasse, adjacent to Schinkel's Theater. This superimposition of an island of modernity brought the contemporary *Zeilenbau* to the heart of the city, and, to a large extent, utilized artistic techniques typical for the polemic collages of Dadaist artists. Deprived of all individuality, Hilberseimer's elementary design, with its stripped-naked walls, strongly resembled the urban architecture in George Grosz' paintings from the same period.

The essentially sober rhythm, emphasizing the definition of regularly articulated space, underscored the factory-like organization of these operational units that were lined up in a uniform scheme derived from industrial organization. With this grim and rather horrifying vision of the modern urban scenario--which, in the words of the late Hilberseimer constituted "a Necropolis rather than a Metropolis"--the threatening nocturnal machine that had been introduced by Fritz Lang's movie *Metropolis* in 1926 found its urban realization in the same year.

Avant-garde projects, like Hilberseimer's Highrise City, proposing an alternative order to the chaotic metropolitan condition as experienced in the American metropolis, were reductive instruments of utopian propaganda. With a crudity similar to the invasion by modern technology of the city's center, these polemic islands of modernism emphasized the radical will to transform the urban environment with contemporary structures, thereby implying that 'modern life' would finally take place. The strategy of the polemic island--conceived of as a city-within-the-city--has its own history and tradition, reaching back in time to the Aerodromes of Henri-Jules Borie from 1867 (fig. 25), and anticipating the projects of Rem Koolhaas, with his Office for Metropolitan Architecture and the Exodus project (fig. 26), dating from 1973, which transferred the Berlin wall to the City of London in order to transform it into an island of maximum urban desirability.

Among the islands of order offered by the history of modern urban architecture, only a few projects embody both the 'metallic culture of the modern metropolis' (Malewitch) with its split-open space and also the sense for a clearly defined space endowed with a classical dignity. In this regard, Mies van der Rohe's late urban projects, like those for New York and Chicago, Toronto and Montreal, represent not *polemic*, but rather *Platonic islands of modernity*, where modern technology is adapted and balanced with a critical mind as a unique urban composition. Contrary to the modernist attempt to turn urban architecture into a "living, cooperating factor of the movement" (Mendelsohn), the modern classical city of Mies establishes itself as an autonomous island of order and calmness, as a stable point of reference within the turbulent ocean of signs. Here, technology and art are married to allow a moment for stepping aside and for reflection *within* the frantic dynamics of metropolitan life.

As in the Federal Center in Chicago (fig. 27), Mies' silent black cubes mediated the facts of modern construction into the laconic splendor of the metal frame, and the disposition of these elegantly proportioned slabs that were well-attuned to one another, formed a careful composition of dislocation, which referred at once to the modern opened-up and the classical closed form. From a certain vantage point, the silent dark slabs fuse and become a massive block that stands in the cityscape as an almost monumental urban cornerstone; but, when one begins to move around it, the composition gradually opens up and the mass separates into two solids of unequal sizes. The process of cutting open the urban space has lost all its violence and become an artful act of gradual unfolding--almost cinematic--motion. Both the moving and the resting eye are given what they desire. As rotating objects, the buildings can be enjoyed on the level of modern cinematic perception; as stable objects in space, they can be appreciated on the level of the classical perspectival view governed by the laws of proportion.

The deliberate rhythm of voids and masses, volumes of bodies and atmospheric volumes, the empty spaces and full spaces, this almost Schinkelesque notion of a cubical city gave Mies' urban islands of reflection their distinctive character. His metropolitan architecture launched a dialogue between modernity and memory which made the stepping back of the Seagram Building from the front of Park Avenue a gesture symbolic of the necessity of distance and space within a highly congested urban world. (fig. 28) At their cores, Mies' Platonic islands were at once modern and traditional. The lofty urban foyers on the plaza level of his highrises were reminiscent of the well-articulated, well-balanced space of the classical city as imagined in the famous prospects of the ideal city painted by Piero della Francesca in the fifteenth century. (figs. 29, 30)

With the return to classical typology and its traditionally constructed space in today's postmodernist urbanism, these 'prospects of the ideal city' have become the popular icons for a neat, nonviolent, and polite urban architecture that supposedly refers to human scale and pedestrian needs. However, it seems to me that today, after the loss of utopia as a horizon for action, and with the disillusionment of postmodernist nostalgia, the necessity for an architecture of programmatic richness, of functional and formal complexity--with solutions not trapped by the oversimplifications of propaganda and narrow ideology--would be a more promising contribution to the architecture of the city. The city as a densely populated artificial landscape of modern civilization has become our second nature.

As an artifact, the city is a technological garden that promises neither redemption in paradise nor condemnation to darkness and despair. As long as the processes of making architecture and building civilization are related to one another, there will be a reason for some modest urban optimism, even for those of us who are architects.

29. Mies van der Rohe, Seagram Building, Photocollage, view from the lobby toward the New York Racquet Club across the street.
30. Piero della Francesca, Prospect of an ideal city, c. 1490.

Responding to Fritz: On Disarming Words and Pictures in the Telling of Teleological Stories

JOHN WHITEMAN
Skidmore, Owings and Merrill Foundation

Responding to Fritz. Responding to Fritz: Fritz has given a paper which in many ways is written around my own biography. I was born in Manchester, not so far from the very mills which impressed Schinkel so much, and whose drawing Fritz showed you. I grew up in Liverpool amid that curious nineteenth century architectural stand-off between Victorian Classicism, in all its pretense at propriety, and the relentless, faceless, repetitious buildings of the factories and warehouses -- which I loved. I now find myself living in a building designed by Miles van der Rohe on Lake Shore Drive in Chicago, where, in order to see his breath upon the cold glass, my young son of eighteen months presses his mouth against the sheer window, a full eighteen stories above the ground; and he is without fear. So, you see, I hope, that the line of my life indeed is inscribed within the narrative which Fritz has told, and I stand here trapped by his account of modern urban history.

Placed here as I am, (and what conspiracy of chaos has brought Fritz and I together at his moment?) I have written a piece which is lovingly called "Responding to Fritz". But, if I respond as I say "lovingly", remember, dear listener, that love is often best understood as a seal or a bargain which is written across a difference which cannot be fully understood or acknowledged by either party: neither he nor I; and, incidentally for the purposes of this response, neither I nor you.

Responding to Fritz: this phrase sounds like the title of an underground movie in a very much above ground entertainment market; a movie in which a beautiful, tedious truth about love between two very decorative but pointless individuals is slowly and evenly revealed to no particular effect over a bottle of expensive carbonated spring water. The camera is focused suddenly on the little metal bottle top, with its potential to cut, to draw blood from the finger which would open it. (The bottle top, like this response is a 'twist off'). This bottle top is the perfect emblem of the social collage which parallels the pictorial collages which Fritz has shown you in his slides. Being social rather than pictorial, it is a process of collage which, while it saturates the scene, goes largely unnoticed. Neither of the two clandestine lovers in our imagined movie, as they sit together in complete boredom, thinks for a minute of the relentless machine which stamps out these bottle tops in their millions, and which is now located in rural Michigan, watched over by a new immigrant worker whose bright-eyed son has just won the spelling prize in the region's schools.[2] As our two distant lovers gaze at each other in an extended and lethargic fit of narcissism, each fails to remark that the scene takes place in the critical but drab colors of clothes from *Comme des Garcons* in a dark restaurant on a wet street in New York, where the residue of motor oil, sliding on the surface of the puddles, obscures the fact the sky, like the human soul, is sometimes blue.

Already I digress.

Or do I? For Fritz, to whom I respond, is much concerned with the sense and feelings of an, or perhaps in his words he would say 'the', urban scene. He too has told you an audio-visual story which takes us from the first urban invasions of modern technology, when trains thunder past the drawing room windows of bourgeois apartments, when the clatter and rhythms of steel rail drown the domestic dispute in which a modest local banker with a neat moustache and a suppressed smile tries to explain away the smell of perfume on his clothes to his wife who has assumed the posture of a public building he, Fritz that is, takes us from this construction of sentiments, a world when the train, despite the alliteration, is newly driven into your dreams, to a new world, a world of "modern urban solids" in which the lover's eye, as in our imagined movie, is colored only by indifference. Grey truth is now our painted toy.[3]

Fritz's concern, sometimes his despair, more often his hope and his infatuation, is to ask how architecture and urbanism can first acknowledge and then build from the new, sometimes terrible world in which they (should I mean 'we') find them- or ourselves. Listen to his own words: "Modern reality is presented in a moment of surprise and violation, which leaves no alternative or escape open."[4]

At first, treating his subject matter historically, Fritz employs language which for me has the aftertaste of terror and destruction. We, as those who listen to his story, are given first the sense of a world lost, a world of hierarchy and order, and subsequently a feeling of infatuation and/or terror as a new world without these qualities overtakes us. Again in Fritz's words modern experience "disturbs and unsettles urban identity"; or again it is said to be "unpleasant and frightening"; or yet again "Like blades the engineer's iron structures chopped up the body of the city, fragmenting the urban fabric, and assaulting its beauty."[5]

So, if I respond to Fritz, and I *do* respond, I hear his words entangle themselves with the words of early modern writers in the early modern times which he redescribes for us. His descriptions of "incoherence and fragmentation", words which writers used then and which we use now to describe our self-imposed plight in history, engender still the doubled reactions of fear and thrill.[6] To make explicit Fritz's near-reference to Nietzsche, he, Fritz, faces the void which the concept of progress imposes upon us, but he is strangely cognizant of (should I say `reticent about'?) the "unpleasantness" and the "unorderliness" of the modern city, the specific qualities of the void itself. So it is significant or rather symptomatic, that Fritz should use such pejorative words to describe our plight and fuel his infatuations with the modern condition. What will I make of this?

Well, listen. When I play Fritz's language back to myself, (and the phrase Fritz's language found a metropolitan abbreviation in my notes as 'Fritz.lang'), language used to describe the modern urban condition at points of its most intense transformation, I hear the failing superlative and the excessive metaphor. So, again in Fritz's own words, "urban fabric" became "metropolitan plankton"; "street life" was transfigured into a "mechanical ballet or unpredictable moves"; and "modern reality (left) behind a violation."[7]

I take it that you can hear Fritz's references to specific modern works in his words. His text is indeed artfully constructed. I hope therefore that you will forgive me for attending to its points of excess and its metaphors. You might think that my paying attention to Fritz's metaphors is a bit like scrutinizing a philosopher's text for its handwriting rather than for the content of what it is saying.

But, responding like this, not so much to Fritz himself as to his language, I have a sense of *deja vu.* In the literary history which I have inherited, Charles Dickens has seen the dissolution of urban fabric in much the same terms as Fritz. I remember a passage in *Dombey And Son*, describing the effects of modern urban technology and its associated construction programme:

> "The first shock of a great earthquake had, just at that period, rent the whole neighborhood to its centre. Traces of its course were visible on every side ... Everywhere were bridges that led nowhere; thoroughfares that were wholly impassable; babel towers of chimneys ... carcasses of ragged tenements, and fragments of unfinished walls and arches, and piles of scaffolding, and wildernesses of bricks, and giant forms of cranes, and tripods straddling above nothing. there were a hundred thousand shapes and substances of incompleteness, wildly mingled out of their places, upside down, burrowing in the earth, aspiring in the air, mouldering in the water, and unintelligible as any dream."[8]

William Wordsworth, the English poet, also saw the modern city in the terms of fear and thrill,

> "All laws of acting, thinking, speaking man
> Went from me, neither knowing me nor known."[9]

He described the city as a "black confusion".[10] I fondly imagine that this phrase finds its equivalent in the contemporary American vernacular as something like `cultural white-out'.

My point in referring to such descriptions is to imply that new urban conditions are often described in terms in which language seems to give out on itself. In speaking like this, at the moment when our words fail us, we exercise ourselves ideologically as subjects of a new world, revelling, we think, in the freedom of a new found chaos.

But these new conditions, which occur to us repeatedly, and which some say are produced by the development, the progress and the application of technology, and which present themselves to us as a 'blank confusion', usually have a sobering side. What was either feared or welcomed (depending on which side you find yourself with respect to the conservative/radical distinction -- a distinction which does work so neatly anyway) -- what was either feared or welcomed as an uncharted, perhaps unchartable tempest of progress often has an order, or rather a structure which for ideological reasons we cannot or perhaps merely refuse to see. Hence the crisis of language, so called.

Another response: this time not by me to Fritz, but of a person to a city, the same English city, Manchester, whose dark satanic mills so impressed Friedrich Schinkel; a response not in the drawings of an architect but in the words of another Friedrich, a social theorist, Karl Marx's benefactor, Friedrich Engels. In *The Conditions of the Working Classes in England*, published in 1844, Engels took a long hard look at Manchester, then perhaps *the* first modern industrial town -- a town which seemed to all who saw it as an unfathomable chaos. In the "great towns" chapter of *The Conditions of the Working Classes* Engels, echoing the sentiments of others, says of Manchester that

> "the disintegration of society into individuals, each guided by his own private principles and each pursuing his own aims, has been pushed to its farthest limit...Here indeed human society has been split into its component atoms."[11]

In such cities, as the German/French poet Rilke says, (and this is a quotation lovingly remembered especially for Fritz), "countless nations (are burned) up for waste".[12] Engels looked searchingly at Manchester, representative of such cities, and managed the difficult feat of reading the illegible. As Steven Marcus has said, Engels revealed in his book that Manchester's apparently unsystematic and possibly incoherent form could actually be perceived as a total intellectual and imaginative structure.[13] Engels showed that in the so-called chaos of Manchester a specific system of exploitation was at work, and he gave us a structural description of what others had seen as an unchartable condition. In doing this, Engels gave us a Classical language for a modern condition. Like all languages it was a bargain with time and therefore doomed to future irrelevance: but for a time it could be said to provide, better to construct, an intelligibility for the modern urban condition.

So part of my response to Fritz is to operate a little skepticism on his teleology, on the temporal structure and sequence implied in his description of a Classical world of integration, hierarchy, and incorporated order, a world which is lost to a new world of "modern urban solids on an infinite plane" *of silence*, I would add. It is my strongest intuition that on such rarefied planes of aesthetic silence the only sound which can be heard is the counting of money. Another quote, remembered especially for Fritz, this time from the German social theorist Georg Simmel: "all things float with equal specific gravity in the constantly moving stream of money."[14]

For me it is not a question of losing one world to another. The Classical world of well-founded order, if ever it existed, is for me a world well lost. Instead I think the urban condition to be more a problem of struggling with the many conflicting and present worlds which we produce for ourselves with the several mechanisms of signification which we put at our own disposal.

As to a Classical world I would ask, following Wittgenstein -- poor Wittgenstein, he is always being quoted in support of the unsupportable -- but I persist in his skepticism, asking rhetorically whether a city or a language can ever be complete. Were towns, were languages complete before the introduction of the regularized patterns of the suburbs with their uniform houses, before the incorporation of the symbolism of chemistry and the notations of the infinitesimal calculus?[15] Such entities, languages and cities, do not complete themselves, but rather run out at horizons which, in being without proper place, can never be reached.

My skepticism about prior completeness fuels another skepticism that I feel with respect to Fritz's teleology, a skepticism as to the idea that somehow the crisis of the modern is produced by a teleology of technology and its application. Thus is our urban difficulty cast for us as a problem of technology and time, a problem that includes the idea of its potential solution -- ie. that 'one day' we might achieve a millennium of urban form. I am skeptical about the force and linearity of such narratives, and prefer to see the urban difficulty as a chronic condition. The city is a condition to be lived not a problem to be solved. Or to use the words of Joseph Rykwert, "the city is not a curable disease".[16]

Let me turn to another point in Fritz's narrative which opens up a specific subject matter through which I can make a further kind of criticism. This is perfectly hypocritical of me -- to point now to a specific place in a narrative which I have done my best to undermine. (What can I say? As Oscar Wilde might have defended himself, "Only the dull are consistent.")[17] But I still want to turn to a specific point in Fritz's account of urban history. This is where Fritz describes the train as cutting through the urban fabric, revealing the back, the dark side of the city. As Fritz describes the situation the "interior becomes exteriorized." (He is speaking of the urban block). Or again,

> "This other, new city consisted of the displeasing, dark side of its interior, since the view was now driven away from the articulated spaces and facades. Instead of a world ruled by Classical order, one could encounter a hitherto invisible urban desert of backyards and voids and fire-walls once shielded from view. This second city crowded with absence, became apparent only as a collection of leftovers and fragments, or unadorned poor buildings, masses of brick and windowless walls."[18] (The windowless wall, the black screen, will figure prominently at the end of my response.)

That the city can now be seen, or rather can be thought to be seen, in its entirety is crucial for the mentality which would construct the urban condition as a problem to be solved. For to construct the city as a mechanical apparatus it is necessary to see how all of its parts work, both 'Queen Anne' front and MaryAnn back. But, in turn, this desire for visibility is not without its own technology and its own difficult metaphors.

If I have my version of Fritz's chronology right, we are in the period 1870-1890. This is the great period of what one might call urban visibility. For a start it is the time, not just of the great Romance with trains, but also of something we now take for granted, the street light. This is the time of the great municipal installation of gas lights, when the urban technology developed in Haussman's office in Paris was disseminated to great cities all over the world, especially London. When Hans Christian Anderson (author of the famous fairlytales) visited London at this time, he remarked that "the great world metropolis was mapped out in fire below me".[19] (Incidentally, when the new American poet and neo-Marxist architectural critic, Michael Hays, flew into Los Angeles two days ago, seeing the city's lights stretching out towards a horizon he could not properly find, he said, "Wow! A-MAZ-ing!" Somehow I think these words equivalent to those of Hans Christian Anderson.)

This is also the time of municipal maps and street signs. The city was being charted in official documents. Soon after this time, in an unmitigated fit of Weberian rationality, all of the street names in Stockholm were changed and reorganized by the city government in order to nominalize and control the city. (I suspect that the government officials were a little too dull to sense the ironies of nominalizing an entire city.) Additionally, it is about this time that the first London A-Z directory of streets was published, and quickly became indispensable to anyone who wanted to find their way about town as everybody suddenly found the need to do.

What I find important about this time is the growing idea that the city can be bent to the human will within a logic of light and the penetration of the intelligence. All can, indeed must, be rendered visible. There is no limit to the transparency that we can impose upon the city, the setting of our lives. The city is simply the scope that can be taken of it. William Blake had earlier sensed this tendency to totalizing rationality in London:

"I wander through each chartered street
Near where the chartered Thames does flow
And mark in every face I meet
Marks of weakness, marks of woe."[20]

Briefly, I draw your attention to two things about this poem which are pertinent to the argument I make here. First, the connection between rationality and misery: the streets are chartered (ie. mapped and known), but this knowledge serves only to reveal the misery which an urban formation operates as the underside of its crowning glories. Second, even, or rather especially, the river, that great sign of the wild, flowing deep within the heart of the city, is also chartered, and thus bent to the human will.

A paradigm for this kind of intelligence is to be found in the detective stories of Arthur Conan-Doyle. Sherlock Holmes is the very model of the clear crystal intelligence which penetrates the dark chaos of society's underworld. It is important to remember that the street on which Holmes lived, Baker Street, is well lit, being equipped with the new municipal gas lamps. He follows his quarry, the London criminal, into the dark underworld, where light is more scarce. But he brings with him a different kind of light, the light of a supreme intelligence to this dark and dangerous underworld and unravels its secrets. Notice further that the story is based on a contrast which is in reality a class distinction with a geographical correspondence, a contrast between the fashionable West-End of London with its street lights and fine carriages and the East-End in which these things are absent and in which it is thought that squalor multiplies to infinity in the murky shadows. The latter is a city of darkness, the former a city of light: and more to the point it is the former, the West-End, which is said to provide models of intelligence by which the darkness of the East-End can be dispelled.[21]

(A remark in passing: too often clarity of thought is accepted without any sense of a problematic as something co-equal to the crisp definitions brought to things by light.)

Fritz implicitly touches on this subject matter when he speaks of Schinkel's concerns with panoramas, for the panorama is nothing if not an attempt to see more of the city than is normally made available to the ordinary person. It is also a privileged view, with specific associations to a totalizing form of intelligence. Of which still more to come.

If I turn then to the logic of light, view and scope, to the panorama of the city, I do so not as a cure for the problems which Fritz raises for us but rather to make them even more difficult, more problematic. I do however want to persist in my disarming of his sense of time, and to do this by problematizing his illustrations.

Responding to Fritz: well, I respond not to Fritz now, and not even to his words, but instead to his pictures.

Tied to our concept of the perfect view is an idea of synchorony in the arrangement of things. Thus a picture, when it is crudely or rather directly constructed or received, by arranging things in relation to one another, may appear to settle our score with history. If there is a right place for things, in either a classical or a chaotic world, things are seen to be in their right place because we have a picture of them, not *visa versa*. Too often it is our fervent and unacknowledged desire that a picture hold us captive.[22] It is noteworthy that such a view of the picture sees the picture itself without irony as something static, as a fixed scene that the eye can roam across, as in a survey or a panorama.

The picture, fixed in a static version of itself, is implicitly tied to the kind of linear narrative which Fritz has told. In this narrative pictures are being used in two ways: first, as evidence to corroborate his story *at a glance* -- the slide seems to confirm what you expect from the words by illustrating them -- you *see* what he means; second, as past or potential versions of an idealized urban world. Only in this latter way, by implying a stasis, a once or future picture of perfection, can Fritz's narrative find its course by positing the twin phantasia of its beginning and its end.[23]

But pictures are full of problems and paradox, and have an annoying habit of not behaving even, especially, at the moment when they seem most compelling as evidence. When Fritz showed his slides, I tried as an experiment to block my eyes to the things to which he drew our attention. Instead I focussed on all that by his account was marginal on the screen: the trees, the shadows, the line of the cornice, the clouds, the mast dividing a picture in two, an so on. My intuition upon looking at the slides in this manner was that these seemingly harmless elements in his pictures were actually performing a crucial ideological function (literally idea-logos,) in sealing over those incoherences and gaps between discrepant parts of the several pictorial schema or regimes at work in each view; thus providing us with his evidence *at a glance* -- a complete picture. Fritz himself pointed to such an example when he described in Friedrich Klose's painting of Berlin (1836) the mast of the boat as cutting an urban scene in two.[24] Here an ideological divide is made conscious in the work and also in Fritz's description of it. My intuition, unsupported since I have only seen his slides for the slight duration of fifteen seconds each, is that such devices are operating in many of his pictures and are the device by which the illustration or picture achieves its unity and its persuasion as corroborating evidence.[25]

Looked at carefully pictures are never picture perfect. We cannot quite get them right in the totalizing way we may wrongly desire. We cannot settle our score with history by (a) vision.

I focus on the problem of pictures like this because I want to respond to Fritz in two more difficult ways. An integral part of Fritz's narrative was an elegantly constructed sub-plot, which in a fit of ugliness I might re-title as *The life and times of the architectural object in the progressive anguish of modernism.* Crudely, he took us from a Classical world of hierarchically centered objects, in which space and object seemed to construct and confirm each other in a mutual and reciprocal relation, to a world of "modern urban solids" in which space seemed (to me) to pre-exist the object. The modern object, in coming later, in finding itself already within a spatial conception and an absolute concept of space at that, acquired (with a bit of word play) both a nomadic and a monadic status. Fritz himself describes modern objects as lonely and solitary or as in "disagreement and disgust with the(ir) given context".[26]

Again this pocket history is a linear teleology, which in summary I have foreshortened somewhat. It is a history which could, indeed would, be extended further than Fritz takes it. The object as such can be dissolved first into its constituent surfaces, so that we live in a world without objects, perhaps a Ruskinian world of surface and color presented directly to the eye.[27] Or, the more radical still, the object can be dissolved altogether in favour of a conception of fields and overlapping qualities. (Philosophically there are some big problems with this conception of the loss of the object, largely concerning the referents of names being denied the status of objects, but as a Romantic urge toward the liquefaction of the world it has its own lovely point of attraction.)

I want to operate the same process of criticism of Fritz's teleology of the object as I did on his history of the modern urban condition under contemporary technological progress. That is to say I want to fracture his teleology down into a chronic condition which we are doomed to repeat blindly.

First I notice that Fritz's history of the object is not so much a history of the object as it is a history of the picture or image of the object. More accurately, I should say that it is a history of verbal descriptions of the picture of the object. (I hope now the relation between twist-off bottle tops and twisted tales is becoming sufficiently clear.) If not, notice that this is a crucial turn of the phrase since a shift from a history of objects to a history of the signification of objects releases me (and Fritz) from a slightly mystical use of physics in a teleology, and allows a more elaborated account of how we fabricate realities for ourselves with a process signification -- verbal, pictorial, constructed, whatever.

Second, part of the problem of the apprehension of objects concerns the placement of effacement of the subject. Too often the mechanism of the picture is utilized to create, on the one hand, a world of externalized objects, and on the other to ensure the effacement of the subject from the world so depicted. The immediate problem is that we cannot take ourselves out of the picture -- just as we cannot take ourselves out of the world. Wittgenstein is wrong, I think, when he says in the Tractatus, that "nothing *in the visual field* allows you to infer that it is seen by an eye."[28] Excepting a purely mystical account of a thing *in a visual field* (which may be his meaning at this juncture of the book), it seems to me that every visual field betrays the subject and the eye that constructs it. Think of horizons, while they can be said not to exist and therefore not to be '*things* in the visual field', they are *in* the visual field, and they are clearly put there by the eye's interaction with the world. Horizons are a line drawn or written, if you like, by the eye across its field of view in order to complete a picture of the world as a picture -- to make that picture complete and compelling as a world. Or think of vanishing points in perspectival vision, not just as an internal device of projective geometry which produces a field of view, but also as the point where the subject tries to write itself out of the picture, and hence out of the world it conceives as existing before itself.[29]

It is my intuition, which in this brief response I merely suggest rather than prove to you, -- it is my intuition that Fritz's teleology of urban form cannot be completed without attention to these structural problems of vision, of the way the city can be seen, can be scene. Part of what is at stake in the construction of any picture is the double difficulty of first constructing a version of the world, or rather constructing a world no less, and secondly acknowledging the fact that, because it is a world we make (sometimes a picture we inherit), but nonetheless a world to which we are subject, we must still act as if we are both immanent and transcendent to that world -- both inside it, encompassed and determined by it, and outside it, somehow free of it. This is why pictures cannot, indeed must not, be completed.

In his doubled reference to the eye and the tongue (the glance and discourse mentioned together in the same phrase), Derrida is right of *both* words and pictures when he says that

> If totalization no longer has any meaning it is not because the infinity of a field cannot be covered by a finite glance or a finite discourse, but because the nature of the field ... excludes totalization ... (I)nstead of being too large, there is something missing from (the field); a center which arrests and founds the freeplay of substitutions."[30]

A picture is never perfect: something is always missing, however hard it is to find.

In the spirit of Fritz's own paper let me by way of ending my remarks (if not my twisted tale) return to the movies, or rather to a metaphor of the movies, or rather to a metaphor of the scene of the movies. Fritz has worried that the modern world threatens us with a reality

> "which is presented in a moment of surprise and violation, leaving no alternative or escape open."[31]

So, in my mind I have returned to the movies. Paradoxically there is showing a movie about being at the movies, when all the exit doors are closed. Each 'Exit' sign reads 'No Exit'. The doors are closed and the screen is blank. (Something like the room which we are all operating together at this very moment). As a subject of this room, facing this blank screen, I hear the faint echoes of those who have faced this terrifying situation before me: of James Joyce, for example, of whose writing Raymond Williams once said that "in a way there is no longer a city there is only a man walking through it," and whose words he described as a "universal isolated language."[32] I think of Beckett who learned not to grieve about the fact that at each moment the cultural inheritance is given as a burden of impoverishment. (Frank Gehry told me after this response that I should have heard the voice of Eric Mendelsohn, whom Fritz also mentions in his talk, and who had stood exactly where I was standing.) In summary I hear a multitude of voices, the voices of those who have in one way or another touched the sensibilities which make me as I am.

And now I wonder how I can take my exit from you, the listener. Perhaps silence is my most graceful recourse, but I am still talking. Perhaps contradiction can be my escape? Shall I speak a silence, say the unsayable, draw the undrawable? And standing here thus accused, must I look you in the eye before I go?[33]

NOTES

1. A response to "The Second Hand City: Modern Technology and Changing Urban Identity" Keynote speech given by Fritz Neumeyer at the *8th Annual ACSA Technology Conference*, held at the University of Southern California, Los Angeles, February 15th-18th, 1990.
2. "The social character of men's labour appears to them as an objective character stamped upon the product of that labour...There is (therefore) a definite social relation between men that assumes in their eyes the fantastic form of a relation between things." Karl Marx, *Capital: A Critique of Political Economy, Volume 1, The Process of Capitalist Production*, Edited by Friedrich Engels, Translated by Samuel Moore and Edward Aveling, New York International Publishers, 1967. From "Section 4: The Fetishism of Commodities and the Secret Thereof." p. 77.
3. See line 4 of "The Happy Shepherd" by W.B. Yeats in *The Collected Poems of W.B. Yeats: A New Edition*, Edited by Richard Finneran, New York, Macmillan, 1983, p. 7.
4. After my response to him at the conference Fritz worried over a glass of white wine (we were both drinking the same kind of wine) -- he worried that I was accusing him of longing for the Classical world which he describes as being lost to us. I hastened to point out that this was *not* my point. If anything I was more concerned with his desires and infatuations as he accelerates into the new world which he describes rather than with his regrets and his despair. More accurately, I am not concerned with either despair or exhilaration, nor with who is feeling which of the two, but with the entire structure of feeling, the opposition of the two that is engendered by the idea of this new word of modern feeling superseding a world of so-called Classical sentiment, the idea that 'this follows that'. It is the teleology in Fritz' story which concerns me. See below p.6.
5. Neumeyer, ibid, pp.1-2.
6. Neumeyer, ibid.
7. Neumeyer, ibid, p.2, p.6, p.8.
8. See Charles Dickens *Dombey and Son*, reprinted London, Penguin, 1970, pp.120-121. Originally published 1848.
9. William Wordsworth, "The Prelude", in *The Poetical Works of William Wordsworth*, Edited by E. de Selincourt and H. Darbishire, Oxnard, Oxford University Press, 1940-1949, p. 286.
10. Wordsworth, *ibid.*
11. See Friedrich Engels, *The Condition of the Working Class in England*, translated and edited by W.O. Henderson and W.H. Chaloner, Stanford University Press, 1958, p. 31.
12. Rainer Maria Rilke, *The Book of Hours*, Translated by A.L. Peck, London, 1961, p. 117.
13. See Steven Marcus "Reading the Illegible" in *The Victorian City: Images and Realities*, Edited by H.J. Dyos and Michael Wolff, London, 1973, Volume I, pp. 257-258.
14. Georg Simmel, "The Metropolis and Mental Life", reprinted in *Classic Essays on the Culture Cities*, Edited by Richard Sennett, New York, Appleton-Century-Crofts, 1969, p. 52.
15. Ludwig Wittgenstein, *Philosophical Investigations*, London, Macmillan, 1953, see remark #18.
16. See Joseph Rykwert, *The Idea Of a Town: The Anthropology of Urban Form in Rome, Italy and the Ancient World*, Cambridge, MA, MIT Press, 1976, p. 188.
17. Oscar Wilde, "The Decay of Lying" in *The Artist As Critic: The Critical Writings of Oscar Wilde*, Ed. Richard Ellman, Chicago, The University of Chicago Press, (1968, original 1891), pp. 306-307.
18. Neumeyer, *ibid*, p. 8.
19. Quoted in Raymond Williams, The Country and The City, Oxford, Oxford University Press, 1973, p. 228.
20. See William Blake's poem "London" in *The New Oxford Book of English Verse, 1250-1950*, chosen and edited by Helen Gardner, Oxford University Press, 1972, p. 484. This version is not quite as Blake's original, which reads, I think, "I wander thro' each charter'd street
Near where the charter'd Thames does flow..."
21. See the brief reference make to Arthur Conan-Doyle's stories about Sherlock Holmes in the context of this thought by Raymond Williams in *The Country And The City*, ibid, pp. 228-229.
22. More apologies to Wittgenstein.
23. I readily acknowledge that Fritz is not so much interested in the end of his narrative and would quickly disclaim such a desire. He must, however, be interested in beginnings, else how can he talk of a once ordered Classical world.
24. The painting is by Friedrich Klose, executed in 1836, showing the Bauakademie. See Neumeyer, ibid, p. 13.
25. See Hubert Damisch, *Theorie du nuages: Pour une histoire de la peinture*, Paris, Editions du Seuil, pp. 11-12.
26. Neumeyer, *ibid*, p.17.

27. See John Ruskin *The Elements of Drawing*, London, Smith, Elder & Co, 1857. Letter #1, impressionist painting.
28. Ludwig Wittgenstein, *Tractatus Logico-Philolophicus*, translated by D.F. Pears and B.F. McGuiness, London, Routledge and Keegan Paul, 1922, Remark #5.633. His emphasis not mine.
29. See Hubert Damisch, "Les Lieux du Sujet" in *L'Origine de la Perspective*, Paris, Flammarion, 1987, pp. 343 et seq.
30. Jacques Derrida, "Structure Sign and Play in the Discourse of the Human Sciences" reprinted in *The Structuralist Controversy*, edited by Richard Macksey and Eugenio Donato, Baltimore, Johns Hopkins Press, 1972, p. 260.
31. Neumeyer, *ibid*, p. 243 & p. 244.
32. Raymond Williams, *ibid*, p. 243 & p. 244.
33. Fritz, in the all too mortal words of Rod Stewart,
"Will I see you tonight?
On a downtown train?
Every day, every day
Seems the same.
All my dreams turn to rain."

CHAPTER 1

Mapping the Post-Modern City: Two Arguments for Notation

STANLEY ALLEN
Columbia University

Why begin a discussion of drawing and postmodernism with Mies van der Rohe? Critical explication of the work of Mies has usually insisted on the primacy of an assertive, constructed material presence which would seem to make drawing irrelevant at best. Mies' laconic statement "We refuse to recognize problems of form, only problems of building," is seen to be emblematic of an architecture which justifies itself entirely by reference to the built artifact. But if the uncompromising use of industrial materials and the clarity of his tectonic means point toward an architecture that begins and ends with construction, there are other aspects of Mies' work,--from his involvement with the avant-garde journal G in the 20's to the radical refusal of form in his later work--which reveal a consistent preoccupation with the "other" of materiality. Nor is this totally inconsistent with the conclusion of the above statement: "Form is not the aim of our work, only the result. Form by itself does not exist."[1]

But to begin with Mies also serves to locate the always shifting term "postmodern" as it is used in the title of this paper. In conscious reference to Andreas Huyssen's formulation,[2] I would propose a notion of postmodernism based not on amnesia--"Where postmodernism simply jettisons modernism it just yields to the cultural apparatus' demands that it legitimize itself as radically new,"[3]--but rather, upon an exploration of the unrealized possibilities of the modern and the self-consciously relational nature of the postmodern. Or to extend this formulation, to rewrite the postmodern as a "countermemory"[4] of the modern: to look not only for what is left incomplete or unrealized in the modernist project, but also to disrupt these stories of origins and to begin to construct alternate histories out of the "other" of the modern itself.

Not surprisingly, in the case of Mies, it is in the drawings (already marginalized by his own declarations) that this other content is manifest. From his early obsession with photo-collage, to his personal sketches or the limpid pencil renderings executed by his apprentices in the 40's and 50's, the drawn work seems to exhibit the exact opposite character to the built work. The architecture in the drawings is emptied out, disembodied and de-materialized. It is an architecture of the intangible. In a collage which refers to the 1942 project, A Museum for a Small City (fig. 1), the architecture as such has all but disappeared, being indicated only by absences: the gaps in the collage. It might be argued that in this example the use of collage signals a heightened attention to materiality. But in this case, it is precisely not the architecture which is made more tangible, and it is photographic representations which constitute the "materiality" of this collage. In these collage-drawings, Mies enters into a complex play of presentation and re-presentation, in which mimetic equivalence is bypassed in favor of a codified play of absences and presences, and in which architecture is primarily implicated by its absence.

1. Mies van der Rohe, Museum for a Small City, 1942.

I would like to argue that what appears to be a paradox or an internal contradiction in Mies' work in fact tells us something very basic about the nature of architectural representation. Mies located materiality very precisely in the realm of building, and never made the conceptual mistake of confusing the materiality of the drawing with the very specific capacities and potentials of building itself. Mies made thematic to his practice an understanding that architects are displaced from the material aspect of their discipline and of necessity work through this disembodied form. Rather than minimizing this difficulty or covering over this split (the classical dream of a perfect mimesis) Mies exploited this distance and elaborated the possibilities of mutual exchange. For Mies, technique is never neutral, and drawing cannot be understood instrumentally. Instead, it is deployed as a highly active middle term in a complicated transaction involving ideas and materiality and provoked by absence as much as by presence.

Architectural drawing, then, is fundamentally impure. Like traditional painting and sculpture, it carries a mimetic trace, a representational shadow which is translated (spatially, across scale), into the built artifact. But it is also notational, like music or poetry. Architectural drawing is based on spatial and material notations which can be translated by means of a code across linguistic boundaries to be read according to known and shared conventions.

Nelson Goodman has proposed a theoretical context within which this question can be given a more rigorous formulation.[5] In his extensive discussion of the question of notation, Goodman distinguishes broadly between two types of art forms. He calls *autographic* those arts, like painting and sculpture, which depend for their authenticity upon the direct contact of the author. However, in music or poetry, the concept of authenticity is described differently. These arts, which have a life distinct from the direct contact of the author, he calls *allographic*. Allographic arts are those capable of functioning at a distance from the author by means of notation. They operate through interpretation and on the basis of convention, and are subject to changing standards of performance. A determinant link is made between the absence of the author and the use of notation: " . . . an art seems to be allographic just insofar as it is amenable to notation."[6] Under strict examination, the link between notation and the allographic arts seems to derive from two significant characteristics: 1) the ephemerality of the work itself (poetry, music) and 2) the collaborative nature of the performance language (dance, symphonic music).

By these criteria, it is obvious that architecture is neither clearly allographic or autographic and Goodman says as much: "The architect's papers are a curious mixture. The specifications are written in ordinary discursive verbal and numerical language. The renderings made to convey the appearance of the finished building are sketches. But what of the plans?"[7] Having called attention to mixed character of architectural representation in general, he goes on to stress the notational character of architectural plans specifically. Rather than understand the plan as a scalar analog, similar to a painter's cartoon, Goodman emphasizes the extent to which the plans participate in a notational language: "Thus although drawing often counts as sketch, and a measurement in numerals is a script, the particular selection of drawing and numerals in an architectural plan counts as a digital diagram and as a score."[8]

But a difficulty arises, tied to the problem of repeatability. What Goodman calls the "compliance class" in architecture is traditionally a unique building. Further, it is also possible to point to the direct involvement of the architect in the process of construction as in someway analogous to the activity of the painter or sculptor. "The work of architecture," Goodman writes, "is not always as surely disengaged from a particular building as is a work of music from a particular performance. The end product of architecture, unlike that of music, is not ephemeral; and the notational language was developed in response rather to the need for participation of many hands in construction. . . . Insofar as its notational language has not yet acquired full authority to divorce the identity of the work in all cases from particular production, architecture is a mixed and transitional case."[9] The radical possibility here--that the work of architecture resides in the design rather than in the realized building--is therefore seen to be compromised by the exigencies of construction and the unpredictability of reality. If architecture is condemned to an "impure" status, what then are the consequences of this condition?

In the case of Mies, this in-between status can take on an explanatory role, and begin to situate some of the contradictions implicit in drawing practice. Kenneth Frampton has called attention to the way in which, in Mies' work of the 20's, the special capacity of glass as a building material to achieve both apparent *and* actual dematerialization was understood as the expression of a new spirituality.[10] This equal co-presence of the real and the virtual is a constant in Mies' architecture. He understood architecture's special capacity to present the ineffable--light, shadow, transparency and reflection--as the paradoxical corollary of building's material presence. This has two implications. On the one hand, it serves to call into question the fixity of the division initially proposed in this paper: that is to say, of drawing as the realm of absence, and building as the realm of presence. It suggests that building itself is in some way irretrievably marked or contaminated by drawing just as drawing cannot help but implicate itself in materiality. And second, by directing our attention toward the intangible aspects of built reality, we are forced to confront the "undrawable":[11] the realm of building which can only be addressed through notation, and which connects architecture to the most abstract arts: poetry and music.

It is at this point that we can propose a tentative answer to the question asked as the beginning of this paper: what possible connection between Mies van der Rohe and the postmodern city? In a certain sense the choice of Mies is unimportant. I would like to suggest that by extending and radicalizing the project of notation articulated in the discussion of Mies, it may be possible to propose strategies to confront the current crisis of representation in the contemporary city. The problem of architecture and the contemporary city is also a problem of the terms representation, of the substitution of the intangible for the tangible, and of the inadequacy of the image as a descriptive mechanism. The rigor with which Mies insists on the notational properties of architectural representation may provide a starting point for an examination of the contemporary city and the postmodern condition.

Historically, the architecture of the city embodied collective memory through a structure of finite definition. A close correspondence obtained between the city as a tangible site on the landscape and a series of representations based on a fixed point of view and static conventions of representation. Today, the technologies of communication, information exchange and war and the concomitant economies of multinational capitalism and global commodity exchange have engendered a condition in which the urban site is no longer clearly geographic. The local, physical difference of cities, from the first world to the third world, is being progressively erased with the exchange of information, knowledge and technique. All cities are instantaneously connected as part of a vast network, in which images, data and money flow freely. And if the advent of mass communication and information technology has undermined the idea of the city as the place of architectural permanence, since 1945, the social value of memory itself has been eroded.

In addition to mass communication, the technology of war has further undermined the residual notion of the city as a protective enclosure. The fracturing and disintegration of the city that began with the perfection of ballistics and the development or roads and railways has been greatly accelerated by the defense requirements of the nuclear age and its supporting technologies. As the only means of defense, dispersion has become the primary tenet of an anti-urban ideology causing further erosion in the public realm. As Paul Virilio has pointed out: "the representation of the contemporary city is no longer determined by a ceremonial opening of gates, by a ritual of processions and parades, nor by a succession of streets and avenues. From now on architecture must deal with the advent of a 'technological space-time.'"[12]

One direct consequence of this has been the marginalization of the discipline of architecture itself. Michel Foucault has noted that "Architects are not the engineers or technicians of the three great variables: territory, communication and speed."[13] This is a situation which is historically determined and unlikely to change significantly as a result of anything that the architectural profession does. But it can also be argued that architects have yet to examine the consequences of this shift, and to ask what it means in terms of representation.

In the rhetoric of the early modern movement, technology was represented in symbolic form. The liner, the airplane or the dynamo acquired ideological value as icons of modernity. Frederic Jameson has remarked that contemporary technology does not lend itself to iconic representation.[14] But this fails to acknowledge that today the artifacts, the new machines, are uninteresting in themselves. More important for the city are the effects of technology: the atomization of information, the splintering of perspectives, the uncontrollable proliferation of "depthless" images. How is it possible to represent the immateriality of networks and systems that comprise the city in the late 20th century without a radical shift in the terms of representation itself? How can architecture address the social and political implications of the shift from artifact to effect?

Any answer to these questions is of necessity partial and provisional. I would like to suggest, however, that a reconsideration of representation that takes notation seriously may provide a starting point. The opening up of architectural representation to the score, the map, the diagram and the script establishes a basis for exchange with other disciplines such as film, music and performance. The score allows for the simultaneous presentation and interplay of information in diverse scales, on shifting coordinates and even of differing linguistic codes. The script allows the designer to engage program and event on specifically architectural terms.

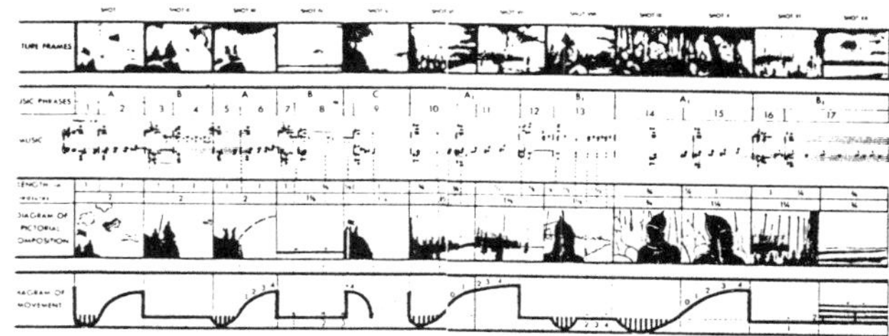

2. Sergei Eisenstein, Alexander Nevsky: Audiovisual Correspondences

Two aspects might be elaborated. If the new technology is understood as a shift from machines of production to machines of reproduction, and if this shift is characterized by the replacement of the analog by the digital,[15] a corresponding shift toward notation in architectural representation seems to follow. To cite Goodman again, "the more we are startled by this, because we think of such diagrams as rather schematized pictures, the more strongly we are reminded that the significant distinction between the digital or notational and the non-notational, including the analog, turns not upon some loose notion of analogy or resemblance but upon the grounded technical requirements for a notational language."[16]

Second, if we allow, along with Paul Virilio, that the life of the city and its experience belongs more today to time than to space ("Now speed--ubiquity, instantaneousness--dissolves the city, or rather displaces it, in time."[17]), the special capacity of notation to make thematic the measurement and unfolding of time takes on a special importance: interval, duration and tempo, acceleration and accumulation are fundamental to notation. And further, in as much as the use of notation signals a generalized shift away from the object and toward the syntactic and the ephemeral, this would seem to open up the possibility of a rigorous, nonreductive abstraction.

At this juncture it seems important to insist that the question of representation in architecture is always a double question. Beyond a discussion of drawing, it is important to call attention not only to the inevitability of architecture itself operating as a representational system, but also to the conceptual problems that arise from this consideration: ". . . in the architectural work the representation is not structurally representational--or it is, but according to a detour so complicated that it would undoubtedly disconcert anyone who wanted to distinguish, in a critical manner, the inside from the outside, the integral from the detachable.''[18] The crisis of representation in the contemporary city is no more than an escalation of an already present conflict within representation. The system which would hold together the conflicting demands of the mimetic (columns as trees, bodies) and the symbolic/linguistic (the whole mechanism of meaning from number to metaphor), is already unstable, and it is brought to crisis in the context of new technologies and urban conditions. What is at stake is architecture's capacity to continue to function as a representational system within an economy of shifting legibility and hyperealized symbolic exchange.

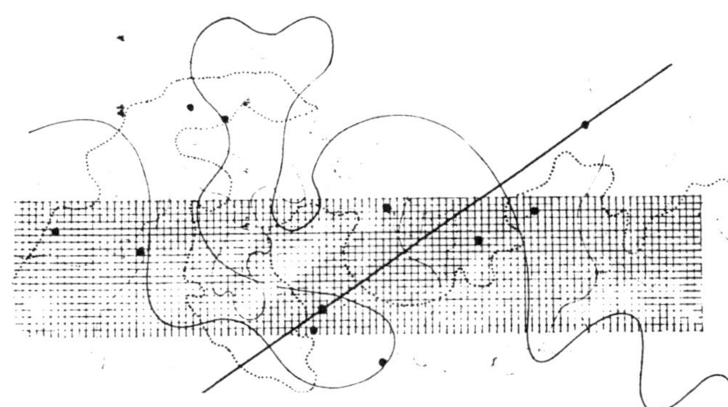

3. John Cage: Score for Fontana Mix, 1958.

NOTES

1. Johnson, Philip, *Mies van der Rohe*, Museum of Modern Art, p. 189 (original from G no. 2).
2. Huyssen, Andreas, ''Mapping the Postmodern'' in *After the Great Divide*, Indiana University Press, 1986, pp. 178-221.
3. Ibid., p. 185.
4. Foucault, Michel, ''Nietzsche, Genealogy, History,'' in *The Foucault Reader*, P. Rabinow, Ed., Pantheon Books, 1984, p. 93.
5. Goodman, Nelson, *Languages of Art*, Hackett Publishing, 1976, pp. 99-174.
6. *Ibid.*, p. 121.
7. *Ibid.*, p. 218.
8. *Ibid.*, p. 219.
9. *Ibid.*, pp. 220-221.
10. Frampton, Kenneth, ''Modernism and Tradition in the Work of Mies van der Rohe, 1920-1968,'' in *Mies Reconsidered: His Career, Legacy and Disciples*, The Art Institute of Chicago, 1986, p. 37.
11. Evans, Robin, ''Translations from Drawing to Building,'' in *AA Files 12*, The Architectural Association, 1987, p. 4.
12. Virilio, Paul, ''The Overexposed City,'' in *Zone 1-2*, Urzone Inc., 1986; p. 18.
13. Foucault, Michel, ''Space, Knowledge, and Power,'' in *The Foucault Reader*, p. 244.
14. Jameson Frederic, ''Postmodernism or the Cultural Logic of Late Capitalism,'' *New Left Review 146*, 1984, pp. 53-92.
15. Halley, Peter, ''On Line,'' *New Observations* 35, 1985.
16. Goodman, *op. cit.*, p. 171.
17. Virilio, Paul, *Pure War*, Semiotext (E), 1983, p. 60.
18. Derrida, Jacques, ''The Parergon,'' trans. Craig Owens, *October* 9, 1979, p. 22.

CHAPTER 2

Technology, the Metropolis and the Avant-Garde Function

SHAYNE O'NEIL
Cornell University

Modernity's witness to the rise and development of the avant-garde may be linked to the emergence of an analogous debate concerning modern technology. The very ambiguity the term 'avant-garde' engenders today, parallels a like uncertainty regarding the definition of modern technology as mere physical process or more generally, as a unique means of rationalized production with its attendant forms of social relations. Indeed, modernity itself may in part be located precisely by the tracings of these multiple trajectories and the critical methods adopted by particular societal groups to seek their reconciliation.

Identified by early 20th century German sociological theory, vanguards or intellectual elites arise in society concurrently with the advent of fully rationalized modes of technological production. Because the production process, according to this account, is the most immediate expression of modern rationality, specific sub-classes come into existence as the necessary guardians of this newly emergent order. However, their role exceeds that of mere historical index. For even to come into being, these groups must first of all be identified as the very agency of historical change itself. Empowered not simply to reflect but to implement this change, they become advocates of the new order.

Along with this definition of the avant-garde as an elite, sociological theory also posits a spatial context for technology's emergence. Since industrial production assumes a highly concentrated network of social relations among those engaged with it, this complexity also finds unique physical representation. Here the city or more specifically, the metropolis characterizes the particular social space typical of technological production. The metropolis, according to this theory, is the spatial locus adopted by a newly defined social structure. Since capitalist modes of production establish social forms analogous to those in the workplace, the metropolis too becomes the formal register of productive processes now transformed urbanistically.

For Georg Simmel, this equation of the social and productive defines the metropolis as the unique place for the exchange and circulation process of a mature money economy.[1] For Walter Benjamin somewhat later,[2] the metropolis becomes the site of commodity exchange and the fetishism surrounding its circulation. For both, the modern city expresses a present uniquely dominated by capital introduced now into the very spatial structure of society itself. But it is the metropolis so termed which specifies the spatial organization unique to the city of modern technology production.

Presented with this new social space, the avant-garde locates itself and its activities directly within the context of the metropolitan experience. Changed with the aim of implementing technology's fullest consequences, the metropolis quite logically becomes the subject and focus of avant-garde attention. Moreover, its every effort to arrive at new formal or cognitive means expressive of modern technological process, makes the metropolis itself the social analogue to these processes. Linked by their very definition, both notions of a vanguard and metropolis, therefore coexist as necessary terms in the sociological analysis of the modern city.

Here however, attempts to isolate an immediate 'theory' of the historical avant-garde and the Metropolis encounter a problem related not surprisingly also with the idea of modern technology. For if sociological accounts ascribe to elites the role of agents of an increased rationality, affirming its forms (including technology) as historically necessary, how might one then join this definition with the no less familiar counter-definition of the avant-garde as a self critical enterprise? Implicit in this 'other' account is the notion of rationality as a kind of self-reflexive activity; an activity aimed at producing enlightenment, of being inherently emancipatory, and finally, having a cognitive content productive of knowledge. Now while affirmation of what is historically necessary may indicate a part of what the avant-garde function entails, self-reflection here would also seem to imply a kind of inquing inherently productive of enlightenment and opposed to what mystifies reasonable self-understanding. Strategies of provocations, protest, opposition or even radical negation might be enlisted in this inquing, contrary to more threatening 'positive' interpretations. Yet at this point, it is important to note that the aims of either an 'affirmative' or 'negative' rationality reveal no implicit contradiction for a definition of the vanguard pose. That is, until one introduces the idea of technology as an unproblematic emblem of modernity's total emergence. For along with this other 'negative' avant-garde, perhaps even defining the object of its very negativity, there is an account of modern technology not as expressed rationality but as a force for structuring social relationships. In this account, reason becomes hostage to principles of productive expediency. Efficiency and the suppression of what impedes the rapid exchange of the commodity comes to define what is reasonable. Technology located within the gambit of contemporary commodity-production thus becomes an instrument of this greater standardization and concentration of social relations. The social alienation which is commonly said to define these relations thereupon traces it's origin to the very abstractness of this new technological rationality.

Now if this increased abstraction and alienation do indeed characterize the social relations of individuals engaged in commodity-production, are not these conditions the appropriate target of vanguard negativity? Again, how might one reconcile an avant-garde's justifiable opposition to these conditions with its other role as an elite committed to rationality's full disclosure in both the productive and social spheres? In sum, how is one to affirm as well as negate technology as mechanistic process and tool for reflective inquiry? Finally, can the metropolis as the site of this reconciliation preserve any sense of modern identity given this equivocal origin? Can the representational activities of the aesthetic vanguard in particular, join the concerns of modern technology with its antagonistic outcome viewed through the metropolitan experience? At last, is art itself capable of synthesizing these contradictory goals?

At this point, it may be helpful to note one form of this technical process specific to modern art. Along with this form and closely joined to it, one may also recall certain strategies or practices which by now have almost come to define early 20th century aesthetics. As originally observed by Walter Benjamin, photography because of its claims to make representation 'scientific,' mimics through its aesthetic function, a process very similar to that of mechanized industrial production. In fact viewed as a mere apparatus, it would appear to collapse the very traditional distinction separating aesthetic and productive realms. Photography's exact rendering of nature enables technology to surpass the artisan, undermining the uniqueness, the 'aura' of the art work through the mass reproducibility of the print image. Moreover, photography acts to 'secularize' the image by making its production generally accessible to a wider audience. Encouraging the practice of amateurs and professionals alike, its very availability reduces artist and public to the undifferentiated status of mere 'users'. Finally, photography's very reproducibility tends to 'democratize' the reception of the visual image by greatly expanding the opportunity of a mass audience to encounter multiples of an otherwise singular object. This equation of production and reception according to Benjamin, introduces the truly scientific approach to objects and their making. The commonality of processes used to produce either industrial or aesthetic artifact thereupon eliminates for him, the basis for art's unique position removed from other practices.

Yet as Benjamin himself was quick to observe the mass culture in which art and technology converge is not just any open context. It is rather a setting radically distorted by the ends of capital expediency which then are reflected in the very structure of social relationships. For art, aesthetic techniques and processes assume the logic typical of other abstracted commodities; for technology, the limitless reproduction of artifacts expands the sphere of a market society, inducing stylistic variation not as manifest technique but as novelty and sales inducement. Here the dilemma of the photograph and the photographic process reiterate technology's own split agenda.

Of course photography has by now been recognized as an essential medium exploited by the early 20. c. avant-garde. This exploitation seems both pragmatic in terms of representational concerns but also dogmatic for its access to the technological process itself. And it is just this accessibility to technology which makes its vanguard use a fulfillment of the avant-guard's mission to implement the new at all cultural levels. However, if the critical role of avant-garde is also to be assumed, how does its embrace of one of technology's foremost instruments, the camera, permit this other function to co-esxist? Specifically, how then does the photographic image (or operations enacted upon it) imply more than its first claim to objectify or rationalize representation.

The German artist, John Heartfield, a member of the Berlin Dada group writes in the late 1920's:

> "In order for the subject to be meaningfully represented, the mere surfaces offered by the photograph must be somehow disrupted. . . the likeness achieved by the photograph refers only to the exterior of the object which does not readily disclose its internal meaning as it manifests itself to the understanding."[3]

Here, Heartfield describes not simply a particular use of the photographic process but outlines a procedure performed upon the photographic image itself. That procedure in fact acts to physically and materially disrupt the photograph proper. Assuming the role of editor, he presents one with a variety of techniques i.e. cropping, captioning, mounting, doubling etc. of image to text or image to other images. Little is noted by Heartfield of the semantic content represented by the photograph. Instead only the syntactic relation of the collected material evidences a meaning greater than the physical act of their being mounted in the first place.

The photomontage procedure which this describes establishes one of the canonical practices of modern art. Not unrelatedly, it also begins to suggest a way in which the positive and negative aims of the avant-garde might be reconciled; that is, how the vanguard role could self-consciously explore the very separate ends of an emerging rationality implicit within the technological process.

Photomontage acts first to problematize photography's very effort to align itself with external reality. It initially would appear to embrace the illusionism of the photographic fragments which it appropriates. Still, it joins these fragments not through the subordination of part to whole according to traditional aesthetic canon. Rather, it depletes their previous meanings through the equalization of their functions as more photographic signs. Through the strategy of juxtaposition, a new meaning is composed in the evident construction of the assembled parts. As Theodor Adorno states, ''montage explodes the veil of pure immanence, and on the other hand, it forces fragments of empirical life to become estranged from their context, subjecting them to immanent principles of artistic construction.''[4] Thus while the elements themselves preserve their claims to be unmediated representations, the editorial manipulation of these elements reveals the contaminated presence of a mediating producer. As Adorno again points out, ''the principle of construction postulates the dissolution of materials and components in art and the simultaneous imposition of unity''[5] and later he again observes, ''in construction the totality makes sure that the discreet elements are combined whether they like it or not. Though imposed from above, the oneness of the modern constructed work is such that it is counteracted by autonomous tendencies in the details.''[6]

Again, one may begin to see how the constructive reordering of photographic material through montage practices may indicate a possible resolution of avant-garde aims. The adoptance by the vanguard of photography seems to affirm its commitment to advance modern technology into all spheres of contemporary life. But once adopted, the aggressive reconstruction of the photo-textual object displays a more ambiguous attitude. Thus while photography's insistence upon verisimilitude appears to remain unchallenged, the fragmentation and simultaneous cognition of its incommensurable parts disclose a possibly subversive intent. If technology is invoked through the process, it seems likewise underminded through particular practices using that process. An uneasy balance may then be momentarily achieved as when Adorno again writes, ''What the technologization of art does is to purge works of art of the immediate language of subjectivity (the authored work). . . what looks like reification is actually a groping for the latent language of things - a language that articulates itself through the radical use of technology,''[7] Photomontage may represent that equivocal articulation. Accepting at first the apparent rationality of photograpy's claims upon the real, it then returns to negate, to do violence to its image as the infragable outcome of that rationality.

However that instant of reconciliation through the photographic process is a fleeting one. Once more, Adorno notes, ''The idea of montage and of technological construction are intimately bound up with each other,'' but he continues, ''together they are becoming increasingly incompatible with the notion of a radically elaborated art with which it used to be identical.''[8] The novelty and shock reflex necessary to the critical uses of technical processes therefore can only persist so long. The cognitive and associational habits which montage sought to destroy through new syntactic operations reemerge in a more sophisticated guise.

The metropolis too, the spatial context for the redress of distorted social relations also begins to lose its provocative sense. Having become the equivocal embodiment of technology's heterodox purposes, its forms represented through montage only reinforce the very 'matter-of-factness' of the now blase' urban dweller. The contemporary city Georg Simmel envisioned as an ''open place disposed to ideological experimentation''[9] becomes not a symptom any longer but an origin for the ongoing conditions the vanguard once sought to resist. Whether reduced to advertising techniques on the one hand or tools of propaganda on the other, montage and the metropolitan social space it invokes threaten in fact to become socially regressive. The vanguard function which photograph made clear thus once again recedes into ambiguity.

While one might conclude that this return to ambiguity marks the end of the historic avant-garde, historicizes its development and final demise (perhaps even forecloses on the further possibility of a 'neo-avant-garde' in the future), there is a more optimistic interpretation. Though particular aesthetic strategies have indeed lost their ability to mediate modernity's divergent ends, this does not mean a return to what Adorno describes as 'mimetic adaption to what is (ideologically) hardened?[10] Viewed critically, practices such as photomontage aside from their more overt disruptive goals may still contain a capacity for radical revision. That radicality now however lies in the very 'essentiality' of the things which aesthetic technique expose - a showing of what is the case. As Adorno again states, 'montage wants to give us facts we can point to... the work of art is supposed to let the facts speak for themselves.''[11] Here, the technological process may be enlisted to determine the appropriate distance at which the eyes might bring the essentiality of facts into focus. This essentialism, this ongoing disclosure however assumes that the art - technology convergence can produce a kind of critical reflection beyond mere shock. It is the ambiguity of this form of reception which may actually undermine the idea of a continuing vanguard. Uncertainty about the conclusions to be drawn from such a confrontation with 'facts' thus seems to assault the very identity of an avant-garde purpose. Yet as Benjamin and later Adorno imply, this uncertainty or ambiguity may be the necessary price to be paid for any ongoing critical function in art. Thus while it may be absurd (and certainly nostalgic) to insist upon a vanguard presence today, it seems that there does remain a rhetorical role implicit to aesthetic/ technical operations - a role sustained between the uneasy poles of disclosure and denial.

NOTES

1. Georg Simmel, *The Philosophy of Money* (London/Boston 1978), pp. 10-16.
2. Walter Benjamin, *The Work of Art in the Age of its Mechanical Reproduction, Illuminations* (Schocken Books, 1969), p. 6.
3. John Heartfield, quoted from *Down Ades, Photomontage* (N.Y. Phaidon 1976).
4. Theodor Adorno, *Aesthetic Theory* (Paul Routledge & Kegan, 1984), p. 365.
5. Ibid., p. 84.
6. Ibid., p. 223.
7. Ibid., p. 8.
8. Ibid., p. 225.
9. Georg. Simmel, *The Philosophy of Money* (London/Boston, 1978).
10. Theodor Adorno, quoted from Peter Burgen, *Theory of the Avant-Garde* (Minnesota, 1984), p. 62.
11. Theodor Adorno. *Aesthetic Theory*, p. 223.

CHAPTER 3

The Roman Latrine: Urban Technology and Socialization

DIANE FAVRO
University of California, Los Angeles

Romanization is synonymous with urbanization. By the imperial period, Roman cities extended from Britain to Mesopotamia. Many were enormous. In the early first century, Rome boasted a population of well over one million, Alexandria over 600,000. As urban environments grew, so did urban problems.[1] Large cities needed huge quantities of water for diverse purposes. Water quenched residents, served public amenities such as baths and gardens, and most important, promoted public health. As early as the Republic, the Romans associated standing water and waste with illnesses.[2] For utility, commodity, and delight, Roman municipal governments funded expansive water networks. A product of water engineering, the public latrine reflected and affected urban social interaction.

In the first century B.C., Augustus established a Water Commission to oversee Rome's complex hydraulic system.[3] Sextus Julius Frontinus, water commissioner in A.D. 98, wrote a history of this office and its duties. According to his careful records, Rome daily received approximately 300 gallons of water per person.[4] Surveying the effects of this input Frontinus claimed, "the improved health of the city, [exists] as a result of the increase in the number of the works, reservoirs, fountains, and water-basins. ... Not even the waste water is lost; the appearance of the city is clean and altered" (*De Aquae* 88).

For maximum efficiency, Rome's Water Commission established a strict hierarchy of usage. After filtering through large tanks, aqueduct water was piped into water towers and then into smaller reservoirs for distribution. Mains at the bottom level of these tanks delivered water to fountains, public baths, and official buildings; pipes attached at a higher level served non-public users.[5] According to Frontinus' careful reckoning, 17% of water within the city was given by the direct grant of the emperor; 44% was assigned to public projects including municipal structures, ornamental fountains, camps, and water basins (Frontinus *De Aquae* 78, 107-8). The remaining 39 % was sold as available to private residences or industries.[6] Roman municipalities also carefully reckoned the secondary applications of waste or 'lapsed' water. For example, they channeled dirtied water from public baths to irrigate surrounding gardens and operate water mills. Run-off from public fountains was directed to municipal uses or sold. However, Frontinus points out private grants were given sparingly to preserve sufficient overflow water "for use in the flushing of the sewers" (Frontinus *De Aquae* 110-11).

Before the establishment of comprehensive water systems, human waste was a major urban concern. Private options were limited. Residents used dry privies in their residences or collected their waste for dumping in public cess trenches or atop festering dung heaps. In addition, open jars of urine stood on many public streets. Fullers set up terra-cotta amphorae (*dolia*) with broken necks to collect urine employed in the cleaning of woolen fabric. These ad-hoc facilities filled Roman cities with noxious odors, nurtured disease-producing bacteria, and contaminated the water table from which well water was drawn. Waste removal became even more troublesome as urban density increased.

Extensive urban water systems alleviated many of these problems. Public fountains fed by aqueducts superceded contaminated private wells. The unabating flow of water through a city prevented the growth of bacteria, minimized odors, and removed waste products through expanded sewer systems. In tall apartment buildings with limited facilities, discourteous occupants unceremoniously emptied their chamber pots out the window, secure in the knowledge that the streets would be cleaned regularly.[7] In the public sphere, *dolia* and communal dumps did not disappear, yet they were supplemented if not supplanted by attractive public latrines.

Public latrines appeared as soon as any Roman city had a complex water delivery network incorporating an ample, continuous flow. Ancient sources allude to the existence of public latrines at Rome in the second century B.C.[8] By this time, the capital had an extensive drainage system, a network of sewers, and city-wide water distribution. At least four aqueduct lines fed the city for a total of approximately 471,086 m^3 of water per day; by the end of the Julio-Claudian era in A.D. 68, the amount had more than doubled and public latrines existed throughout Rome.[9] Municipal governments sited public latrines in relation to both density of use and water networks. The first latrines in any city usually appeared near the forum in the city center. A Roman forum was at once a gathering point, functioning municipal center, and symbol of municipal pride. Great effort was made to keep such environments clean and well-drained. In addition, as gathering points for governmental activity fora attracted the cities' most important citizens who in turn required appropriate facilities.

Bath buildings also frequently incorporated latrines. Appearing in the early empire, large public *thermae* competed and eventually superseded private baths. Made possible by the expanded aqueduct systems, *thermae* daily employed thousands of gallons of water. Most citizens attended the baths, but only wealthy upper-class members could spend several hours each day in the lavishly decorated imperial facilities.[10] They needed appropriate rest-rooms. Fortunately, the *thermae* had ample run-off water to cleanse large latrines. For example in the Central Baths of Pompeii the latrine was flushed with water from the large swimming pool in the main court (fig. 1). Rather than restricting use to those who paid for bathing, cities opened bath latrines to all urban residents. Most had two entrances, one from the street and another from within the *thermae*.

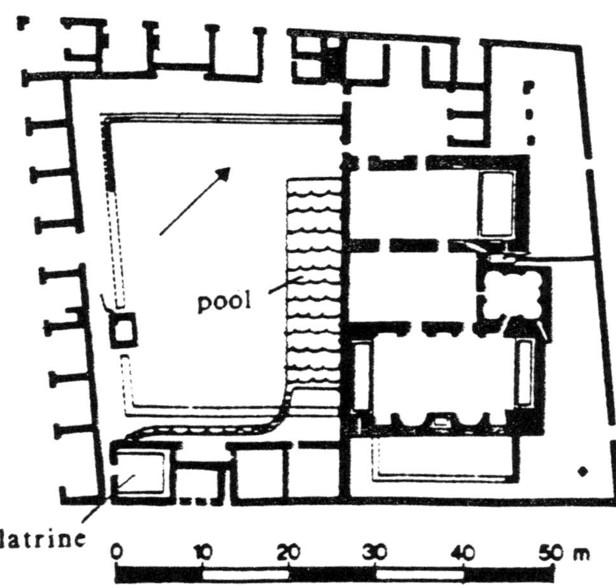

1. Central Baths with latrine, Pompeii (after H. Eschebach)

Large latrines appeared in other public locations only when high use was accompanied by easy access to water. For example, the marble-clad Flavian market building at Puteoli had capacious latrines connected to the municipal water system feeding the central fountain of the complex.[11] In other public gathering points such as the theaters, citizens had to rely on *dolia* or portable commodes, or else wait until they went home or to a location serviced by a public latrine.[12]

To save money, municipalities built a few large, multi-seat latrines rather than numerous small facilities. According to the publication known as the *Regionaries*, Rome in the fourth century had a total of 144 public latrines.[13] With a population hovering around one million, the capital had approximately one public facility per 600 residents. Each could accommodate numerous users at a single seating. Preserved examples confirm that many Roman latrines had seats for over twenty users.[14]

Roman public latrines were usually rectangular, with benches for sitting along three sides. Semi-circular, U-shaped, and trianglar rooms also existed (fig.2). The benches, often of marble, had simple circular or spoon-shaped openings. Under the seating, running water carried refuse in slanted troughs to the main sewer and from there out of the city to a nearby river or the ocean. Most latrines were designed to encourage entry yet prevent unwanted stares from passers-by. In the forum of Pompeii this was achieved by having a vestibule with staggered doors between the street and the seating.

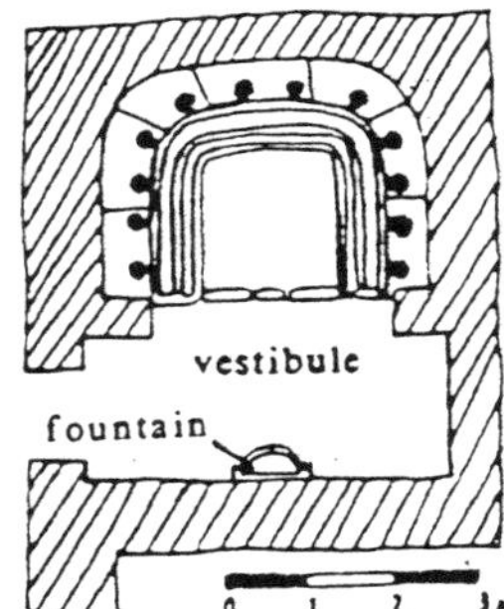

2. Public latrine, Thugga, North Africa (after M. Grassnick)

Though unappealing to modern sensibilities, the group seating of latrines was not considered immodest by Roman standards. According to contemporary writers, the Romans frequently and openly discussed bodily functions.[15] A visit to a privy was as natural a visit to the dining hall, and just as conducive to conversation. In fact, latrines were ideal for socialization. They occurred in important locations in the city and comfortably accommodated numerous people at a time. Furthermore, their elaborate appointments encouraged dalliance.

Today, public facilities are starkly functional. The preserved examples from Roman sites display rich decorations and ample amenities. The latrine near Caesar's Forum in Rome was heated; that in the forum at Timgad had dolphin-shaped armrests. Most included playful fountains. Elaborate decoration covered every surface. Decorative mosaics spread over the floors; mosaics or wall paintings faced the walls.[16] The double latrines of Puteoli had marble-covered surfaces, large windows, and niches for statuary. Some latrines even included shrines. An inscription from Ostia identifies the deity worshipped as Fortuna, goddess of health and happiness.[17]

Literature confirms the popularity of latrines for socialization. Martial in the first century tells of a certain Vacerra who spent his day dallying in public latrines hoping to wrangle a dinner invitation (Martial, *Epigrams*, 11.77). In another passage, he chides a fickle friend who no longer searches for him "in warm baths, and in theaters, and in every latrine" (5.44). The passage implies these three urban places were where a man of leisure lingered.

The siting of latrines provides further clues to their social uses. Located in fora, public facilities were frequented by senators and other politically-minded citizens who found latrines ideal places for networking. The Trajanic latrine off the Clivus Argentarius in Rome was readily accessible from the Senatehouse, Forum Romanum, and Forum of Caesar. In addition, this attractive facility had hypocaust heating.[18] On days when the cold in the forum was unbearable, senators could gather in the large, warm latrine. Evoking the couches of philosophers, curved seating further encouraged discourse.[19]

The lobbying and intrigue of the latrines may have been the impetus for a proclamation of Tiberius. This unpopular emperor declared it a capital crime to carry a ring or coin with his image into a privy in an attempt to prohibit or curb subversive talk.[20] A contrasting motive may underlie the construction of a public latrine in the previous generation. After the dictator Caesar was murdered in the Curia of Pompey, the room was closed. Subsequently, the claimants to Caesar's power transformed the space into a public latrine (Dio Cassius 47.19). This action can be viewed as an attempt both to wash away the memory of the assassination and to present a non-dictatorial image by providing a public, and especially senatorial, facility.

The accessibility of public latrines remains a question. Modern sources repeatedly refer to fees, though evidence for pay facilities is inconclusive. In a famous passage, Titus chided his father Vespasian for taxing urine; his father responded by holding a coin under his nose and asking if it smelled (Suetonius *Vespasian* 23). While this can be interpreted as referring to a fee for using public conveniences, it more likely applied to the urine jars collected by fullers. Other references imply public latrines had regular attendants. A small fee or the presence of a tip-hungry attendant would have deterred poorer city-dwellers from using public latrines, yet well-established social hierarchies probably served the same purpose.

Latrinae publicae served a select group: the governing male elite.[21] All members of the citizenry frequented the fora and baths of cities, yet only the members of the patrician class did so on a consistent basis. Equally important, this group avidly sought decorum in all aspects of their lives. In the late first century B.C., Vitruvius argued that the homes of "persons of high rank ... should be provided princely vestibules, lofty halls" and other features appropriate for their stature (6.5.2). Such men likewise desired suitable environments in the work sphere.

Roman technology and organization made possible the transferral of huge quantities of water to cities. Availability of water in turn encouraged urban growth and improved urban health. Yet other, non-Roman cities thrived without superfluous water.[22] Roman developments in urban water distribution reflect unique social priorities. Even the appearance of multi-seat public latrines was not for the "general" good. More than utilitarian urban amenities, Roman latrines served and encouraged socialization among a specific, elite clientele.

NOTES

1. On the population of Rome see John E. Stambaugh, *The Ancient Roman City* (Baltimore 1988) 89.
2. Varro, *De Re Rustica*, 1.12; Columella, *De Re Rustica*, 1.5.
3. Leon Homo, *Rome imperiale et l'urbanisme dans l'antiquite* (Paris 1971) 186-198.
4. Frontinus' records present some difficulties as he based his figures of volume on pipe diameters without considering the rate of flow; L. Sprague De Camp *The Ancient Engineers* (New York 1960) 213-214.
5. Pipes placed higher had a slower flow and were the first to suffer if the water level dropped; Frontinus *De Aquae* 113.
6. Frontinus records that the sale of water brought Rome a yearly income of nearly 250,000 sestertii (*De Aquae* 118).
7. Juvenal warned pedestrians in the streets of Rome, "You can but hope...that they may be content to pour down on you the contents of their slop-basins" rather than the entire vessel; *Satires* 3.276-277.
8. C. Titius in Macrobius, *Saturnalia*, 2.12.
9. Stambaugh, *The Ancient Roman City*, 128-133. Pliny in the first century described Rome's sewers as "the most noteworthy achievement of all;" *Natural History* 24.104.
10. On the Roman baths see Jerome Carcopino, *Daily Life in Ancient Rome* (New Haven, 1971) 289-300.
11. Stefano De Caro and Angela Greco, *Campania* (Bari 1981) 46.
12. Wealthy Romans were accommpanied by slaves carrying commodes; Horace, *Satires*, 1.6.109. The only other large facilities in Romans cities were to be found in barracks for soldiers or police, yet there is no evidence the public could use these latrines; R. Meiggs, *Roman Ostia*, (Oxford 1960); 2nd ed. 1973) 305-306.
13. H. Thedenat, s.v. "Latrina," in *Dictionnaire des antiquites grecques et romaines d'apres les textes et les monuments* (1877-1919) 988.
14. For example, two examples from Timgad and three from Ostia had over twenty seats.
15. Petronius, *Satura*, 47; Suetonius, *Lucan.*
16. Thedenat, *Dictionnaires*, 987-991.
17. An inscription naming "Fortuna sancta" was found in the latrine of the vigiles; Meiggs, *Ostia*, 305; *CIL* xiv, Supplement, I, 4282.
18. C. Ricci, "Il Foro di Cesare," *Capitolium* (April 1932) 365-390.
19. In latrines a curving shape was preferable for the underground troughs to keep waste from collecting in corners.
20. In this proscription Tiberius also included brothels, another place where politicians were likely to express seditious thoughts; Suetonius, *Tiberius* 58; cf. *Lucan.*
21. There is no evidence women frequented public latrines; the existence of double latrines, as at Puteoli, indicates a large number of male users, not separate facilities for each gender.
22. Bryan Ward-Perkins, *From Classical Antiquity to the Middle Ages* (Oxford 1984) 120-122.

CHAPTER 4

Pandora's Black Box: The Cellular Prison in France, 1830-1860[1]

DAVID VANDERBURGH
University of California, Berkeley

INTRODUCTION

Most discussions of prison architecture note the popularity of cellular prisons and the Philadelphia System among mid-nineteenth-century prison reformers. Niklaus Pevsner goes so far as to call John Haviland's Eastern State Penitentiary of Philadelphia, opened in 1829, 'the model prison of the nineteenth century' (Pevsner, p168). Yet in France the Philadelphia System was hotly disputed, in England it was unevenly applied (Evans), and in the United States it lost ground steadily to its competitor, the Auburn System, which called for isolation only at night. Even where cellular prisons were built, they seldom followed the system for long: as prisoner populations mounted, cells built for one often came to hold two or more inmates.

The idea of the cellular prison clearly caught the imaginations of many, even those of its detractors. But it remains to establish the limits of its influence, and to locate that influence in practices and built form. A major purpose of my dissertation research is to look at what happened to the idea in France, via the Interior Ministry's standardization program of 1836-53, and more particularly at how patterns of action and reaction among various groups can tell us what its real meaning might have been. When framed in this way, the problem becomes one not only of architecture, but of public policy, professionalism, and social change. It is for this reason that Michel Foucault (1979) considered the cellular prison a kind of social technology, with ramifications far beyond its walls. Most historians, however, find it hard to apply Foucault's analysis to specific problems of history. For this paper, I have turned instead to the work of a historian of science, Bruno Latour.[2]

THE CELLULAR PRISON AS SOCIAL TECHNOLOGY

Latour's *Science in Action* (1987) discusses the spread of scientific and technological advances using the metaphor of the 'black box.' In Latour's view, the aim of any innovator is that her product, whether a new machine or a scientific fact, should be adopted by others as such a black box, leaving aside questions of how or why it works. Once these black boxes are adopted, 'no matter how controversial their history, how complex their inner workings, how large the [social] ...networks that hold them in place, only their input and output count'' (Latour, p3).

It may not be obvious why I would draw my analysis from the history of science and technology. Aside from the clear importance of some of the innovations associated with the cellular prison, notably in mechanical systems and the use of iron, there are questions that seem to belong more to social or architectural history. I suggest two reasons for my choice: first, that the search for solutions to the problem of crime in nineteenth-century France was a quest for just such a mechanism or black box as could be set in motion like a machine, operating efficiently and trouble-free; and second, that despite failures and setbacks, there was a successful 'paradigm shift' (to borrow a term from another historian of science, Thomas Kuhn) in conceptions of crime and punishment, creating a new, more predictable kind of criminality that Michel Foucault (1979) has termed 'delinquency.' Thus, the first case calls for a technological metaphor, the second for a scientific one. More generally, we must view the cellular prison in its wider context of a nineteenth-century concern with innovation and progress. The best argument for using Latour's model is that the people we are studying considered themselves scientists and engineers of society, explaining and altering its nature, trying to make it work.

The spread of the cellular idea cannot be accounted for as a steady diffusion outward from centers of innovation. It was much too uneven a process, contested at every step. Indeed, Latour argues that the diffusion model is too simplistic to account for *any* adoption process, even one as apparently straightforward as electric power or the theory of relativity. Instead he proposes that the innovator engages in a process of 'translation,' whereby she persuades others that their interests will be served in adopting her black box without further question. Then, once convinced, these others must be controlled, so that their actions are predictable and continue to serve the innovator's purposes (Latour, p145-76).

Latour uses examples ranging from Pasteur's development of the microbe theory to the recent invention of the micro-computer. In each of these cases, it is not just that a concept or machine wins acceptance because it is true or it works; it is also that concepts become true, and machines functional, by being accepted. To create a successful black box is to work both inside and outside the laboratory to corral all the human and non-human resources necessary for its maintenance.

Rephrased in Latour's terms, then, the problem facing the French Interior Ministry in its standardization program was as follows: in order to make the cellular prison function as a black box whose inner workings were no longer open to question, the Ministry needed to translate its own interests into terms acceptable to the relevant political and social actors (the notion of translation is important in a literal sense here, as French was a second language in many regions until the twentieth century). The implications of this schema are particularly rich since, for the present context, 'relevant actors' would have to include not only officials and architects but the prisoners themselves. Without the cooperation of all, the program would be a failure, as by some accounts it was. Elements of persuasion, coercion and control were present all the way down the hierarchy, and were indeed part of the technology itself.

THE PROGRAM'S PROGRAM

In the discipline of architecture, the word 'program' is given a special meaning, that of a list of requirements to be fulfilled in the design of a building. In wider usage, the word refers to any set of structures and procedures intended to support a statement of policy, as in a 'government program' or a 'social program.' This double meaning belongs at the center of my discussion, because the case I present here was, in effect, both. Embedded in the policy statements of Interior Minister Duchâtel were strong implications for the architecture that might embody them; likewise, embedded in the architectural program for the new prisons were physical manifestations of the Ministry's social goals.

There isn't space enough in a short paper to reproduce the architectural program in its entirety. Following are some key passages, freely translated (Duchâtel, pp13-16):

> Article 1. ...The prison shall be surrounded...by two perimeter walls, entirely isolated from each other and from the prison building...
>
> Article 2. ...Each ordinary cell shall satisfy the following conditions: Dimensions: at least four meters long, 2.25 meters wide, three meters high; walls between cells to impede communication at normal volumes; a window high enough to keep the prisoner from looking out, without restricting the entry of daylight or air; some means of recirculating air without opening door or window, and without allowing communication between cells; some means for the prisoner to signal for a guard; some means for the prisoner to answer the call of nature without leaving the cell, or causing an undesirable odor; some means of communicating with the prisoner without opening the cell door; some means for a guard to observe the prisoner without being noticed; some means for prisoners to follow the religious services from within the cells [fig. 3]...; heating of the cells to a degree sufficient to prevent suffering from the cold...
>
> Article 11. ...The arrangement of buildings should allow the warden to observe, from a single point and without being noticed by the guards, all the different parts of the prison...
>
> Article 14. ...The architect should abstain entirely from anything which is only of an ornamental nature. He should similarly realize that he is not designing a monument to art. He should further keep in view that the good disposition of the buildings and the central point of surveillance allow him to dispense with that lavish employment of grillwork, of bolts, latches, and doors, of enormous walls that constituted the old-style prisons. He should, finally, build not only for the present, but also for the future, and allow for the addition of an upper floor should the need arise...
>
> Paris, August 9, 1841.
> [Interior Minister] T. DUCHATEL

It should be clear from the foregoing that the social and technological programs are inextricable. Each element cited has implications in the environments of policy-making, administration and building maintenance. In order for the black box to remain 'closed,'[3] i.e. successfully adopted, each guard, each warden, and each prisoner had to play his (or, rarely, her) part. Note, for instance, that the program assumes prisoners will not shout--how sure could anyone have been that they would not? But all this presumes that such a prison had actually been built. In a system of nearly 400 local prisons, only about 60 of these cellular prisons were constructed during the period I am discussing. For some understanding of this situation, we must look to the architects.

PARIS VS. THE PROVINCES

The architect most associated with the cellular prison was Guillaume-Abel Blouet, a Prix de Rome winner and member of the Conseil des Bâtiments Civils, France's elite advisory board for public architecture. It was his visit to the United States in 1836 (Demetz and Blouet) that had made detailed drawings of the American penitentiaries available in France. And it was he who had drawn the most influential of the model plans to go along with the ministerial program. Blouet was appointed to the Conseil as an expert, an event that signalled an evolution in the Conseil's role, from broad competence in technical, budgetary, and aesthetic matters toward a restriction to fewer domains. Indeed, soon after his dismissal in 1848, most functional criticism of public projects became the task of a more specialized committee of 'Administrative Service Inspectors' (Archives Nationales, F[21]1848).

Blouet was a member of a close-knit, privileged, Beaux-Arts-trained fraternity. Most provincial architects, on the other hand, were trained through apprenticeship or other practical experience. And most would still have held to the model of the architect as generalist, in contrast to Paris' developing culture of experts. Provincial architects' talents and aspirations varied, but resentment of Parisian hegemony was widespread. In a period when architects everywhere were beginning to organize as a profession, France's first professional organization, formed in Lyon in the late 1830s, was a direct attempt to weaken the power of Paris (Archives Nationales, F[21]1817). These architects correctly saw that the practice of sending Parisian architects out to design and supervise large provincial projects served not only to keep central control over construction budgets, but also to reinforce the secondary status of provincial architects. It would take a particularly adept 'translation' to convince them that their interests were being served.

Perhaps it is these tensions between center and periphery that gave rise to the curious mixture of messages in the architectural program. While, on the one hand, it is deliberately vague as to the means by which some of the provisions are to be satisfied (as in its use of the phrase 'some means of...'), this velvet glove of vagueness conceals an iron hand of specificity: there were in fact few alternatives for resolution of these details, and the opinions of experts were strong and well publicized. Blouet's accompanying drawings were closely emulated in many of the projects realized, at least where site dimensions permitted (fig. 1-3). When they did not follow Blouet's model, most cellular projects followed another highly-regarded model prison in Tours, in which Blouet's involvement was at least that of close advisor, if not designer. It seems that the choice for provincial architects was to adopt the black box whole or do nothing, and many chose the latter.

The program, viewed in this light, was for the provincial architect simply another chapter in the story of Parisian domination. Not only did its provisions leave little room for invention, but its Arcticle 14, by specifically proscribing ornament and the 'lavish employment' of materials, deprived him of any opportunity to show his talent or enhance his status. If we are tempted from our vantage point to see the program as an early statement of functionalism, or to fit it into the French 'rationalist' tradition, we must also try to see it as its audience did. For provincial architects, this particular exercise in translation would not have been convincing: not only would their interests not be served in adopting Blouet's black box--they would actively be undermined.

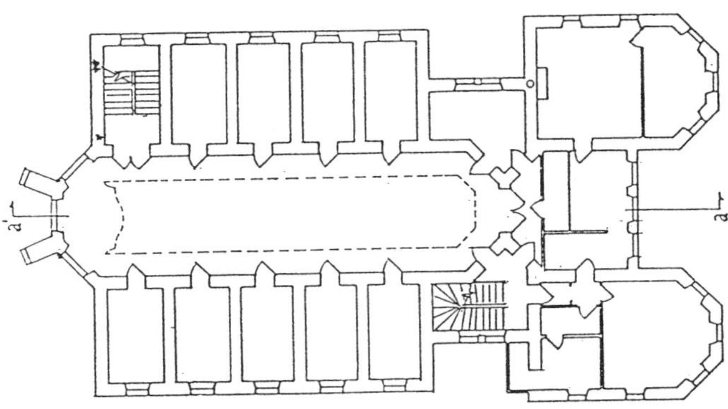

2. Second floor plan, Coulommiers Prison, as of 1986. Author's drawing.

1. Exterior view, Coulommiers Prison (1845-53, architect unknown). One of many projects that were virtual copies of Blouet's model designs for the 1841 program. Author's drawing.

3. Central 'nave' of cell block, Coulommiers Prison, showing altar at first gallery level. Cell doors all open toward the altar, and can be locked partly open to allow visual access to it. Author's photo.

CONCLUSION

Though another cellular standardization program was to be attempted in the 1870s, the first one was dismantled suddenly and definitively in 1853, by a brusque memo (Moreau-Christophe, pp285-6) from Persigny, a new Interior Minister under Napoleon III. Citing the resistance of provincial officials (and by implication, architects), budgetary constraints, and general non-compliance, Persigny declared a new era of penitentiary realism. Because those regions which had not built cellular prisons had likely done little or nothing to upgrade their prisons since the Napoleonic era, Persigny hoped that lowering the standards would induce them to do at least something. Most did not, and a modified cellular program of 1875 was another attempt to raise the ante.

The cellular prison steadfastly refused to become a black box. Instead, its complex inner workings were examined and criticized throughout the last half of the nineteenth century, securing its status as a compelling model with limited practical impact. In successive efforts to engineer its adoption, the French government decreed, cajoled and fumed while the provinces resisted, complained, and temporized. But the black box is nevertheless a useful metaphor for the prison: for most of us, as for most nineteenth-century French citizens, its inner workings remain obscure, but its input is well known and its output if anything more so.

NOTES

1. Most of the research for this paper, and for the dissertation of which it is a part, was undertaken with the assistance of the French Ambassador's Châteaubriand exchange program during academic year 1988-89.
2. I thank historian Robert L. Frost, of the State University of New York at Albany, for introducing me to Latour's work.
3. Though space does not allow me to discuss it here, I wish to note the interesting parallel between Latour's open/closed dichotomy and the "transparent/opaque" dimension discussed in Peter McCleary's article "Some Characteristics of a New Concept of Technology" (*Journal of Architectural Education*, Fall 1988, pp 4-9)

REFERENCES

Archives Nationales, Paris. Series F13 (*Travaux Publics*), F16 (*Prisons*), and F21 (*Beaux-Arts*).

Demetz, F. and Blouet, G.-A. *Rapport...sur les pénitenciers des Etas Unis*. Paris, 1837.

Duchâtel, T., Ministre de l'Intérieur [with G.-A. Blouet and others]. *Instructions et programme pour la construction des maisons d'arrêt et de justice. Atlas de plans de prisons cellulaires*. Paris, 1841.

Evans, Robin. *The Fabrication of Virtue: English Prisons, 1750-1850*. Cambridge U. Press, 1982.

Foucault, Michel. *Discipline and Punish: The Birth of the Prison*. Vintage Books, 1979 [orig. published as *Surveiller et Punir: Naissance de la prison*. Paris: Gallimard, 1975].

Latour, Bruno. *Science in Action: How to follow scientists and engineers through society*. Harvard, 1987.

Moreau-Christophe, M. *Code des Prisons ou Receuil Complet...Tome II. De 1846 à 1856*. Paris, 1856.

Pevsner, Niklaus. *A History of Building Types*. Princeton, 1976.

Van Zanten, David. *Designing Paris: The Architecture of Duban, Labrouste, Duc, and Vaudoyer*. MIT, 1987.

CHAPTER 5

Designing the Inaccessible Plaza

ANASTASIA LOUKAITOU-SIDERIS
University of California, Los Angeles

PRIVATIZATION OF PUBLIC SPACE: AN OVERVIEW

The privatization of public space, the passing over of its production, management and control to the private sector, is a relatively recent form of private involvement in public open space provision. Traditionally, public open spaces would be publicly acquired, created, owned, controlled and managed. They would be accessible to the public and available for individual or community activities (Scruton, 1984). In recent decades, however, the onus of providing public open space has been increasingly shifted to the private sector. In the 1970's and 1980's urban plazas built with private money, usually in downtown areas, became the modern American version of public space.

Public space privatization can be attributed to three interrelated factors:

a. The desire of the public sector to utilize private resources and find an alternative that could relieve its economic burdens and increasing financial retrenchments. Skyrocketing land values and construction costs, tax cuts and declining municipal revenues have resulted in the reluctance and inability of the public sector to maintain existing public spaces or create additional ones at a rate consistent with the growth and expansion of the urban population.

b. The responsiveness of the private sector to development incentives and its willingness to participate in "public-private partnerships" and incorporate public spaces within private development projects. The early New York precedent of incentive zoning was copied widely by other cities throughout the country in the 1970's and 1980's. Developers were quick to respond to the opportunities of incentive zoning and ensure increased floor area ratios of valuable commercial space in exchange for the provision of some public amenities. Developers also grasped the fact that the enrichment of their projects with public space could be profitable if the space was in close connection to commercial facilities and private services.

c. The existence of a market demand from certain sectors of the population for the facilities and services that the privatized settings have to offer. The "urban pathology" of traditional public spaces, the perception that such spaces represent the locus of urban problems, and the desire of the middle and upper classes to separate from treatening groups opened a market for privatized spaces.

Thus, increasingly in-town commercial developments are organized around interior or exterior courts, shopping plazas, and internal pedestrian "streets" and "boulevards." These spaces are supposed to be open and accessible to the general public. Most of the times, however, plazas provided by the private sector display symbolic and physical characteristics that are drastically different from traditional public settings (Loukaitou-Sideris, 1988). Their design and offered services are programmed to appeal to some segments of the public. These new forms of public environments tend to be subservient and an appendage to private purposes.

Control is the operating principle in privatized spaces. "Coercive" control targets the elimination of certain undesirable elements through the employment of private security officers and the use of regulations that prohibit certain things or allow them only after the issuance of permits, or through programming, scheduling and leasing. "Inducive" control focuses on symbolic restrictions through the lack of facilities that could appeal to certain people or encourage functions deemed undesirable (public restrooms, food vendors, sandboxes, etc.), and through the utilization of design cues that seek to achieve a "subtle closure" and a screening of the undesired elements.

Both types of control practices are exercised by the private producers and managers of privatized settings (Kim, 1987). However, in this paper I am particularly interested in exposing inducive control practices and more specifically exploring the role of architecture in the promotion of design cues that are consistent with the goals and purposes of private enterprise. My discussion will focus on two specific types of privatized space: the corporate plaza and the shopping plaza. During the last decade these two types have offered the most significant amounts of new public space in the downtown areas of American cities.

PUBLIC SPACE AS AN IMAGE GENERATOR: CORPORATE PLAZAS

The urban form and character of the American city has changed dramatically after the 1960's. Urban renewal schemes fueled by public and private capital, have left significant imprints, especially in downtown commercial districts. Whole city blocks, once occupied by a multitude of different shops and small buildings, gave way to corporate megastructures. Diverse and animated street life was replaced by inwardly oriented buildings with blank facades and segregated land uses. It has been argued that the memorable decline of the life and variety of urban streets has paralleled the rise of corporatist economy of the city, the shift from mostly small to mostly big business in the contemporary American capitalist economy after the second World War (Relph, 1987).

The rebuilding of central business districts has been assisted by corporate desires for high visibility, display of power, enhancement of image and identity and high returns on corporate ownership of central city real estate. Each new office tower represents a corporate flagship that demands recognition through prominent location, building height, distinctive or unique design. In this game of rivalry for power, public open space often has been perceived as a device for the enhancement of corporate image. Corporations saw in the legal mechanism of incentive zoning the possibility of increased real estate profits, but also the potential to use open space, so as to bring more prestige and invite more attention to their buildings.

Thus, in the last decades hundreds of plazas have been built in front of high-rise office towers, merely seeking to complement the buildings and accentuate their importance and self-assertion as unique elements within the surrounding city grid. The design of these plazas borrows heavily from the modernist doctrines. After all, the Modern Movement style dominated corporate building in America until quite recently.

A common plaza pattern is that of a rectangular area of concrete, with rectangular flower beds, fixed benches, a modern sculpture, perhaps some water element. Colors are drawn from a limited palette of dark grays or browns and pale greens. The fact that the plazas are built to satisfy some instincts for corporate power and grandeur leads often to the employment of some kind of abstract ornamentation, as a limited attempt to break away from the standardization and universality of the modernist design scheme. This usually takes the form of swirling whirlpools, concrete cliffs, or tumultuous cascades (Laurie, 1978).

The design of urban plazas needs also to convey the image of ''serious business.'' Hardscape materials are, thus, overwhelmingly preferred than softscapes, the latter being associated with messiness. Hardscape materials are also preferred as easier and cheaper to maintain. Most plaza layouts display formal, austere and rigid design. Nothing is left to chance or can be easily modified. Serious business atmosphere requires also the elimination of external distractions, the editing of the noise and dirt of the surrounding city. Design seeks to achieve a complete break from the outside environment, by producing corporate plazas which are introverted and zealously territorial. Control of access is obtained through a variety of design means: Enclosing walls, deemphasis of street level accesses, skyways, building of plazas above or below the street level. As Grady Clay (1987) suggested, corporate plazas represent ''zones of confinement,'' consciously designed to antagonize and rival the surrounding context and their competitor buildings.

In general, plaza design obeying the whims of corporate clients, produces an inflexible, sanitized, and ordered environment, which becomes incidental to mere beautification and image generation. The rigidity of design, that aspires to a certain level of monumentality, counteracts spontaneous and intimate use of space by the public. Created as by-products of private development, corporate plazas are more like public relations gestures than urban spaces intended for use (Jensen, 1979). Signs of ''no drinking,'' ''no littering and loitering,'' ''no tresspassing,'' combined with the more subtle but equally effective design features mentioned above send clear messages to potential users.

PUBLIC SPACE AS A CONSUMER GOOD: SHOPPING PLAZAS

The idea of inserting a shopping plaza into urban rather than suburban contexts was initiated after certain shifts occurred in development trends and important zoning incentives were offered to private developers. City planners saw in retail the opportunity to revitalize downtowns, developers the potential for profit. The attraction for developers was heightened by the increasing saturation of the suburban market and the largely unexploited purchasing potential of the downtown white-collar office worker. Thus, in the 1980's many downtown development projects included commercial facilities which were surrounding plazas and courts and were linked by pedestrian paths.

Let us examine some of the purposes and objectives of the private enterprise as related to shopping plazas and see how these are served through design.

Shopping plazas are there to serve the consumer, to attract the public, expose it to an array of goods and services. But not all potential users are welcome. The development of shopping plazas is based on the ''target group'' concept. These settings aspire to fulfill the needs and values of only the part of the public that is most likely to consume the private services offered. The rest are undesirable elements. From personal interviews with developers, managers and security guards of many new plazas in Los Angeles it became quite clear that the undesirable population includes not only criminals, drug dealers or dangerous individuals, but also harmless derelicts and homeless, ''bag ladies,'' ''hippies,'' street vendors and musicians, noisy teenagers and children, and in general anyone who does not conform with the management's standards of appropriateness, or whose presence might damage the image of a clean, "proper" and safe environment (Loukaitou-Sideris, 1988).

In order to serve the purposes of the developer design most often aspires to create settings for an exclusive class of consumers. Chic architecture, stylish and highly ornamental materials intend to attract, impress and at the same time promote the feeling of affluence in a materialistic, capitalist society. Many new shopping plazas are dressed with a postmodern costume. The stylishness, superficiality and impression of affluence that postmodernism seeks to achieve as an aesthetic result blend well with the purposes of commercial enterprises (Benson, 1987). Shopping plaza postmodernism uses a pastiche of colors, stylish and decorative materials (marble, travertine, brick, stone, chrome, brass) and design elements borrowed from various styles. This type of design treats space as a commodity to be consumed. In an attempt to make the design product all the more appealing for the targeted consumers architects often reproduce parts of settings from popular places of the world. In general, the layout and design of shopping plazas attempts to create and enhance several purposes:

A FANTASY-ORIENTED ENVIRONMENT is created through design so as to support the shopping-as-an-entertainment theme. Projects are injected with themes that aspire to keep the public entertained and amused. These can take the form of Italian piazzetas, exotic landscapes with palm-tree vegetation, country-western motifs, or images from "small-town, U.S.A." Design emphasizes a strong element of escapism from reality and messy details of everyday life are carefully edited from view. It has been actually argued that his type of public space represents an idealized projection and version of the public realm, an optimal image of urban life (Dale and Pieprz, 1986).

A GOOD-BUSINESS ATMOSPHERE is a prerequisite for good business. Developers want the plazas to be perceived as both attractive and safe. All uncertain and unwanted elements that trouble traditional public spaces are eliminated or screened (noise, traffic, violence, ugly surroundings). A high degree of control allows the monitoring of activities, events and type of clientele. The public space of plazas is orchestrated in such ways so as to be viewed passively. Nothing encourages spontaneous initiatives. Circulation elements are so arranged to induce the user to move past the maximum number of shop frontages. Seating is often under private jurisdictions, associated with food establishments, cafes and delicacy stores.

INTROVERSION AND INWARD-ORIENTATION characterizes most shopping plazas. Their public space is often surrounded by blank walls and impenetrable street frontages. Not much of the exterior gives a clue to the space within. Major entrance points to the plazas are usually through parking structures. Doorways and openings that provide a direct link to the streets are systematically deemphasized. As with corporate plazas the intention of design is to create a sharp contrast between the grey exterior space and the bright interior courts and atria.

EPILOGUE

Privatized spaces such as corporate and shopping plazas have become in the 1980's an artificial substitute of the public realm (Goldberger, 1989). Developers are given bonuses to create public places for the benefit of the public at large. But only a selected part of the public actually uses these spaces. Plazas are characterized as more successful if they bring certain parts of the public in, but also if they can keep other parts of the public out. This is in reality a stratified success, since it does not cut across class lines (Stephens, 1978). The cross section of the public that uses them is quite skewed with more higher-income people, more professional white-collar adult population, and fewer blue-collar workers, fewer minorities, children and elderly (Loukaitou-Sideris, 1988). Very few of these spaces provide the appropriate settings for children to run freely, couples to lie on the grass, big groups to congregate and picnic.

The visual language of design and architecture is often utilized to promote cues consistent with the purposes and goals of commercial or corporate developers. The design characteristics commonly present in urban plazas built under private auspices, are introversion, fragmentation, escapism, orderliness, and design rigidity. These are congruent with private objectives for control, protection, social filtering, image generation, elimination of external distractions, and manipulation of user behavior.

Clearly privatization of public open space is not the architect's fault or responsibility. It is a result of major social, economic and political events that have colored the American urban context in the last decades. However, it is quite obvious that architecture has chosen to take sides with the developer, the "nominal client" so to speak, rather than with the general public, its "substantive client," to draw on the distinction suggested by Mera (1967). The social role of the profession has been conveniently forgotten, in light of generous commissions by developers. Architects seem to have become more and more ignorant and disconnected from the larger social problems facing the city. As Paul Goldberger (1989), the New York Times architectural critic, complains, the recognition that architecture cannot solve all urban problems is seen as justification for saying that social problems are therefore not architecture's concern at all. Gone, of course, are the heroic days when architects with manifestos and polemics were ready to change the world. Today they know better. But are they ready to succumb to a servant's role? Or is it more worthy and socially responsible to search for ways that the profession can make the public environment of the city a better place for all segments of the public?

REFERENCES

Benson, R. (1987), ''Regional Shopping Malls and the Future of Public Architecture,'' in *Common Ground: The Built Forms of Public Life*, Proceedings of ACSA, Ames Iowa.

Clay, G. (1987), ''Why Don't We Do It in th Road?,'' *Planning*, Vol 53, No 5, pp.18-21.

Dale, J., Pieprz, D. (1986), ''Sunday Architecture,'' *Space and Society*, Vol 30, December, pp.18-29.

Goldberger, P. (1989), ''Beyond Utopia: Settling for a New Realism: Can Architects Serve the Public Good,'' *The New York Times*, Sunday, June 25, 1989.

Jensen, R. (1979), ''Dreaming of Urban Plazas,'' in *Urban Open Spaces*, New York: Cooper-Hewitt Museum.

Kim, J. (1987), ''Public Processes and Private Influence: Privatization of Public Open Space,'' in *Common Grounds: The Built Forms of Public Life*, Proceedings of ACSA, Ames, Iowa.

Laurie, I. (1978), ''Overdesign Is the Death of Outdoor Liveliness,'' *Landscape*, Vol. 39, November, pp.485-486.

Loukaitou-Sideris, A. (1988), *Private Production of Public Open Space: The Downtown Los Angeles Experience*, Ph.D. dissertation, University of Southern California.

Mera, K. (1967), ''Consumer Sovereignty in Urban Design,'' *Town Planning Review*, Vol. 37, No 4, pp.305-312.

Relph, E. (1987), *The Modern Urban Landscape*, Baltimore: The Johns Hopkins University Press.

Scruton, R. (1984), ''Public Space and the Classical Vernacular,'' *The Public Interest*, No 74, Winter, pp.5-16.

Stephens, S. (1978), ''Introversion and the Urban Context,'' *Progressive Architecture*, Vol 59, No 12, December, pp.49-69.

CHAPTER 6

The Construction Drawings of a Blind Architect

MARCO FRASCARI
University of Pennsylvania

This is a tale, a philosophical short story. It is a fable narrating of a born-blind architect and of her construction drawings. This is a technological tale, an allegory showing how imagination operates in architecture.

THE STORY OF CAPO MAESTRA

> "... architecture has limits--and when we *touch* the *invisible* walls of the limit, then we know more about what is contained in them."[1]

The name of our virtuous hero is Capo Maestra.[2] She was born ''three hundred miles and more from Chimborazo, one hundred from the snows of Cotopaxi, in the wildest wastes of Equator Andes. There lies that mysterious mountain valley cut off from the world ... the Country of the Blind.''[3] When Capo started to study architecture she knew that the prospect of becoming a successful architect was nearly impossible. She had realized that the proverb stating ''In the Country of the Blind the One-eyed Man is King'' was the leading principle in the profession of architecture, a profession where most of the judging was done from the monocular point of view of the brilliant colors of a CAD.[4] She also knew a utopian and amazing short story written by H.G. Wells. In this fiction,[5] by putting his finger on the problem of a language dominated by visual metaphors, Wells has demonstrated that in the lost Nation of the Blind the two-eyed man is not better than a one eyed man. A non-blind man has an unformed mind, a terrible disability which can be cured only by making him a visionless person.[6] The fashionable dean of a major technological school in the Southern part of the States turned her application down when Capo asked to be admited to the college of architecture. Nevertheless she felt that her dream could become real and she keept on studying architecture as an autodidact. Volunteers read on tape for her the writings of the great autodidacts of architecture, Leon Battista Alberti, Francesco di Giorgio, Filarete, Francesco Colonna, Daniele Barbaro, Vincenzo Scamozzi, Ribart de Chamoist and L.I. Kahn. From listening to their words Capo learned that the symbolic dimension of architecture always originates in its instrumental representations, which are haptic demonstrations. She learned that when properly understood, these pedestrian representations are powerful technological figures. These are metaphorical representations displaying streams of images, which are able to elicit feelings. Capo also learned that technological representations are regarded as a necessary but not important part of the architectural process, since many professionals farm out their construction drawings, as a mundane production. In their offices, they produce only design and presentation drawings. In the country of the blind, however, presentation and design drawings do not exist, since blind persons merely feel the architecture around them by inhabiting it.[7] Capo learned that the world as perceived by vision and the world as perceived by touch are equally valid, equally rich, but they are by no means identical. She knew that blind people do not have abnormal sensitivity to sounds and touches, but simply they perceive things that go unnoticed by the visual person.[8] Paying close attention to certain types of sensory information, it is possible to notice things that the others miss. Recognizing subtle differences between stimuli that are confused by the seeing others, a blind person perceives obstacles and objects up to several meters. [9]

From listening the word of the philosopher George Berkeley, Capo Maestra learned that touch is the only sense that provides the mind with spatial information. Vision is a learned ability which is initially dependent on a haptic space perception. The dominant aspects of haptic perception are three. The first one is an emphasis on substance and shape properties rather than on form. The second is based on the integration of successive impressions, and the third is the ability to capitalize on the mobility of the hand and the body.[10] In her practicing of architecture, Capo Maestra draws tactile pictures embossing wet paper. She designs by drawing only sections and plans which, by the way, are horizontal sections. She feels her designs, but the visual architects sees only the shadows of them. Based on ''feeling'' her construction drawings are a technological procedure where constructing and construing merges. In these representations are embodied technological thoughts which do not see but feel the architecture which is around them. From this point of view, feeling has a cognitive dimension which can be expressed in drawings outlining the construction of buildings.[11] In her drawings the world as perceived by vision and the world as perceived by touch are integrated in a technological fiction; her drawing fingers do the walking.

Construction drawings, the graphic expression of technology, are the basis of architectural imagination and of its constructive reality since feeling as Ricour has pointed out, "... have a very complex kind of intentionality. ... Feeling is not contrary to thought It is thought made ours."[12] Technological thought finds its poetic expression in this feelings which are then demonstrated in a set of construction drawings, an assimilation of the constructed world. In their embossed drawings blind people use metaphorical devices, such as drawing a wheel with curved spokes to show that is rolling or a man with very long legs to show that a man is running. For them drawing is not simply a way of duplicating objects but a way of expressing ideas. In construction drawings lines stands for visible and invisible edges. These are physiognomic outline drawings which cannot be visually perceived but can be tactually perceived by blind people.

Horizontal and vertical sections are one of architecture's most puzzling enigmas. Plans and sections present the entire building by simplifying its reality, yet at the same time, they manifest a more complete view of the building's interacting parts by showing more of what is visible. A section presents the invisible aspect of architecture, representing an original in a way which can never be seen. In a section, the building's technological nature is manifested in a outline: three-dimensional extensions are represented on a two-dimensional plane.

The content of the section incorporates that which is present in the visible building, but is itself invisible. Metaphorically speaking, the drawing of a section represents the coalescence of architectural imagining. Architects can draw a section of a building just by walking through it; they reconstruct the section of a demolished structure; or they can devise a section for a future building. The common denominator in all these graphic procedures is the making visible of that which is invisible. Through a peculiar and curious procedure of de-composition, selection and re-composition, through a polysemic use of simple marks on paper architects use a game to trace rooms whose functions become self-evident in the composition of the section. Sections guide the construction of a building as well as the construing of it as it is, will be, or has been. Sections make apparent the rooms' spatial relations, which will never actually be seen in the constructed building. A section presents the inner and outer spaces simultaneously and reveals the many temporal sequences of architectural perception. The building is represented in its entirety but there is no likeness between a sectional representation and the original, the section produces it poetically. It is in this poetic dimension that the enigmatic beauty of the section lays. In it is embodied the emotions of architecture.

A trivial psychology of feelings make us to talk of emotions a bodily disturbances. The reality is that by emotions we live our body in a more intense way, we are under the spell of it. We emotionally undertand architecture by moving through it and the schema of it is drawn by the hands in a design. "Feelings complete imagination in the act of schematization. This schematization is an insight in the like and unlike proper to similarity." Capo's drawings are not simulations of construction, but rather "predicative assimilation."[13]

When she goes on the site to feel how the work is constructed her long white cane becomes in her gloved hands the measuring rod of the Gothic master builder, a tool for helping her imagination to draw the two modalities of technoloqgical association: contiguity (metonomy) and similarity (metaphor).[14]

> Now hear how light and shade should be used in order to show a thing in a drawing... . When you draw a thing, you have only the form of that thing. Then you must study it carefully part by part, as light *touches* it ...[15]

But this is another story.

NOTES

1. L.I.Kahn, *What Will Be Has Always Been*, p.89; my italics.
2. "Who wants to express the power of the said name in vernacular, he will say chief-mistress (capo-maestra) ... the dignity of architecture is close to wisdom: and as heroic virtue she dwells among all the arts ..." Daniele Barbaro, *I Dieci Libri dell'Architettura di M.Vitruvio, tradutti e commentati da Monsig. Daniele Barbaro*, Marcolini, Venice 1556, p.7, 1.58.
3. H.G. Wells,"The Country of the Blind," *28 Science Fiction Stories of H.G. Wells*, New York, Dover, n.d..
4. Brunelleschi was the one who really started this one-eyed vision of architecture by designing the Baptistery in front of Santa Maria Novella, using a peep hole. However, he warned us by having a philosophical novel telling us of a practical joke he played on his friend, the Fat Carpenter (*Il Grasso Legnaiuolo*).
5. *Fictor cum dicit fingo figura imponit* (The image maker when he says I shape puts a figure on the thing), Varro, *De Lingua Latina* 6.78.
6. At first the valley was open to the world and several families of Peruvian half-bread came here seeking refuge from a tyrannic Spanish ruler. However, a few years after their settling, a geological event cut off the valley from the rest of the world. All the inhabitants are blind, since after their separation from the world a disease broke out and blindness became hereditary. "They forgot many things; they devised many things," and they built a city to fit their condition. Only one man is said to have visited the country, which he arrived

in by accident. When he realized that everybody in that valley was blind, he thought he could become the king of the country because of the obvious advantage of having eyesight. In reality that was quite an handicap and he had to run away before they could blind him to make him ''normal.''

7. As Benjamin traces in his discussion of the role of a work of art in the age of mechanical reproduction, architecture is appropriated by habit in a twofold manner--by touch (use) and by vision (perception). As the making of buildings has become increasingly a complex technical enterprise, professionals have become increasingly isolated in their designs, both from the bodily presence and the embodiment of human habits in edifices. They are only interested in what Benjamin called a tourist appreciation of architecture. (Walter Benjamin ''The Work of Art in the Age of Mechanical Reproduction,'' *Illumination*, New York, Harcourt, 1969 pp. 240-241) Professionals are not interested in the tactile and invisible dimensions of architecture; for them, the visible range is dominant, since it is the only one which can be photographed and used for increasing the range of their market potential; they forget that, as Loos pointed out, good architecture cannot be photographed. The photographic presentation of buildings on the pages of magazines and newspapers does indeed make the market for architectural services more effective. It would seem that this effectiveness is valid whether or not the professional knows anything about the theory of architecture, and even at times whether or not they know why the designed solution works. The image of the buildings devised in the professional's practicing of architecture is a finished image like the current image of the human body. This image of the body does not have any ambiguity in it. The beginning is the beginning and the end is the end. No sign of the lower stratum or of the corporeal functions is visible in this deodorized and untouchable body image. The origin of this conception is in the Neoclassical image of the body. It is like a sculpture of Canova, where no part or member is shown in its carnal nature, none of the excrescences and orifices are demonstrated on the finite surface of this absolute body which can be nude but not naked. The image of the buildings devised by the professor in his practice of architecture is an unfinished image like that of the grotesque body. The basis of the grotesque imagery is a special concept of the body as a whole and of the limits of this whole. In grotesque architecture, the *limina* between bodies and buildings differ sharply from the Neoclassical models as well as from the naturalistic picture of the human body. The grotesque body is a body in the act of becoming. It is never finished, never completed; it is continually built, continually created; and it is the principle of others bodies. It is a body which can only be understood in the pitch-dark of a grotto. The logic of a grotesque image ignores the smooth and impenetrable surface of the Neoclassical bodies, and magnifies only excrescences and orifices, which lead into body's depths. The outward and inward details are merged. Moreover, the grotesque body swallows and it is swallowed by the world. This takes place in the openings and the boundaries, and beginning and end are closely linked and interwoven.

8. Hollins Mark. *Understanding Blindness*. Hillsdale, Laurence Erlbaum Associates, 1989, p.43.

9. Hollins Mark. *idem* p.46-47. This is the so called obstacle sense. A naming devised by Diderot, the 17th century encyclopaedist, called this sense ''facial vision,'' and thought was based on a detection of air currents, a 1940 Cornell University study demonstrated hearing provides the mainstay of obstacle sense.

10. Hollins Mark. *op. cit.* p.46. & p.59

11. John M. Kennedy, ''What Can We Learn about Pictures from the Blind.'' *American Scientist*, 71, Jan-Feb 1983, pp. 19-26.

12. Paul Ricour, ''The Metaphorical Process as Cognition Imagination and Feeling,'' *Critical Inquiry*, 5, Autumn 1978, p.156.

13. Paul Ricour, *idem*. p. 155-157.

14. Roman Jakobson (''Two Aspects of Langauge and Two Types of Aphatic Disturbances,'' *Fundamentals of Language*, The Hague: Mounton, 1956, pp. 239-259), in a seminal study, reduces the system of tropes to two which then he organizes on the two fundamental axis of language: the paradigmatic and the syntagmatic axis. Metaphor is a substitution done on the paradigmatic axes *in absentia*, whereas metonymy is a substitution done on the syntagmatic axes *in presentia*. This theorization was drawn by Jakobson in discussing the two tropes--metaphor and metonimy--on the observation of two types of aphatic disturbances of language. Aphasia is a loss of using of words resulting from a brain lesion. Apraxia is a loss of object manipulation developing also from a brain lesion. Following Jakobson's indication, a similar theorization is possible for the objects of architecture, considering two types of space disturbances, the constructive and distributive apraxias.

15. Filarete, alias Antonio Averlino, *Trattato d'Architettura*, Milano, Polifilo, 1961; my italics.

CHAPTER 7

Drawing Out of Architecture

JAMES P. WILLIAMSON
Georgia Institute of Technology

The authority of artists or architects with regard to their work (drawing, painting, building) has been assumed. Indeed, society often favors the signature, and we require by law that architects pay for a stamp and brand their drawings signifying as much as the signature the authorship and authority which they exert as producer. The drawing, as artifact, has been forgotten as the place where the architect operates; the drawing is the space of the poetic act of architecture. If, however, we consider the authority of the architect as subsumed by the authenticity of the drawing, then drawing is no longer a neutral representation or artifact. We might make note that both words, authority and authenticity derive from the Greek *auth* or one who acts on his own authority and are akin to the Sanskrit word *asus* meaning life, especially of the soul.[1] This non-neutrality initiates a series of hermeneutic circles which elicit the dismantling of current practices in both the production and use of architectural drawings. This dismantling has a rich heritage which was manifested in both art and architecture in the twentieth century.

Twentieth century art, in particular early twentieth century painting, revolutionized pictorial representation by advancing an art and an attitude toward artistic production in reaction to (and out of) a critique of perspectival and instrumental modes of spatial and pictorial representation. One of the legacies of this extraordinary event is the liberation of the artist from an assumed loyalty to certain conventions and, more importantly, the liberation of the ambiguous and contradictory--if not often *non-sensible*--space of representation. Among these conventions one finds depictions of the world and experience faithful to objective, scientistic, and *realistic* codes of representation. Artists, coming to the realization that these were neither sufficient nor relative to their experience of the modern world, reacted by questioning these conventions. Consequently, these codes, (perspective and projective systems and notions which are faithful *to how the world looks*) were found to have little grounding in one's experience, especially when that experience was indexed to the modern world. Thus, artists reacted by ignoring, inverting, denying, and subverting the conventions. Through the reactions, however, a perhaps unforeseen phenomenon occurred; drawing opened up to criticism, to science, to psychoanalytical readings, to memory, to dream, to apparently meaningless gestures, to the ambiguity of spatial and temporal relationships and a new body of work was created.

It is inaccurate to suggest that modernism presents a consistent body of work. We cannot point to a Modernist Manifesto; however, we cannot deny that there was a phenomenon which unveiled with the reinventions, reaction and reappropriation of pictorial representation as an engagement of surface or page that is plastic and open to any kind of interpretation. This *plasticity of the surface* opens up the drawing to an unusually rich realm of interpretation, and ultimately implicates the artist, viewer and the drawing in a complex hermeneutic. *The mode no longer has authority, but the artist assumes that authority.* Blanchot gives us the consequence of these phenomena when he states: "The image requires the neutrality and the effacement of the world, it wants everything to return to the indifferent depth where nothing is affirmed, it inclines towards the intimacy of what still continues to exist in the void; its truth lies there."[2] Blanchot's notion of the truth of the drawing also reminds us of the paradox which forms as a result of the artist or architect assuming authority. Once the artist takes hold of drawing again so that mode no longer constrains or operates as authority, the artist's authority demands a relinquishing of authority, yet another opening up; it is an authority which allows the relinquishing of authority. This paradox then reveals to us one of the hermeneutic acts to which I am referring. Or, in Marcel Duchamp's words: " All in all, the creative act is not performed by the artist alone; the spectator brings the work in contact with the external world by deciphering and interpreting its inner qualifications and thus adds his contribution to the creative act. This becomes even more obvious when posterity gives its final verdict and sometimes rehabilitates forgotten artists."[3] We have a world where the interpreter's role within a Peircean triangle gives way to both imaginary constructions and constructions of the imagination.

We have been describing the revolution in modern painting; however, in what we might call early modern architecture this also occurs. It is neither a late development nor latent revolution, architecture is part of the complex, coincidental and coimplicative; architects engage in the revolt with as much vigor as the artists. The phenomenon manifests in architecture in the constructivists drawings, in de Stijl, or in the paintings of Le Corbusier. However, the consequences for building have not been explicit to date. It has seemed enough to know that the plasticity of the surface was also occurring in modern architecture. But in considering early modern architecture, we can see the impact of constructions of the imagination upon architecture is significant in many ways, and for the purposes of this presentation, most importantly upon the constitution of a construction drawing in architecture and in a change in the role of drawing and technology or the process of building.

The constructions of the imagination which then form construction drawings from which a building may (or may not) be constructed are still too often thought of as representations which must conform to building standards. What we inherit from the modern movement is that the drawing must be thought of not as a representation but as an authentic technology whose ambiguity, plasticity and openness must be embraced by the building. To think otherwise is to revert to the closure of the reading of drawings. We can consider two noteworthy constructions which would not have been possible without the hermeneutic engagement of the drawings. Hoesli's work on the purist painting of Le Corbusier, shows a direct relationship to the Villa Stein. Another example involves the preparatory drawings (as well as the unassociated abstractions) of Rietveld's that lead up to the Schroeder House. The drawings refer specifically to the house and the de stijl style--the spatial relationships inherent the painting are played out in the house.

These are two isolated, though not sole, examples which are indeed constructions of the imagination. The point being made is that without the architect's willingness to engage in the plasticity of space and suspend the conventional drawing to building process, without the suspension of the realist images' privilege within the process of architecture and the willingness to allow image making or drawing to open up the drawing of architecture to the same artistic possibility (sensuality, psychoanalysis, dream) and possibility of nonsense initiated by the modernists, these projects could not have been possible. In other words, without the willingness to engage architecture with the same openness and the impossibilities of architecture in drawing, then the buildings, the Schroeder House and the Villa Stein, would not be. Suddenly the drawing as an ambiguous, open vague, contradictory signification has both authenticity and authority. The architect is no longer authority over the drawing...the drawing is set free and in this negative freedom a new hermeneutic has taken shape. Other architects who have understood this hermeneutic include Carlo Scarpa and Mies van der Rohe. Scarpa's sketches and van der Rohe's collages demonstrate how the traditional role of the drawing which describes a building to be constructed reverses; architectural drawings seen as imaginary constructions and as constructions of the imagination present a drawing which the building must faithfully embrace in all of its ambiguous and (imag)inary wealth. This, of course, then requires a very different understanding of and approach to construction drawings in architecture.

This different approach to construction drawings grows out of those architects' work such as Corbusier's paintings and Rietveld's abstract drawings. When we realize that we can call these construction drawings, and that after executing the drawings and then setting these drawings free from authority, we can understand that the architect upon deciding to build, engages in yet another hermeneutic. He or she now engages in the construction of imagination as the hermeneutic act of building;, the architect takes up the role as interpretant. In the buildings we have discussed thus far, Rietveld and Le Corbusier discarded the mask of architect/ image maker and embraced the ambiguity of the drawings in order to execute faithfully a building which could indeed issue from such construction documentation or drawings.

We might now consider a contemporary architect. John Hejduk's recent work reveals a man whom I believe has fully inherited these ideas and extended them not just to drawings but to the notations of drawings as well--we have constructions of words and images. To give them a historical modern base, there are drawings and disassociated narratives not at all unlike the sketches and notes for the Large Glass of Marcel Duchamp. We have a construction of words, the actual construction itself, and the drawings all of which operate within the same sphere.

Hejduk invents an architectural program through telling stories: by making a fluid construction of words and images, thereby rejecting orthodox functionalist programming. Words become eponyms as well as truncated narratives and are then identified with images. When he constructs this kind of program, he builds a myth and this myth becomes a new language for the program in which the various subgroups of characters within the fable can be named like the various characters in a small town. When one engages this new language as program, constituted by an infinite complexity of morphological and visual elements, one must acknowledge that there resides in it a certain enigmatic quality that relies more on what is *not* said in the text than what is said. The hermeneutic circle opens. When one looks at the Masque projects, the real myth that is fabricated resides less in the specifics of the text (words, images and narratives) than in the imaginative space that exists between them and the interpretant. They myth distorts and displaces, but it does not disappear. It creates a space that is activated and produced through one's participation in the *presented fragmentary world*. A threshold is created at which we must pause and reflect. There is neither a fabrication of mixed metaphors, nor references, nor the simple integration of narratives and design constructions; but all of these things constituted at once so none is the sole embodiment. "They exist nowhere, yet they have created their place....they are liveable because they use imageable things--things with direct associations, memories, thoughts impressions, etc." [4] in a construction of the imagination.

These things and construction of the imagination are coupled with a kind of new drawings which he has provided in some of the mask projects which he calls x-ray drawings. We can draw from Hejduk's own writings to enhance our understanding of his notion of the task of the architect and drawing.

> 1 That architectural tracings are apparitions, outlines, figments. They are not diagrams but ghosts. 2 Tracings are similar to X-rays, they penetrate internally. 3 Erasures imply former existences. 4 Drawings and tracings are like the hands of the blind touching the surfaces of the face in order to understand a sense of volume, depth and penetration. 5 The lead of an architect's pencil disappears (drawn away) metamorphoses. To take a site: present tracings, outline, figments, apparitions, X-Rays of thoughts. Meditations on the sense of erasures. To fabricate a construction of time. To draw out by compacting in. To flood (liquid densification) the place-site with missing letters and disappeared signatures. To gelatinize forgetfulness.[5]

These x-ray drawings are those in which plan, elevation and section are superimposed upon one another to exist simultaneously on the surface. The form, an (imag)inary construction is plastic, open to interpretation and the project resides mostly in drawing. The narratives and drawings form an architecture of psychic geo\graphy.

In order to enter the hermeneutic of an architecture of psychic geo\graphy, "...one moves in and out of imaginative absorption...One abandons the imaginative mode from time to time to reflect on the work and one's response to it." [6] It is only in giving way of the architect's authority over drawing that there can be any hope for the future of architecture. It becomes crucial for the mode of representation to be evaluated and understood and for new modes of representation to be allowed in order for architecture to sustain itself. Further, as the interpreter's for architecture to be built, we must engage in hermeneutics of the drawing and in their extraordinary reality--in the words of Octavio Paz in their *radical strangeness.* If we don't allow architecture and ourselves to break out of the chains of realistic representation, then the drawn original can never appear original, because it will itself be a metaphor in the process.

NOTES

1. Eric Partridge, *Origins: A Short Etymological Dictionary of Modern English* (New York: Greenwich House, 1983) 33.
2. Maurice Blanchot, *The Gaze of Orpheus*, trans. Lydia Davis, ed. P. Adams Sitney (Barrytown, NY: Station Hill, 1981) 79.
3. Craig E. Adcock, *Marcel Duchamp's Notes form the Large Glass: An N-Dimensional Analysis* (Ann Arbor: UMI Research Press, 1983) 8.
4. Raoul Bunschoten, "oTOTEMan or 'He is my Relative'," *AA Files*, 13 (1986): 73-82.
5. John Hejduk, *Victims* (London: Architectural Association, 1986) 3.
6. David Novitz, *Knowledge, Fiction & Imagination* (Philadelphia: Temple University Press, 1987) 85.

CHAPTER 8

Automatic Determinism or the Devil in Mr. Meyer

PRESCOTT MUIR
University of Utah

In Robert McCarter's essay "Escape from the Revolving Door,"[1] he suggests that the appropriate resolution to the insoluble opposition between the technological and the architectural can be found within marginalized practices, which implies the intellectual higher ground. This is a proposition that the only appropriate resistance to the vicissitudes of production can be sustained from a level of cultural simulation extant in an avant-garde or the parasociety of the academy. McCarter's position constitutes a perpetuation of the mystique of an aesthetic spirit separated from work.

Gropius's Bauhaus model was to find a structural field for the social intervention of art. The idealized proposition posited an integration between the spirit of inspiration and the praxis of implementation. Hannes Meyer, while endorsing the deterministic aspect of industrialization, exposed the impossibility of such a merger, at least as formulated by Gropius. A marginalized practice demonstrates, if not a total disengagement, then a visceral relationship with social and evolutionary processes.

Mimicry of invention and production is arguably a greater concession to the consumptive pressure of capital than the historical process of technique and the formulation of a popularized artifact. Mary McLeod's assessment of the current architectural condition, although singling out deconstructivism, could be applied to a neo-machine aesthetic. "Decomposition lacks the faith in social regeneration that the modern movement had . . .emphasizes formalism which makes Russian constructivism as a source with its political and social programs incredibly ironic."[2] The current regeneration of the Rousseauian myth of a rarified object of inspiration justified by the isolated suffering of genius has assumed the level of parody. In its attempt to reconcile the critique of the avant-garde with the cultural determinism of his time, the work of Meyer should be measured against the current debate.

The harsh treatment of Meyer by the myth of modernism was the result of Gropius's desire to codify the representation of his position and thus mobilize capital in pursuit of career enhancement. Gropius wrote "Meyer was a treacherous character which I did not recognize . . .his downfall was his denying of art as such,"[3] or at least his denying of the myth that Gropius had perpetuated. Meyer's work was characterized as the heretical fringe. Yet, in reality, the work was inexorably linked through the positions of the avant-garde in response to the social upheavals of the period. The work, in responding to the rapidity of social transformation, was the more normative position than one conditioned by media-engendered image making.

Meyer's position is a unique mix of Goethe naturalism motivated by proletarian incentives balanced by a predilection toward an intellectual critique of the political and aesthetic avant-garde. Meyer faced the dilemma of determining a socialist position within a capitalist society.[4] Medieval architecture was an example of the return to authenticity based on the "cooperative character of medieval guilds. . .in order to understand [and absorb the new] functional forms of the middle ages."[5] Scholarship at the turn of the century supported the assumption of a collaborative medieval building industry. A collaborative utilitarianism, as formulated by Pugin and as implemented by Morris without the religious ideology, became a discretionary restraint on the perceived breach between capital and its social contract. The disjuncture between object and its determinant process could be closed by a return, albeit naive, to craft. If the worker could only get his hands (literally forced, as Loos would have it) into the industrial process, then the loss of a responsive product and a quality 'work' could be reconciled.

The myth of a preindustrial organic social harmony would be used to impede industrialization. "At best their [Morris's] work could be valued for achieving an appropriate relation between the character of a product and the process that had produced it."[6] Yet Morris's position denied the inclination toward standardization and the effects of Taylorization on the craft persona. So on the one hand Morris subscribed to a natural determinism of labor, while still insisting on the autonomy of intuitive spirit. The Arts and Crafts movement actually perpetuated the schism it attempted to close.

Art Nouveau sustained the disjuncture by its insistence on

"the ideal of a holistic Nietzchean artistic culture to be set against the [further] advance of a positivist scientific civilization."[7] The advancement of a positivistic production process continued its linear course immune to much deflection from the `higher ground' of the avant-garde, which personified the aspirations of the 19th century middle class. Whereas Morris was able to influence an early industrialism by establishing a standard for quality, Art Nouveau was hopelessly out of synchronization with a more sophisticated industrialization and thus relegated to iconography and ultimately was consumed as image. The permutation of intent reinforced the vulnerability of the intellectual position.

The divergent positions of critique and praxis were to reach a stage of catharsis in the Dessau Bauhaus and the comparable workshops of the Moscow Vkhatemas. The crisis of the Constructivist experience was an aberration of the dilemma, "a model based upon the legitimacy of form derived from craft, craftsman engendered process and it disenfranchised feudal labor pool with the prospect of a mature Western industrialization."[8]

Loos posed the first sustainable opposition to the eccentric proposition of Art Nouveau but, because of the cynicism that pervaded the disintegration of the Austrian Empire, Loos relegated architects to the marginalized position of technocrats. Schumacher and Rathenau, taking advantage of Van de Velde's vulnerable theory, called for the artists to "abandon personal inclinations and contribute through production to the enobling of `work' and thereby enoble entire society."[9] The denial of art and authorship except as a model for collaboration established a critical position to be adopted by an avant-garde disillusioned by the ravages of the First World War and expatriated in Zurich.

The Dadaists' manifesto, emanating from Zurich in 1916, declared a negation of art and supplanted it with the industrial commonplace. The objet-trouve after Duchamps's ready-mades constituted a symbol for the repositioning of art to that of the organizing connoisseur. Although the Swiss Dadaists were apolitical, the subsequent French Surrealist's movement of Bretons assumed a political commitment.

The Surrealists subordinated the position of the individual artist to a process whereby social determinism and psychic automatism could emerge. Objet-trouve, photo montage, and spontaneous poetry were early manifestations of the loss of authorship and an art reduced to a zero position. The movement insisted on a commitment to personal anonymity. There was a collective working method, the use of abstracted technique and a psychic method to release by chance Freudian symbology disassociated from cognition

"True poetry comes only from the unconscious act of desire to incorporate Freud's experiments."[10] Any image making associated with career or personal style constituted heresy. Lissitzky's photomontage was an exploration in photogram where images where introduced `accidentally' in subsequent generations of the photo without concern for scale juxtapositions. Then the artist is engaged to organize and infuse an ideological content. XYZ in the photograph represented the Swiss *ABC* publication on which Lissitzky and Meyer collaborated. The mechanical compass from line to eye links the artist within the literal gears of the publication process. This photo was the frontispiece of the Vkhutemas yearly publication in 1927, the year that Meyer proposed a student exchange with the Dessau Bauhaus. However, Meyer would have considered the use of self-portraiture as self-indulgent.

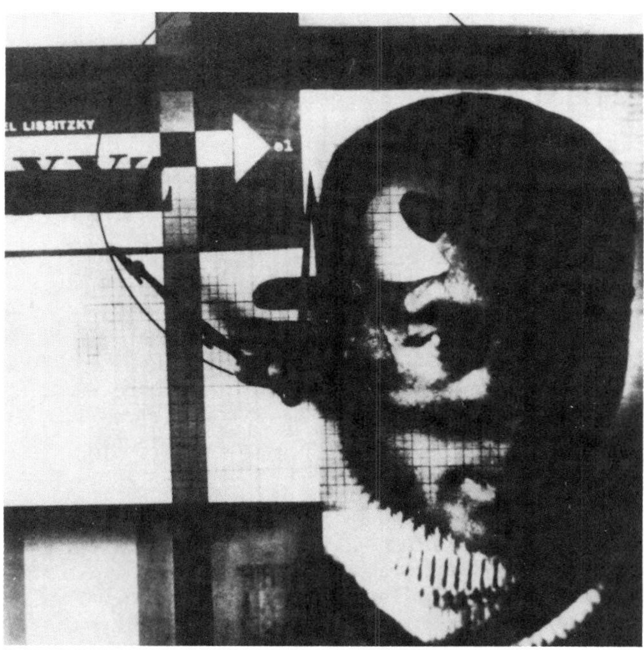

"Self Portrait: The Constructor." El Lissitzky, 1924

As the aesthetic diversion of Surrealism began to lose the stimulus of discovery and recognized its inability to influence social change, their work, to regain legitimacy, absorbed a political ideology. Gropius, while rhetorically incorporating the social and collaborative inclinations of the avant-garde, maintained a commitment to the consanguineous line of Rousseau - that of an industrial process guided by inspiration. Again the Ivory Tower was reconstituted as the keeper of the sacred aesthetic. Gropius characterized the Bauhaus as "a diversity of individuals who are willing to cooperate without relinquishing their identity."[11] The derivation of prototype was to be incubated within the laboratory and through edict became an overlay on the social process. The legacy of the monk as common laborer on the medieval construction site was transformed to serve the needs of the 19th century middle class.

"And it is this game of hide and seek between necessity and freedom that nullifies the Nietzschean discovery of the free acceptance of the necessary as the unique and supreme freedom."[12] Gropius pursued the Sachlick that, once articulated, could be metered out as a career intensive mechanism that might direct and improve society, but at least would enshrine the inventor. Thus the work would have a direct engagement with the amorality of capital irrespective of necessity. If capital is the sole motivator, the resultant product will be immune to social transformation because it is historically dysfunctional and fixed in time.

Gropius's structure of the Bauhaus seems more "the ultimate proof of a 'flight from the world' attempted by an intellectual coterie anxious to protect itself from urban anguish than the logical premise to what would later become the mystical aspect of the Bauhaus."[13] The myth assumed the universality of representation that defied local social stimulus. Meyer labeled the provocative images of the Weissenhof project "a far cry for an 'international architecture' in this age of national self-sufficiency and awakening of colonial peoples . . .is a dream of those building aesthetics who, anxious to be thought in the forefront of fashion, conjure up for themselves a uniform world of buildings . . .detached from social reality . . ."[14] This represents the evolution of an original position of conceding the international component of standardized technology to a position refined by experience within "local circumstances."[15]

The architectural process as opposed to art cannot be a pure search for signs as metaphor for the spirit of the new world. It stands instead as a confrontation with reality. The only possibility for understanding and legitimization lies within reality itself. The need to break down an Ivory Tower embodied in the social simulacra of the academy and to accept reality was the only option for Meyer, a zero position for architecture itself. The formulation of 'school' and 'architecture' became an impossibility.[16]

Similar to Gropius and Le Corbusier, Meyer initially relied on proportioning for mitigating the influence of rationalized etiology. The Bolshevik uprising of 1918 in Switzerland gave rise to the first experiments in cooperative housing. Meyer's Freidorf housing estate near his office in Basle was his first attempt at a reconciliation between standardized spacial configuration and the regulating effects of classical proportioning. Meyer was able to immerse himself in performance by living in the project and acting as the Building Commissioner for seven years. The lessons of this experience convinced Meyer to abandon abstract regulating strategies in favor of a scientific methodology.

Kenneth Frampton has argued that Meyer's early attempts at an automatic determinism, exemplified in the Petersschule and League of Nations competition entries, constituted a "random empiricism in which a utilitarian iconography does not assume optimum utility."[17] Meyer's designs for these projects, inherited from the Freidorf, experience a willingness to subordinate the author's desires to a deterministic social process, similar to avant-garde attempts to negate the artist. Because these two projects were competition entries and the League of Nations particularly was international in character with no cultural locus, they did not provide Meyer with the benefit of a social condition, thus they played to the advantages of the laboratory. Similar to Siza's refusal to participate in the Bienalli, Meyer should have avoided these projects for their implicit contradiction. Meyer's personal disassociation from his work implies its anonymous naturalism, which neutralizes any self-criticism.

The problem of transforming an artistic activity into an inert position within the productive organism made the proposition of maintaining the status quo in the Bauhaus for Meyer an impossibility. The school "whose reputation vastly outran its power of achievement . . .the object of unprecedented publicity . . .[left him with] the need to fight against the Bauhaus style."[18] By 1927 the Bauhaus had a greater inclination toward de Stiyl than the influence of production as implied by Gropius's rhetoric. The simultaneous downturn in the German building economy signaled an increase in political pressure against the school. To improve this situation, Meyer introduced the brigade method of instruction (a greater shift toward collaboration) and the direct involvement of the architecture students within the workshops. The Bauhaus under Meyer's direction became more production oriented and for the first time was directly engaged in the design of public works. The school became much more financially independent than under Gropius.

Meyer's class based antiformalism created tensions between his new regime and the remnants of the Gropius era. Meyer's desire to incorporate the convictions of the avant-garde left, that of a collaborative determinism open to the chance proclivities of social change, could only lead toward an ultimate dismantling of the school. Faced with the pressures of mass unemployment brought on by the world-wide depression and the concomitant political emergence of the radical right, Meyer was forced out. Mies subsequently brought a return to spiritual isolationism of the academy with its incumbent financial dependence on a highly volatile political state.

While Meyer had riled against the formalism of the Bauhaus style, in the Soviet Union he found a polarized situation of two dominant camps "each of no use: that of the more or less romantic realm of empiricism and that of the artificial universe of the avant-garde."[19] Both conditions were incapable of reconciling the disparity between the model, held up by the Proletkult before it was restrained by Lenin, of an industrialized social utopia with the primitive status of Soviet labor and technique. The method of realizing the social agenda had to be carried out at the lowest level.

Vopra, the pro-Stalinist association of proletarian architects, had attacked OSA and SASS for their eccentric positions of deurbanization, utopianism, and mimicry of western technology. Meyer joined Vopra because of their commitment to working within the existing capabilities of the Soviet system and their desire for action. Meyer characterized the remnants of constructivism as having "abandoned architecture to the arbitrariness of the new formalism and who have created a new fetish of bare walls."[20] Meyer brought the brigade system to Vasi and actually committed the students to job site experience in contrast to the mere simulation through the workshops of the Bauhaus. He directed a town planning brigade that dealt with the transformation of existing medieval cities into the socialist ideal.

This was carried out by an integration of rationalized site planning within the extant medieval framework.

Engels's desire to suppress class distinction and the Constructivist laboratories of architectural experimentation gave way to the central position of Vopra's dialectical materialism. Lenin's had acknowledged the need to assimilate existing culture before a new system could evolve.[21] Although Vopra's position eventually led to the emergence of social realism, its original position acknowledged the psychological and social ideological potential of utilitarian determinism. The Bauhaus determinism never assumed an ideological position. Meyer sought a specific but not fixed architecture. ''Society determines the content of its own life and thus the content of architecture within the framework of a specific social system within a specific period of time with specific economic and technical means . . .in a real situation . . .once separated from its age and society it becomes an empty sham.''[22]

After social realism became the orthodox state position in the Ukase of 1932, Meyer remained in the Soviet Union until foreigners were denied further commissions in 1936. During this time he never adopted the affectations of classicism but maintained a commitment to the appropriateness of a rationalist position. Subsequently, Meyer was asked to direct the Mexican Institute of Urbanism and Planning by the Cardenas administration. There Meyer found the same isolation of architects within the Tower and thus an inability to derive a socially grounded response to the specific Mexican revolution. He allied himself with the Muralists because of their sympathy for folk iconography and their ability to create an imagery responsive to a national imperative. Meyer's work insisted on a technological concomitance to local labor, cultural iconography, and socially conditioned materials. Art was merely the organizational implement for a social condensed industrialization.

Meyer's denial of authorship resulted in the fusion of art and work. Art was then reconstituted in the honorific status of the manufactured object. The loss of authorship invited the introduction of the unpredictability of social determinism into Meyer's architecture whereas Gropius had always remained committed to a singular architecture.[23] The contradiction in Gropius's position became clear in the mystification of the heroic pursuit of an intellectual project isolated from implementation. Moholy-Nagy's piece, which was constructed by dictation to a technician over the telephone, is a demonstration of this attitude. To regain a functional perspective, Meyer surrendered to the immediate historical process.

Architecture, in accommodating industrial technique while maintaining a social legitimacy, must perpetuate the principles of work by accepting the anguish of the social condition and recognize the futility of preconception. Architecture must avoid the ''murderous capacity of images to destroy the real . . .''[24]

We are left with Benjamin's continuing question ''What is the attitude of a work to the relations of production of its time . . .the position in them? This question directly concerns the function the work has within the literary relations of productions . . .it is concerned directly with the literary technique of works.''[25] To reconcile spirit with work, the former must be subsumed within a work directly responsive to use. Only through this consortium will the spirit be manifest in the object while accommodating the vagaries of social transformation over time. The spirit will be rendered inert if frozen in sequence through a concession to the image making capacity of technique and its protagonist, the cult of personalities.

NOTES

1. Robert McCarter, ''Escape from the Revolving Door: Architecture and the Machine,'' *Building Machines*, (N.Y., Princeton Architectural Press, 1987), p. 8.
2. Mary McLeod, ''Architecture and Politics in the Reagan Era,'' *Assemblage 2*, (Cambridge, Massachusetts, MIT Press, 1986), p. 45.
3. Walter Gropius, ''Letter to Editor,'' *Architectural Review*, (March, 1963), p. 6.
4. Massimo Scolari, ''Hannes Meyer e la Scuola di Architettura,'' *Controspazio*, (Aprile-Maggio 1970), p. 86.
5. Claude Schnaidt, *Hannes Meyer: Buildings, Projects and Writings*, (Zurich, R. Weber, 1965), p. 57.
6. Stanford Anderson, ''Modern Architecture and Industry: Peter Behrens and the Cultural Policy of Historical Determinism,'' *Oppositions II*, (Cambridge, MIT Press, 1977), p. 55.
7. Ibid., p. 56.
8. Scolari, op, cit., p. 89.
9. Anderson, op. cit., p. 57.
10. Helena Lewis, *The Politics of Surrealism*, (N.Y., Paragon Press, 1988), p. 18.
11. Hans M. Wingler, *The Bauhaus*, (Cambridge, MIT Press, 1969), p. 9.
12. Manfredo Tafuri, *The Sphere and the Labyrinth*, (Cambridge, MIT Press, 1987), p. 119.
13. Ibid., p. 129.
14. Gillian Naylor, *The Bauhaus Reassessed*, (N.Y., Dutton, 1985), p. 173.
15. Wingler, op. cit., p. 153.
16. Francesco Dal Co, *Hannes Meyer, Scritti 1921-1942 Architettura o Rivoluzione*, (Padova, Marsillo Editori, 1969) pp. 43, 44.
17. Kenneth Frampton, ''The Humanist versus the Utilitarian Ideal,'' *Architectural Design*, V. 38, March 1968, p. 135.
18. Naylor, op. cit., p. 171.
19. Tafuri, op, cit., p. 169.
20. Christian Borngraber, ''Foreign Architects in the USSR,'' *Architectural Association Quarterly*, Vol. 11, 1979, p. 58.
21. Anatole Kopp, *Town and Revolution*, (N.Y., Braziller, 1970), p. 212.
22. Schnaidt, op. cit., p. 55.
23. Dal Co, op. cit., pp. 16-18.
24. Jean Bandrillard, ''The Precession of Simulacra,'' *Art After Modernism*, ed. Brian Wallis, (N.Y., Godine, 1984), p. 256.
25. Walter Benjamin, ''The Author as Producer,'' *Understanding Brecht*, (London, New Left Books, 1973), p. 222.

CHAPTER 9

Technological Advances Affecting Architectural Representational Methods

OMAR FAWZY
University of Pennsylvania

DRAWING PRODUCTION

Perhaps the earliest drawing medium used by architects in laying out their designs was in fact the site itself. The ancient architect, after conceiving the design, would transfer whatever conception he had of the building onto the site by means of stakes and ropes, thus producing a delineation of the outline of the building on the ground. And hence these ropes and stakes were in fact the architect's "drawing" instruments as the statue of the ancient Egyptian architect Senmut of the XVIII Dynasty portrays.

Vitruvius in "De Architectura", mentions a similar procedure when discussing the fundamental principles of architecture under the heading "arrangement" (Book 1. Ch. II). He describes three tools for composing the building: Ichnographia (ground plan), orthographia (elevation or upright) and skenographia (a form of perspective). His definition of ichnographia, however, is rather ambiguous but taken literally would imply the geometrical setting out of the building on the ground, i.e. the foot print of the building. This is corroborated by another passage where he discusses the importance of geometry in the architect's curriculum because it "teaches the use of the rule and compasses, by which we specifically acquire training in making plans for buildings in their grounds" (Book I, i,4). Elsewhere he mentions the square, the level and the plummet; all tools used for site delineation. Such was the conception of the architects instruments.

For centuries, the notion of the site as drawing medium persists. This is what Guillaume d'Auvergne, 13th century Bishop of Paris, describes as a kind of mental procedure or "Cogitatio" where the ground plan, which was conceived in the architect's head, would be transferred directly onto the site using it as a full-scale drawing board.[1]

While the examples cited so far have been limited to full scale projections, there is no doubt that ancient architects have produced reduced drawings on different drawing media. From the few examples that have survived, it is possible to categorize such drawings according to drawing medium into: rigid and pliable. Of the former, stone panels and clay tablets were the most used. The statue of Gudea, Babylon in 2130 B.C. depicting a ground plan of a temple inscribed upon it; the clay tablet from Tell Asmar (later third millennium B.C.) containing an incised house plan; and the fragmental marble plan of Rome which was set up in the Templum Sacrae Urbis by Vespasian and afterward by Severus, are a few examples. Because of obvious handling difficulties it is clear that these incised slabs could not have been used for communicating the architects' design instructions, and should therefore be regarded more as records of existing buildings than as means to new achievement.

Both rigid and pliable drawing media were in use in the Middle Ages. Understandably, the one that required manual labor was the one reserved for craftsmen, the other for scribes and scholars. Of the rigid type, the usage of slabs of plaster as drawing medium took place in the masons' lodge practice of the medieval workshops. Through a geometric progression of a basic figure, numerous markings were made on a slab of plaster. Unlike ancient practice, these seemingly unintelligible markings were indeed construction drawings in a sense that they provided information on the size of every element within the building.

A pliable type of drawing medium that existed since antiquity, but was formerly used almost exclusively in manuscripts, is parchment. Parchment was manufactured from sheep or calf skin. As a drawing medium parchment had the limitations of high price and size. It was expensive to the extent that it was recyclable, causing the erasure of design upon that material in order that it may be reused.[2] Because of size limitations, different views of the building had to be drawn on separate sheets. Quite often several separate sheets were needed for the creation of a single drawing. An example is the celebrated plan of St. Gaul 800 A.D. which was made up of five separate sheets of calf skin sewn together. By the 12th and 13th centuries, successful selective breeding of sheep resulted in an increase in the size of parchment.[3] However, the increase in size was not of a magnitude to affect its usefulness for architectural purposes. For this one had to await the advent of mechanically produced paper which apart from its larger size allowed for the use of a less tedious drawing technique than was necessary with parchment.

To produce a drawing on parchment, a stylus (a blunt pointed instrument) was first used to score lines on the material. These lines were then inked in freehand using a quill pen. From ancient times until the 16th century, the stylus was made of horn, ivory, hardwood or metal. During the Middle Ages lead styli were used.

With the introduction of paper-making in Europe in the 13th century, paper soon replaced parchment as the popular drawing medium. Paper, which was manufactured centuries earlier in China, was at first hand made. Soon afterwards, it became mechanically produced. By the 14th century, paper mills driven by water power were spread all over Europe. At first, paper was water absorbent. But sizing treatment by impregnation with animal glue soon made paper smooth and non-absorbent. As mentioned above, drawings produced prior to the introduction of paper were prepared using a scoring instrument. This practice continued with early hand-made paper. From the 16th century onwards, however, drawings began to be prepared using quill pens, metal point, charcoal and crayon.

The introduction of the graphite pencil in the 16th century was of great significance. Unlike charcoal and lead, the marks of a pencil were erasable and could be inked following erasure. In addition, it helped alleviate some of the inconvenience of using pen and ink. Drawing pens had the disadvantage of clogging and the lack of a constant ink flow prior to the invention of its waterproof forms in the late 18th century, had the drawback of smudging and the and the length of its drying time. The modification of the ruling pen, an instrument in use since antiquity, to produce lines of constant thickness helped evolve a series of new drawing convention. It became possible to differentiate between the various views by virtue of their different line thickness.

The advent of mechanically manufactured paper had far reaching effects on drawing production. Paper became less expensive and therefore more extensively used for drawing purposes. Drawing production was also much facilitated by the substitution of the dual process of scoring with a single step of drawing in ink or pencil directly on the drawing medium.

However, paper still had the disadvantage of being opaque, a fact which made it impossible to make overlays. This, of course, had to wait till the introduction of some kind of transparent paper. Various forms of transparent paper were commonly available in Europe from 1700 onwards. Tracing paper was widely used for copying drawings in the mid-19th century.

DRAWING REPRODUCTION

One of the earliest methods for providing copies of drawings was to make a duplicate of the drawing using dividers. Each dimension would be taken off separately from the original and transferred to the copy with the points of a pair of dividers, marking the drawing medium (parchment and later on paper) with a prick. Prick marks would then be connected to form the copy. This, of course, was a tedious method, but it remained in use until it became more or less obsolete once tracing paper became the accepted means of copying.

The introduction of tracing paper in the 18th century had a great impact on the graphic process. For the first time in architectural history it enabled the architect to superimpose different views of the building (plans, elevations, sections), thus opening up the possibility for a broader and more comprehensive understanding of the design. Tracing paper supplanted oil-paper which was neither transparent enough to permit the tracing of drawings nor a particularly convenient surface to receive well the stroke of a pen or the marking of a crayon or pencil. With tracing paper, no longer was it necessary to send the original paper drawing to the work site for the workmen's use. Instead, tracings of the original were made for that purpose. Tracings were done by 'tracers'-draftsmen or office boys with little or no background in architectural training and who were thus prone to inaccuracies.

With the broadening of the field of architecture in the beginning of the 19th century, it became evident that such a procedure that depended on single copies of drawings was unrealistic. By mid-century, a new photographic process used in publications was becoming popular in architectural practice especially on large scale projects. Drawings were delineated with an autographic ink and then photolithographed, or traced on lithographic tracing paper and transferred to stone or zinc from which a large number of copies can be taken.[4] Such a photographic process was expensive and its use therefore had to be justified, as in the case of Charles Garnier's Paris Opera.[5] The wide application of this process was hampered by its cost-effectiveness and was therefore shortlived.

The invention of the ferro-prussiate or blueprint process in 1840 and its use in graphic reproduction in the 1870s revolutionized the process of drawing-production.[6] Not only did it provide an inexpensive and fast means of producing copies,[7] but it also virtually eliminated the inaccuracies involved in tracing out individual drawings. Now it was possible to provide identical drawings to all those involved with the building process.

The implications of the use of the blueprint process were far reaching. Prior to its use, the logical sequence of operations in the design production process involved the making of an accurate inked-in original on a heavy drawing paper from which tracings could be made. The introduction of the blueprint process, however, eliminated one step in this procedure. It obviated the necessity of inking-in the original drawing by making an inked tracing over the first pencil drawing on paper.[8] A later development was that it obviated the necessity of an original on paper in the first place. With the further improvement of the process, it was possible to dispense with inking-in as well.

The introduction of the blueprint process had a significant effect on certain drawing conventions then in vogue, especially in France and Germany- namely, the practice of using shadows on drawings; and the use of color to indicate materials. These highly finished drawings such as those for the Paris Opera, were intended as both presentation and construction drawings. Copies sent to the workforce were traced without shading.[9] Both tinting and shading were eventually abandoned because of obvious reasons, although the former persisted longer by virtue of the fact that a differentiation between building materials was indeed needed. Therefore instead of coloring the original, all copies were individually colored. However, hatching and cross-hatching, in addition to the standardization of most if not all the symbols used for indicating materials in section, have entirely supplanted coloring.

The above discussion focused on only a few of the key technical advances that affected drawing representation. Other innovations that provide fertile ground for further study include the developments in the drawing board, the T-square, the compass, the scale-rule, protractors, and the use of graph paper. As for drawing reproduction, the influence of the early 14th and 15th century treatises, the 17th and 18th century handbooks and patternbooks, 20th century text books and catalogs have not been discussed. This paper also did not address current practices especially computer-generated graphics.

NOTES

1. Spiro Kostof. *The Architect: Chapters in the History of the Profession.* New York: Oxford University Press, 1977.
2. Wyatt Papworth. ed. ''Drawing'' in *The Dictionary of Architecture.* London: The Architectural Pub. Society, 1853-92. Vol. ii, D-65.
3. Jean Gimpel. *The Medieval Machine:* p. 45.
4. R. Phené Spiers. *Architectural Drawing.* London: Cassell & Co. Ltd., 1887. p. 45.
5. T. L. Donaldson. ''Description of the Working Drawings of the New Opera House in Paris'', *Transactions of the Royal Institute of British Architects.* (4 April 1864) p. 121.
6. The process was invented by the British astronomer Sir William Herschel in 1840 and was used for scientific purposes. Its introduction in office practice in the 1870's was through the engineering profession.
7. By the 1890s in the United States it was estimated that tracing would generally cost ten times the amount of blueprinting. Christopher Gray. *Blueprints: Twenty-Six Extraordinary Structures.* New York: Simon and Schuster, 1981, p. 7.
8. ''The 'Blue' Copying Process'', *The American Architect and Building News.* (Aug. 3, 1878), vol. iv, 136, p. 44.
9. R. Phené Spiers. ''Remarks on the Foreign System of Shading and Tinting Drawings'', *Transactions of the Royal Institute of British Architects*, n.s. 1, 1884085, p. 89.

REFERENCES

''The 'Blue' Copying Process,'' *American Architect and Building News*, 4, (Aug. 3, 1878), vol. iv, no. 136, p.44.

Booker, P.J. *A History of Engineering Drawing.* London: Chatto and Windus, 1963.

Briggs, Martin S. *The Architect in History.* New York: Da Capo Press, 1974.

Bucher, Francois. ''Design in Gothic Architecture,'' *JSAH*, 27, (March 1968), pp. 49-71.

Gimpel, Jean. *The Medieval Machine: The Industrial Revolution of the Middle Ages.* New York: Holt, Rinehart and Winston, 1976.

Hambly, Maya. *Drawing Instruments 1580 - 1980.* London: Sotheby's Publications, 1988.

Harvey, John. *The Master Builders: Architecture in the Middle Ages.* New York: McGraw-Hill Book Co., 1971.

Jensen, J. Norman. ''The Early History of Blueprinting,'' *Architectural Record*, 71, (May 1932), p. 335.

Kostof, Spiro, ed. *The Architect: Chapters in the History of The Profession.* New York: Oxford University Press, 1977.

Papworth, Wyatt. ''Practice in the Last Century'', *The RIBA Journal.* n.s., ix (1892-3), pp. 3-6. 2 Oct. 1892.

Spiers, R. Phené. *Architectural Drawing.* London: Cassell & Co. Ltd., 1887.

Spiers, R. Phené. ''Remarks on the Foreign System of Shading and Tinting Drawings'', *RIBA Transactions* n.s. 1, p. 89.

CHAPTER 10

Modernity, Technology and Caricature: The Representational Qualities of Erich Mendelsohn's Sketches

KENDRA SCHANK SMITH
Georgia Institute of Technology

Erich Mendelsohn's sketches both reflect and caricature a view of a streamlined utopian future of his modernity. His sketches are visual interpretations revealing his personal fantasy. He uses exaggeration, deformation and ridicule to transform and interpret the world around him and to define his image of architecture. These transformations hold elements of caricatures. I wish to demonstrate how perceiving his sketches as caricature can give us insight into his designs. I want to first touch on the environment in art and architecture prevalent in his early experience, to examine influences which may affect these sketches.

Mendelsohn completed his education at a time of severe turmoil. The pre-World War I Europe was changing culturally and socially. We can identify a few movements and activities of which Mendelsohn was undoubtedly aware, but their influence on the development of his architectural style can be debated. Bruno Zevi acknowledges his ''position in the context of the expressionism of the *Bruche*''[1], but he believes in Mendelsohn's unusual originality: ''His cultural and artistic development, without patronage or the influence of major teachers, so free of outside influence that he might be called `the only true revolutionary of his generation'.''[2] Looking at his work we can draw relationships, real or imaginary, between the work of Mendelsohn and influences such as German Expressionism, Futurism, Antonio Sant'Elia, and changes in the building technology of his time.

It is common to connect Mendelsohn to the German Expressionists.[3] In 1912 Erich Mendelsohn graduated from the Technische Hochschule of Munich in Architecture.[4] The German Expressionist movement was at its height from 1904 to 1912, as a student, Mendelsohn was aware of its ideas and influence. He met Paul Klee, Franz Marc, and Vasily Kandinsky in Munich, and their influence on him is noticeable, ''...for his first references to art as a biological phenomenon'' begin at this time.[5]

Bruno Zevi evaluates expressionism and Mendelsohn's sketches: ''Expressionists are those who react, fighting for liberty, for atonality in music and in the arts. 'External rules do not exist. Everything is permitted which is not repudiated by one's inner voice'', pronounced Theodor Von Hartmann. Mendelsohn's sketches reflect this state of affairs, enjoying the most unrestrained fantasy.''[6]

A highly publicized movement of the times, was the emergence of the Italian Futurists, whose premise was ''to aim directly and deliberately at a mass audience.''[7] Through it, Filippo Tommaso Marinetti was able to communicate his dynamism and violence across Europe.[8] Essays by Mario Morasso were circulated from 1902 to 1905, with titles as ''The Aesthetics of Speed'' and ''The Heroes of the Machine''.[9] He writes that the modern artist must:

> ''Know and love...[machines] and grasp their energies and great destinies in order to render their spirit and beauty, which should evolve from their function: `a racing car will be called beautiful when it appears as light and nimble as possible...[and] the more it approaches the ideal form of a knife cutting through the air'.''[10]

Mendelsohn most likely saw ''the Futurists'' exhibition on show in either Munich or Berlin in 1912.[11] Two years later Antonio Sant'Elia exhibited his fantasy drawings, which were was not conceived under any affiliation with the Futurists, but he was soon adopted by them and he was instrumental in the ''Manifesto of Futurist Architecture''.[12]

Erich Mendelsohn is most often compared to Sant'Elia, because they both caricature a future of industrialization and motion. Sant'Elia used monolithic forms: designing not just buildings but whole cities in a new age of factories and electrical power stations. In the Manifesto of Futurist Architecture, Sant'Elia provides his view on the architecture of the new urban condition:

> ''We no longer feel ourselves to be the men of the cathedrals, the palaces, and the podium. We are the men of the great hotels, the railway stations, the immense streets, colossal ports, covered markets, luminous arcades, straight roads and beneficial demolitions.''[13]

The drawings for a "New City" were dynamic, powerful and contained extreme action. Mendelsohn, similar to Sant'Elia, was rendering a future of monumental buildings with the efficiency of machines.

The machine was symbolic of "...industrialization from which would arise not simply a modern style, but an entirely new way of life."[14] It had a powerful impact on the twentieth century and Mendelsohn was certainly familiar with the captivation of motion. "...The intoxicating aim of Futurist art was not the painting of states of minds,...but the search for *the style of movement*."[15] This fascination with speed and machines affected not only styles of building but society and culture.

Another factor which helps to paint this impressionable period for Mendelsohn, in the immediately pre-World War I and post war era, is that of socialism and its accompanying mechanism. The Russian revolution, Marxism, and the changing of society immediately relative to industrialization all had reciprocal influence on areas of society and culture.

With all the social and political uncertainty, another influential indication of the times which affected and was effected by industrialization was the production of new materials with which to build. Mendelsohn was definitely excited about the possibilities for architecture in the use of these new materials.

At this time, Mendelsohn was undoubtedly aware of new construction in Germany and also throughout Europe and America. The Crystal Palace, the Galerie des Machines and the Eiffel Tower, buildings by Bruno Taut, Peter Behrens, Adolf Loos, Otto Wagner, Frank Lloyd Wright and bridges by Robert Maillart employed lighter materials, longer spans and utilized advanced technology. How much each of these buildings directly influenced the work of Mendelsohn is difficult to know, but these examples create the architectural climate of his times.

Most of Mendelsohn's sketches evoke a fluidity which creates a need to build with reinforced concrete. The fantasy sketches, free and abstract, display incredible spans and great curved mullions reflecting his interest in steel and concrete. These materials allowed the fantasy of his imagination to be united with a desire for these projects to be realized. "...Mendelsohn intended his revolutionary designs to be as practical as they were imaginative."[16] This technology was technically available to architects, but when building the Einstein Tower, Mendelsohn was forced to employ brick and plaster because of concretes limited availability in Potsdam. In this interesting paradox, the building looks to the future to encompass a new age, and in fact it is an example of traditional building techniques.

Having put Mendelsohn in context, it is now possible to propose how caricature in these sketches reveal his position as both representative and innovative. Utilizing caricature, I want to introduce how Erich Mendelsohn manipulates images. Exploring aspects of caricature in his architectural sketches, such as his views of the future, the machine age, the human body, building technology and buildings by other architects allows us to perceive his cunning visualization.

Caricature is a relatively recent art. Ernst Gombrich and Ernst Kris have pursued the most comprehensive study of caricature recently. They see a distinct beginning of caricature, versus humorous art, when they write that portrait caricature was not known before the end of the sixteenth century. At that time, the artist was newly valuable, sought after, and possessed "the supreme right of the poet, to form a reality of his own."[17] The work of art was "...considered as a *projection* of an inner image."[18] These fanciful ideas and combinations came from the imagination of the artist himself. This idea of 'projection of an inner image' is very similar to the ideals of Expressionism. I find it very interesting that when Gombrich speaks of the Expressionists, he writes, "Caricature had always been 'expressionist'..."[19]

Important elements of caricature are; exaggeration, deformation, transformation, simplicity and ridicule. For caricature, the "...conscious distortion of the features of a person with the aim of ridicule..." paradoxically allows us to see the truth beneath this distortion.[20] Gombrich and Kris write:

> It was in the first place a discovery concerning the nature of likeness. To put it briefly, it was the discovery that similarity is not essential to likeness. The deliberate distortion of single features is not incompatible with a striking likeness in the whole. True caricature in this new sense is not content with drawing a long nose just a little longer, or a broad chin just a bit broader. Such partial distortions are characteristic only of superficial or immature work. The real aim of the true caricaturist is to transform the whole man into a completely new and ridiculous figure which nevertheless resembles the original in a striking and surprising way.[21]

The role of caricature in revealing a truth has occasional affinity to a monster.[22] Demonstrating and employing the new combination "to show", the monster seems to present the future and act more as a soothsayer in the role of architecture. A caricature stresses one aspect of a concept, and more of the image is involved. Both caricature and monsters recombine ideas and forms into new compositions. These compositions bring a new meaning to the understanding. The caricature uses emphasis in deformation to show the state of affairs, to find the inner meaning to a specific personality, or, most often, to ridicule. It takes important aspects of the character to the extreme so that character is easy to recognize as a visual image. Caricature is dependent on the image and the transformation of features. When we understand the meaning, we are surprised by the recognition, simplicity, and its quickness.

Similarly, the switching of interpretations is an example of the grotesque. Nonnons also, are "absurd objects, shapeless, pockmarked, mottled, knobby things which, when placed before a distorting mirror become handsome and sensible.''[23] The ''grotesqueries'' are literary or visual occurrences which ''call into question the adequacy of our ways of organizing the world, of dividing the continuum of experience into knowable particles.''[24] The grotesque resembles caricature by revealing a new truth in the reality it displays. They both exhibit intelligence; often through paradox. The recognition is immediate, as in caricature, and is contingent upon interpretation.[25]

We can recognize the features of caricature in sketches by Erich Mendelsohn. In two imaginary sketches done about 1915 for conceptual halls, we see a series of three gigantic ''wings''. In one they look similar to three dorsal fins; in the other they are akin to modern day airplane tail fins. Our first impression is one of extreme motion. The great wings seem functionless except to caricature great speed. This is reinforced in words by Mendelsohn himself; revealing the world around him, he writes:

> ''...there is the influence of speed which dominates our lives. Speed is hostile to detail. The man in a motor car, or in an aeroplane, with his tense vision, has no longer any leisure to notice details and petty decoration. He requires great masses and bold lines.''[26]

The fluidness of these buildings, so vividly in motion presses us into the fourth dimension. ''In the expression `of a brief sign', `of a single outline', Mendelsohn...evokes an obsession of Borromini and Gaudi...''[27] This is a caricature, exaggerating action in an object as stationary as a building.

In these 'wing' building sketches, Mendelsohn is ridiculing scale. The buildings are scaleless, without people or trees, they could be two stories or ten. Without clues, the long fluid lines seem to make us believe ten. He also exaggerates scale to give the buildings monumentality, and to multiply the motion. The thinness of the fins, accentuates the lack of function.

Mendelsohn always spoke of creating buildings which could be realized; these winged buildings caricature what reinforced concrete will do. Although it is possible to build these structures, he is stretching the possibilities judging from what had been built by 1915. The motion of these fins and their separation, makes them seem machine-like possibly similar to turbines or radiators. Mendelsohn is manipulating these imaginative sketches to ridicule an industrialized society.

The drawings are strikingly simple, both in the way they are fully constructed with only a few lines, and are devoid of details. Because these imaginative drawings are loose and simple, the architect does not need to be concerned with the intricacies of connection. As with a caricature, the austere, vague forms allow the artist to combine a human's body and a goat's head. Here we see fins attached to a low horizontal structure. Simplicity is essential to caricature. The simple and unfinished qualities of this drawing do not keep us from understanding the connection.

Mendelsohn's sketch of a grain elevator, drawn in 1914 is strongly reminiscent of Otto Wagner's Postal Savings Bank in Vienna of 1904.[28] The grain elevator is covered with large bolts, a very distinctive element of the Postal Savings Bank. Here we see exaggeration of the quantity and scale of these aluminum bolts. In this sketch, the grain elevator bolts, are huge. Those near the doorway appear to be three per story or several feet in diameter. Their exaggeration exhibits Mendelsohn's interest in their metallic quality. In this sketch, he is caricaturing the work by another architect, Otto Wagner, and the use of immense metal panels as a new building material. This substantially similar image becomes a caricature of the original, not a replica, but a transformed, new combination. Gombrich and Kris attempt to define the role of transformation in caricature;

> ...whereas the artist, although the most alive of all men to external stimuli, is nevertheless a person who elaborates, plays with and reshapes sensory experience under the influence of internal and affective states. With the turn of the century came a new means of grasping the way in which the mind plays with elements of sensory experience and out of them shapes new patterns.[29]

Mendelsohn transforms visual images, especially those of architectural elements, rearranging and 'reshaping' to make new configurations. We see similarity to Expressionism. The 'internal and affective states' helps him to rearrange and caricature architecture.

Mendelsohn caricatures buildings by other architects in his sketches. In a sketch for an industrial building, he seems to be combining elements from many buildings. He combines vaulted windows, cylindrical ribbon windows, small punched windows, light terraces and massive monumental forms with strong vertical elements all in one building. The most obvious elements show a resemblance to the Larkin Building done by Frank Lloyd Wright in 1903. The monumentality also seems to caricature the fantasy sketches by Antonio Sant'Elia.[30] This sketch by Mendelsohn has three elements crucial to caricature; transformation, ambiguity and condensation. He is recombining forms as artists rearrange figures for emphasis.

Surprisingly this sketch, as well as the 'House of Friendship', speak of the human body. They create voluptuous buildings. It appears as though a person is enclosed in a cloth bag, and we are seeing parts of a body protruding. Architectural elements protrude as knees, elbows, heads, arms and noses, which give these fantasy buildings an organic, and life-like quality. Seeing the forms inside gives us a sensation of movement. In his book, ''Erich Mendelsohn Opera Completa'', Bruno Zevi describes Mendelsohn's sketches of people as Art Nouveau or Doric.[31] Zevi is stressing the way their clothes are treated. Mendelsohn draws not only the figure, but bodies draped in clothes. The falling of the fabric, vertically propagates an analogy to a Doric column. This veneer is demonstrated, especially, in the sketch ''House of Friendship'', which reveals a bent arm complete with five bent fingers. We detect the horizontal folds in the strong ribbon windows he uses so often. Alternative sketches for the Einstein Tower look both as a spinal column and a face. We are reminded of a very literal expression of the idea of cladding in writings by Adolf Loos. We are also reminded of robots, and the biomorphic machines of the 1920's. Where humans attempt to simulate life in the machine, looking to their own body images. In his sketches, Mendelsohn's architecture caricatures the human form, and buildings by other architects.

In these examples we see how the architect caricatures other buildings or drawings. Kris and Gombrich support this idea when they explain how artists caricature a figure. "He [the artist] consciously alters his model, distorts it, plays with its features, and thus shows the power of his imagination - which can exalt as well as degrade."[32]

We have seen how Erich Mendelsohn caricatures his times and also his vision of new technologies for the future. He surely is a man of his current condition: fascinated by forthcoming industrialization, involved in avant garde movements, conscious of architecture happening around him, but he is also a forerunner with an incredible imagination ready to expose and ridicule, to set the pace for an exciting and expressive future. He is an original with an unique understanding of the future, and his vision entices us into this future. Studying Erich Mendelsohn's sketches as caricature gives insight into his perceptions, especially those of the technology of his modernity.

NOTES

1. Zevi, Bruno, *Erich Mendelsohn*, Rizzoli (New York), 1982, p. 9.
2. Ibid., p. 9.
3. Zevi and Wittick confirm this, (Whittick, Arnold *Eric Mendelsohn*, Faber and Faber Limited, London, 1940).
4. Zevi, op. cit., p. 198.
5. King, Susan, *The Drawings of Eric Mendelsohn*, University Art Museum, (University of California, Berkeley), 1969, p. 16.
6. Zevi, op. cit., p. 34.
7. Tisdall, Caroline and Bozzolla, Angelo, *Futurism*, Oxford University Press (New York and Toronto), 1978, p. 7.
8. Ibid., p. 121.
9. Martin, Marianne W., *Futurist Art and Theory 1909-1915*, Clarendon Press (Oxford), 1968, p. 42.
10. Ibid., p. 42.
11. King, op. cit., p. 12.
12. Ibid., p. 12, also see Tisdall and Bozzolla, op. cit., p. 125.
13. Tisdall and Bozzolla, op. cit., p. 121.
14. Wilson, Richard Guy, Pilgrim, Dianne H. and Tashjian, Dickran, *The Machine Age in America 1918-1941*, Harry N. Abrams, Inc. (New York), 1986, p. 16.
15. Martin, op. cit., p. 127.
16. King, op. cit., p. 9.
17. Kris, Ernst and Gombrich, Ernst, "The Principles of Caricature", *British Journal of Medical Psychology*, 17, (1938), p. 331.
18. Ibid., p. 331.
19. Gombrich, Ernst, *The Story of Art*, Prentice-Hall, Inc., (New Jersey), 1985, p. 447.
20. Kris and Gombrich, op. cit., p. 319-20.
21. Gombrich, Ernst and Ernst Kris, *Caricature*, King Penguin Books (Great Britain), 1940, p. 12.
22. Definition of monster from an architectural seminar by Dr. Marco Frascari, February 1989, Georgia Institute of Technology, Atlanta, Georgia.
23. Harpham, Geoffrey Galt, *On the Grotesque; Strategies of Contradiction in Art and Literature*, Princeton University Press (Princeton, New Jersey), 1982, p. 21.
24. Ibid., p. 21.
25. Ibid., pp. 18-22.
26. King, op. cit., p. 59.
27. Zevi, op. cit., p. 13.
28. King, op. cit., p. 16-19, Susan King makes a comparison between this building by Wagner and the sketch by Mendelsohn, but not in terms of caricature.
29. Kris and Gombrich, op. cit., p. 319.
30. Publications were circulated in Europe which included works by Frank Lloyd Wright, specifically the 1910 and 1911 Wasmuth folios, King, op. cit., p. 14, and works by Antonio Sant'Elia were exhibited in 1914, King, op. cit., p. 12, but especially noticeable are his sketches for a 'New City'.
31. Zevi, Bruno, *Erich Mendelsohn Opera Completa*, Etas Kompass, (Milan), 1970, p. 51. Passage kindly translated by Dr. Marco Frascari.
32. Kris and Gombrich, op. cit., p. 338.

CHAPTER 11

In Transitu: Material Simulation in the Design Studio

PETER WONG
University of North Carolina at Charlotte

Holographic building image.

INTRODUCTION

Architectural representation, specifically drawing, has been thought to exist in two basic forms. We can describe the first as illustrative, where the representation is imaged after the architecture it presupposes. The second is documentational, where the representation is an instructional plan that suggests how the building is to be made. Seldom do we encounter a drawing that embraces both these qualities, an observation that frequently leads us to the question of the integrity and wholeness of our craft. In many ways this concern is inherited from a larger macrocosm of issues that has burden Western civilization for the last 200 years. The pealing away of aesthetic concerns from technical means has left a void between our notions of art and science; craft and technology; and man and machine. This dichotomous relationship has unfortunately affected the practice of many trades and vocations, especially those that rely on conceptualization and production. Our architectural representations are direct descendants of this schism and therefore present themselves in a two-faced manner.

This paper acknowledges this duality as a point of departure, and will attempt to address a narrow band of this dilemma as it pertains to the representation of design and construction. The subject of simulation will be used as an aid for the discussion of a possible technique that seeks to expose the reciprocal nature of the design process and the procedures of construction. In mapping this investigation, this discussion will first address the definition of technology for the purpose of underpinning our perception of craft and its relationship to art. It will then survey the current notions of simulation, and posit an alternate reading of this field of inquiry. Lastly, it will suggest a means for viewing this representational attitude, and project a graphic technique that aims to reconcile the distance between our notions of making and thinking.

REDEFINITION OF TECHNOLOGY

Martin Heidegger has identified the ancient Greek word, *technè*, as a term which bears two essential meanings: (1) the knowledge of the activities or skills of the craftsman; and (2) the appreciation of the fine arts, and the arts of the mind.[1] If we accept this definition we might conclude, from a traditional viewpoint, that any division between art and technology fails to exist. The notion that art and technology are coextensive for the knowing (*episteme*) of; material, form, belief, and effect; calls forth the emergence of an "essence of technology." An understanding that values the showing of truth (*aletheia*), rather than the mechanical or manufactured qualities of a thing. This bringing forth of the pervading characteristics of the technological device was commonplace for the ancient Greeks. The process, termed *poiesis*, was the way of making present the true nature of a given thing. An observation by Louis Kahn, may help illuminate our understanding of this relationship:

> *One day waiting for a friend, I watched the crane lifting heavy (concrete) members at the (Richards) Medical Building at the University. On previous days, watching its movement, I resented its presence - a red painted monster, out of scale with the buildings and the members it was lifting into place. It imposed its image on every progress photograph, but because I had to hang around it, it gave me a chance to reflect on its meaning*

and I realized that the design of a building could have a direct bearing on how capable is the crane. I thought of columns a few hundred feet away from each other carrying great spans. No longer did they appear as columns really but as stations, a composite grouping of service rooms composed of large prefabricated and intricate parts ... the column formed a space itself designed to serve the greater space ... Because the members were so big, weighing even more than the crane before could carry, I imagined that I would demand bigger cranes and forget resentment ... suddenly the crane became a friend.[2]

Kahn's reflection bolsters the shared dependence of art and technology in the field of modern construction. His reverie illuminates the inherent limitations (or freedoms) of a mechanical device and its constructional possibilities, and therefore, simultaneously projects a poetic horizon as well as a logic of building on which architectural design might arise. Kahn witnesses the performance of *technè in situ*, as he appraises the site before him.

Although Kahn's insights are revealing, not all architects have the opportunity or capacity to stand before a construction and muse its essence. Designers are typically suited to a milieu that they were trained in - the design studio. This is not to negate the value of on-site participation, but it may serve us well to concede that, like the craftsman, the architect finds prudence in the familiarity of a disciplined locale. Thus the question to be raised is to what degree can the understanding of technological essence be brought forward in a controlled setting - that is, the *in vitro* nature of the design studio, a place that focuses primarily on representational techniques such as drawings, models and writings. It may be appropriate to state that the studio setting is not unlike the environment of a laboratory - where the investigator can speculate, experiment, model and simulate his craft in a secure atmosphere.

SIMULACRA AND SIMULATION

The laboratory has traditionally been a place for the practice of *in vitro* techniques. Experimentation in the physical and life sciences has relied on the modeling of real world circumstance for the purpose of improving the conditions that affect man and nature. Perhaps one of the more interesting, if not arguable, form of this research lies in recent studies into the notions of simulation. This particular branch of study can be best characterized by its capacity to represent a hyperreal situation of real conditions or events. Current work in the areas of flight simulation, robotics, artificial intelligence, psychobehavioral research and holographic imaging are just a few of the areas being investigated.

Perhaps one of the most intriguing branches of this research is in the field of artificial intelligence. Here scientists are attempting to model computers to represent (and possibly exceed) human intellectual patterns. This research makes an appeal for an ideal model of the mind by synthesizing its complexities through the building up of small theoretical elements of thought.[3] The attempts to replicate human thinking leads to an investigation that ultimately intends to get beneath our mental capacities. Although highly fascinating, this science has yet to reconcile the universe of meaningless facts (i.e. the nature of our physical surroundings) with the world of meaningful human concerns.

In the behavioral sciences, researchers are also mapping the human intellect but for an altogether different purpose. Their interests lie in the objectification of human preferences by means of highly simulated situations. Subjects are exposed to artificial environments that vary from pastoral and urban scenography to the extremes of wind, snow, and other severe climatic stimuli. These subjects are monitored by sensitive neurological devices that measure and analyze psychophysiological response.[4] The ultimate purpose of such scientific investigations is to gather data so that environmental design criteria can be established to ensure "positive human response" in real life situations. Yet, like the artificial intelligence researcher, the behavioral psychologist has been unsuccessful in ordering the subjective nature of mortal concerns and the diversity of human preference.

Jean Baudrillard has observed these phenomena and has assigned it the word "simulacra." He refers to this term as an artificial construct that is obliterating our readings of actual things and events, and therefore alters our concept of reality.[5] Baudrillard's observations imply an inversion to the meaning of reality, and points out that contemporary simulacra no longer refer to a person, thing, or event but instead is an entity that precedes, and ultimately replaces, our understanding of any connection to the real. This therefore, nullifies the coextensive nature that exists between the use of our representations and the meaning of actual experience. With this, Baudrillard has stated that simulacra,

... is rather a question of substituting signs of the real for the real itself, that is, an operation to deter every real process by its operational double, a metastable, programmatic, perfect descriptive machine which provides all the signs of the real and short-circuits all its vicissitudes. Never again will the real have to be produced ...[6]

Perhaps the idea of simulacra is most evident when we consider the production and build-up of our nation's strategic arsenals, particularly as this relates to the concept of nuclear deterrence. A notion that erects symbolic boundaries and artificial fears for the purpose of negating the possibilities of an actual military conflict. This concept is an extreme example of the problems that face the current use of simulational discourse.

If simulacra or simulation is to hold any relevant degree of meaning for the discipline of architecture, then the use of this term must not be linked to a precursory or hyperreal attitude, but rather, it should be demonstrative and reflexive of the conditions to which it refers. Perhaps a reflection of the word simulate would better serve this point.

The word simulate is linked to the Latin term, *simulare*, which means "to make like." With this understanding it could be said that the origins of the word attaches itself to the notions of assemblage, construction, craft, and production - activities that are necessary to the making of architecture. Further interpretation of this definition implies that the word "like," implies the condition of something which is near or approximate. When we say that something holds the "likeness" of another thing we are referring to two separate entities which embody a degree of semblance (e.g. think of two people who hold similar facial characteristics). Therefore, two things which are similar can be conceived as embracing the qualities of sameness, but simultaneously, be similar due to their inherent differences.

This definition may at first seem oblique to our question regarding simulation and architecture, but it gives rise to an important query into the making of design and the making of a building. If we return to our initial question regarding graphic representation - and resist the notions of an exclusive, precursory reference - then we might begin to sketch a connection as to the possible value of a simulational discourse in the field of architecture. Such a discourse would imply a certain degree of artifice. What role does artifice contribute to the realization of a building via an architectonic technique? What are the intentions of such a technique? Joseph Rykwert has written,

> *There cannot be design ... without intention; and it follows, since intention is a voluntary function, that there cannot be design without artifice.*[7]

He further states,

> *This artifice of transforming brute matter into a built statement must therefore be subject to the rules of some game: clearly it is in some way a syntactic procedure of disposing elements according to some rules.*[8]

From these remarks we can conclude that the effect of a built statement necessitates a cause that is connected to intention, and that to employ the aspects of a game is to unfold and make evident those intentions. Artifice calls ingenuity into play and this play must model or simulate itself after the realities of some phenomena. This to and fro relationship leads us to a field were the artificial and the real remain distinct yet have the opportunity to meet. This domain is the arena of representation.

THE DILEMMA OF REPRESENTATION

Our current practices in the representation of architecture, in both the design studio and the professional office, has been typically guided by a process of transforming programmatic criteria into a document that alludes to the realization of some buildable artifact. As mentioned above, the designer seldom has the opportunity for exploring the techniques of the trades that he or she is to anticipate and is therefore restricted, to a degree, to the locale of his craft.

To minimize these demands, the architect has employed a variety of strategies. Unfortunately, many of these methods involve the reallocation of his time and efforts away from the trade with which he is most familiar. The architect is obligated to modify his craft in an effort to expedite his investigations so that he might find time to research other responsibilities (i.e. marketing, product research, etc.). Representational techniques such as standard nomenclature, templates, typical details, and the computer are often used to imitate, copy and repeat information so that which is represented can be accurately and quickly described. This method of description often increases the distance between the architect and his craft. In addition, the architect has further complicated matters by replacing his understanding of construction with a catalog of standard building practices. This reduced status weakens the architect's understanding of the techniques of representation and the ultimate goal of construction.

If we are to accept this as a plausible problem, then we must pin-point our understanding of the relationship between the representation and the thing which it aspires to represent. To say that a representation is a "picture" of reality is to acknowledge and accept its isolation from its original (i.e. the building, detail or material). This is not to infer that the original acquires a new, more real mode of appearance via the picture, but instead suggests that because of the original, the picture ultimately takes on its own reality.[9] This transitive ontological relationship between the original and its representation functions like a mirror to reveal a simultaneous linkage between a building and its graphic picture. When a building shows itself as an original it must fulfil the expectations that the drawing inspires. In what way can this be accomplished? The following examples demonstrate a means by which the nature and technique of materials simulated in the studio act as a point of departure for an *in transitu* relationship to the material which it depicts.

MATERIAL AND ITS SIMULATION

In the making of architecture we manipulate and transform (as Rykwert has noted) brute matter into a built statement. Materials such as stone, concrete, wood, steel and plaster embody distinct characteristics in terms of their workability, connective possibilities, finish, and weathering qualities. The specific nature of these materials allow variations in their use, form, and expression. Steel can be beaten into panels, stamped into sheets, and extruded into structural shapes. Wood can be sawn into boards, laminated to form composite sections, and rotary cut to yield veneers; while concrete can be cast into complex shapes requiring the aid of heavy machinery to lift it into place, or it can be formed into individual units and placed patiently by the human hand.

The strategies for connecting these various materials range from screwed to splined, linked to lapped, and wedged to welded. The resulting finishes of these materials can be honed, perforated, waxed, scored, painted, or polished. Lastly, the affects of age and weather on a particular surface can stain, fade, warp, erode or patina a material. The possibilities of these strategies appear limitless.

In practice, the designer must represent these material characteristics through limited means. His materials are less honored than those present in reality, therefore the architect is bound to an array of papers, films, liquids, and adhesives. By the same token, the range of suitable techniques are less extensive than of those of the craftsman. The architect finds himself restricted to drafting, fixing, cutting, washing, smudging, and erasing. Studio media are employed ubiquitously, that is, they are used to whatever means deemed necessary for the documentation and depiction of the real material they are attempting to represent. Consequently there is little room for understanding the use of this media and how it might assume a connection to what is built. As Marco Frascari would state, there is in effect no construing over the methods of construction.[10]

To address this question students in their second year of design at the University of North Carolina at Charlotte were assigned a project that addressed this problem. The intention of the project was two-fold: (1) to increase their skills of architectural delineation; and (2) to make a conceptual and graphic connection between the methods of the studio and the techniques of construction.

The student was first asked to design a small room that was composed of one entry, two vertical wall openings, one table, two chairs and a place to burn wood. The student was left free to render and depict materials with standard studio techniques. This portion of the project lasted one week and was juried The students were then taken to a construction site where they observed the use and application of methods and materials *in situ*. They were then asked to collect various graphic media and building materials for discussion. Both of these materials groups were examined for their characteristics, potential forms, use, method of application and expressive possibilities. Similarities were drawn between the two groups with the explicit intent of negating the visual similarities of outward appearance - i.e. texture, color and shape. Alternatively, the students made conceptual and procedural connections between the studio media and constructional materials, and therefore based their findings on application, technique, and constructional procedure.

These observations were then applied to the second portion of the project, in which the students were asked to outfit the interior surfaces of their designs according to an "explanatory narrative" that suggested the use and means of graphic media to that of the building material. The students were encouraged to select building materials for their interiors and then asked to construe and simulate those materials with an appropriate media. Alternatively, the students were allowed to anticipate actual building materials after establishing a narrative that centered on the capabilities of their studio media. By the same token, the student was also left free to work simultaneously in conceptualizing their simulation, and to therefore work in a transitive mode between the representation and the represented.

Figured panel simulation.

The process of these investigations led the student into an involved search for a "procedural story" on which to base their graphic and constructional intentions. Instead of contriving an explanation of experiential sequence to attach meaning to their designs, the students raised the issue of architectonic character through the explication of a constructional intention. These narrative techniques gave rise to an array of engaging scenarios. The use of freehand pencil simulated wood which was rough cut and embodied a surface with varied characteristics. Drafted pen and ink simulated the precision of standard steel shapes. An ink wash simulated the layering and plastic characteristics of a plaster/lime wash technique. The weathering of a copper panel was simulated by soaking cut paper in water, then allowing it to dry. Eradicating selected areas of a charcoal layer applied to the surface of mylar simulated the tooling of joints in a concrete block wall. Pre-cast or manufactured panelized elements were simulated by photocoping patterns onto swatches of paper to represent the repetitiveness of systematized constuction. The cutting and removal of the top (paper) layer of foamcore simulated the scoring of a horizontal poured-in-place concrete surface or a vertical plaster wall.

The exercise generated a high level of dialogue between the students as to the appropriateness of their individual representations as it related to actual building techniques. Often the exercise assumed the possibility of projecting a novel technique or alternative method of construction previously unknown to the student. The project was most interesting when unfamiliar construction techniques arose from the narration of studio techniques. Of course, such alternatives can carry inherit limitations, but the significance of conceptual thought as well as the level of the student imagination significantly outweighed these difficulties.

CONCLUSION

The findings of this project brings forth the possibility for an artifact to be born out of a transitive relationship between reflexion and making. Such investigations underpin the technological implications of a built world which is tied to building materials and graphic media, and equally as important, the conceptual narrative that drives technique. The full exposure to our understanding of *technè* is possible if we direct the way for an aesthetic experience that links itself to technological strategies (and vice versa). This proposition should be understood as a means rather than an end for architecture's ability to illuminate and promote poetic content.

The question of whether our designs should arise from the artificial constructs of a theoretical discourse, or by the innate experience of phenomena, is a conflict that offers no simple or direct conclusion. Yet, in light of this dilemma, it might be significant to answer that thought and being can survive in a mutual alliance that calls forth changing positions of command.[11] If our mortal endeavors for essence are to be granted, then we must be-thought the manoeuvering of our technological ways in a manner that allows for this exchange.

NOTES

1. Martin Heidegger, "The Question Concerning Technology," *Basic Writings* (New York: Harper & Row, 1977), 294.
2. Except from Richard Saul Wurman, ed., *What Will Be Has Always Been: The Words of Louis I. Kahn* (New York: Access Press & Rizzoli, 1986).
3. Early researchers in artificial intelligence attempted to isolate simplified blocks of the human thought with the hopes of gradually building up a more complex model for thinking. For the complexities of this type of representation reference Hubert Dreyfus, "Artificial Intelligence: The Problem of Knowledge Representation," *VIA 9: Re-Presentation* (New York: University of Pennsylvania & Rizzoli, 1988), 91-101.
4. Recent environmental simulation research by behavioral psychologists claim that "well-being" can be achieved as a product of our visual responses to artificial scenes. See Roger S. Ulrich, "Natural versus Urban Scenes: Some Psychophysical Effects," *Environment and Behavior*, Vol. 13, No. 5 (London: Sage, 1981), 523-556. One can only question the consequences of such simulational investigations, and how this research is falsely pecking at accumulated data and behavioral criteria for generalizing the urban environment.
5. Jean Baudrillard, *Simulations* (New York: Semiotext(e), 1983).
6. Ibid , 4.
7. Joseph Rykwert, "The Necessity of Artifice," *The Necessity of Artifice* (New York: Rizzoli, 1982), 59.
8. Ibid. The element of play is a central to Rykwert's explanation of artifice, and has been discussed extensively by Johan Huizinga in his book *Homo Ludens: A Study of the Play Element in Culture* (Boston: Beacon, 1950).
9. Hans-Georg Gadamer, *Truth and Method* (New York: Crossroad, 1985), 119-127.
10. Marco Frascari has identified the architectural detail as the element on which these two terms are ultimately joined. Reference Frascari's essay "The Tell-The-Tale Detail," *VIA 7: The Building of Architecture* (Cambridge: University of Pennsylvania & MIT, 1984), 22-37 [Dr. Frascari had inspired the Author's concept of simulation during graduate studies undertaken at University of Pennsylvania in 1984].
11. Fragment VIII by Parmenides elegantly states this changing relationship: *Thinking and the thought "it is" are the same. For without the being in relation to which it is uttered you cannot find thinking. For there neither is nor shall be anything outside of being, since Moira bound it to be whole and immovable. For that reason, all these will be mere names which mortals have laid down, convinced that they were true: coming-to-be as well as passing away, Being as well as nonbeing, and also change of place and variation of shining colors.* From Martin Heidegger, "Moira (Parmenides VIII, 34-41)," *Early Greek Thinking*, trans. D. F. Krell and F. A. Capuzzi (San Francisco: Harper & Row, 1975), 79-80.

CHAPTER 12

The Model Represents a Measure of Modernity

ALBERT C. SMITH
Georgia Institute of Technology

Measuring, the determining of dimensions, capacity or quantity of a thing, has historically been essential in the development of our technology. This paper will discuss how measuring is developed through our machine-like models.

The history of measuring begins about 10,000 years ago and follows the development of western civilization. The weights and measures systems and standards of the ancient eastern empires in the Tigris-Euphrates Valleys were adopted by the Greeks and passed on to the Romans. The Romans in turn extended their measurement practices throughout the European continent. This heritage was not to be challenged until new forces of unification brought forth the metric system in the 18th century.[1]

By understanding the measure, we are offered a standard, an acceptable measure of comparison for quantitative or qualitative value by which something intangible is determined or regulated. In other words, measuring is important in our search for understanding.

> Measurement begins with a definition of a quantity, condition, property, or other characteristic that is to be determined. These definitions of measure may be conceptual or operational definitions in preparation for measurement. That is, they must be defined in terms of a sequence of steps or operations that describe a procedure for accomplishing the measurement. The measuring instrument is an embodiment of these operational steps. If the measurement is not fully defined the measurement process becomes, itself, an essential part of the process.[2]

Each measurement of an unknown involves a comparison with a carefully conserved known. In the development of measurement several steps, not always apparent, are involved: 1) an unknown is measured by comparing it directly with a known device, for example, in architecture an architectural model may be compared with an existing building or series of buildings; or 2) the measuring device or instrument has been previously developed to agree with reference measurement standards. These reference standards are calibrated from time to time by comparing them with a higher-level, generally agreed upon reference standard, such as a temple against, say the Parthenon or man against God.[3]

"Measurement is the process used to answer the questions: how many? how much? Measurement, broadly defined, can be made by the unaided human senses and brain - for example, in estimating distances dimensions, temperatures, and weights; identifying and matching colors; estimating roughness by touch. In general, however, man's capabilities need be both extended and refined by instruments."[4] These instruments for measuring are manufactured through our machines.

The definition of the word machine generally means to us something with a practical purpose, a device that substitutes for or extends man's own forces. The word itself has the same root as might. Machines, unlike tools, have an important ability to take on a life of their own. This is why, historically, machines have often been regarded as toys or agents of magic, marvel and fantasy. For philosophers, they have served as symbols and metaphors.[5]

Measuring devices such as rulers, scales and various kinds of meters are manufactured to be in accordance with an exemplar model or ideal. It is through our attempts at measuring the exemplar model that we create not only measuring devices such as inches, liters and pounds but also our philosophies needed for measuring and defining the interpretive narrations of the small copy model. The small copy model offers us an understandable surface (framework) upon which we can project and develop our measures of the exemplar model. What each of us sees reflected in our attempts of measurement is our current relationship with this exemplar.

The word *model* comes from the Latin *modulus* a diminutive of *modus* which means to measure. A model is typically a small object, usually built to scale, that represents another, often larger object. It can be a preliminary pattern serving as a plan from which an item not yet construct will be produced. A model can also offer a tentative description of a theory or system that accounts for all of its known properties.[6] Architectural models operate in both of these areas.

Vitruvius, in the *Ten Books of Architecture*, devotes the entire last book to the study of machines. It is within this last book that Vitruvius discusses models. A machine can be a structural or constructed thing; which is why many architects consider a building a machine. The architectural machine model is typically a small scale machine offering a representation of a possible future of a larger machine. In other words, the machine model is a scale device, which helps us extend our intellectual might in an attempt to understand and define the measure a complex whole.

The architectural model is a mechanism for creating definition, mediating between perceived chaos and man's designs. Sitting between lifelessness and the uncanny, the model is cast in the role of being a measuring machine, offering us the opportunity of an understandable scale within which we can develop our narratives, myths, buildings and finally cities. Myths, legends and fairy tales, Machine models themselves, contain within them attempts to measure a seemingly chaotic world. I have created a myth about the first model machine that I use as a description to explain how the machine model measures. This myth offers us one extreme example of the beginnings of measuring through the model. The cathedral, which I will discuss later, offers us a machine model perceived to be more developed measurement. I believe that it is important to look at these extremes in our attempt to find a more balanced and understandable relationship with our machine model.

Long ago, before anyone built a first primitive hut, there lived a very intelligent human. One day the human was walking in the woods and found a marvelous stick. The stick was long - about as long as the human. It was straight, strong, and pointed at one end. There was something about this particular stick that made the human want to pick it up and keep it. Rather quickly the human found that the stick could be used as a staff to ease his walking. It was also useful in digging for delicious roots and helpful in knocking down berries from high branches. Once the human was attacked by a vicious animal and found that the stick could be used for defense. The human realized the stick made a wonderful and controllable extension of the hand. The stick was a tool and a most prized possession.

Still wandering, the human arrived in a large pleasant clearing and decided to rest there. Finding no close-by tree against which to lean the stick, the human decided to drive it directly into the ground. All day long the human rested and watched the shadow of the stick change. The once-controllable stick was beginning to raise wondrous, but not necessarily easily understandable, questions about the universe. The stick took on a life of its own; it presented a more understandable scale model of the sun opening questions about a vast chaotic universe. It changed from being a tool to a machine model and seemed to offer the possibility of understanding the measure of things.

From then on, whenever the human met other humans, the stick would be ceremoniously thrust into the ground. They, then, were also compelled to think about their relationship to their universe and make a variety of attempts at explanation. The stick, model, machine possessed the most interesting and powerful ability to take on a life of its own.

As I have mentioned earlier, there are two types of models. The first is the exemplar (the ideal) and the second is the small copy (our attempt at reproducing the ideal) or the machine model. It is through our attempts at measuring the exemplar that we create the analogies (framework) needed in developing the interpretive narrations of our small copies. In other words, the measurer's relationship with the exemplar is important in defining the measurement through the machine model small copy.

Chartres Cathedral is similar to a machine model and offers an example of a thinking machine. The cathedral towers over the town dominating the life of the people. It is a machine model for measuring the exemplar Catholic religion. Though it certainly offers a wonderful example of medieval engineering, when used as a model, the machine qualities of the cathedral become more apparent. The building creates a strong feeling of the presence of God. The builders have carefully controlled the quality and the quantity of light. Your eyes are forced to focus upwards on the brilliant stained glass windows. The sound inside is hushed reminding you that you are in a sacred place. The relationship of the parishioners to the church hierarchy is carefully controlled. Even the damp humidity and the faint smell of eight hundred years of pilgrims reinforce the feeling of awe and history.

The Catholic religion itself is measured through the cathedral. The building offers through sculpture and stained glass windows the story of medieval Catholicism to an illiterate population. Each door and window defined the religion in a simple direct way to the reader. The building became a device for thinking about the measurements of the church. The cathedral has taken on a life of its own and thus is an example of a model machine.

The stick and cathedral offer a model machine with which to project the user's thoughts in the development of the measure. They are models, both mediating between the order of the known and the chaos of the unknown. The possibilities of measurement offers the beginning of a small amount of control to its user. Nevertheless, like a crystal ball, tea leaves left in a cup, or smoke in an alchemist's tort, the user could never be sure of how he or others would interpret the message of the model machine on any given day. The small copy model presents us with an understandable surface (framework) on which we can project and define our measures of the exemplar model.

I would like to illustrate this point further with the following concerning the projection of the measurers unconscious imagery. This imagery is the reflection of our unconscious from our machine models.

Our relationship with our machine model is a strange blend of religious science and scientific religion combining a scientific pursuit of nature's secrets with a religious quest aiming at measuring ultimate nature. The machine model has thus an exoteric or *scientific* aspect and an esoteric or *mystic* aspect. In explaining the strange development of esoteric or *mystic* measuring one encounters the psychological phenomenon of projection and the universal law that nature abhors a vacuum. As our age-long investigation of order plunges us them into a dark void, the darkness was finally defined by the groping psyche of the measurer who projected thoughts onto the model. Thus, through the indirect way of projection and free association the measurer came to activate the unconscious which allied itself to their work in the form of hallucinatory or visionary experiences.[7]

Christianity looks for a tightly-controlled measure offered in a specific way. A process using a machine model that appears to deal with *such unexplainable* as alchemy or magic would appear suspect in such a controlled environment. A machine model offering a more tightly controlled narrative is much more acceptable.

The cathedral, though operating as a machine model, maintains much greater control over its user projections than the stick. The church did not necessarily wish the parishioners to jump to too many wrong conclusions. The Catholic religion offered the reader a relatively tightly controlled narration because the church offered a specific solution to what the unknown was. No wonder competing exemplars such as myths, legends, witchcraft and modern science were frowned upon. The church did not offer the reader much opportunity for misinterpretation of the measure.

There are those who are suspicious of the measures of modern technology. Some say this condition has developed because of another machine stick that sits in a concrete silo in Montana. There seems to be a great deal of questioning of even the most basically accepted control over our measurements.

Errors in measurement may result from imperfect operator performance. Measurement, it would seem to be developed from the corporal or human measurement, for the human measurement. When you remove the imprecise human factor to create seemingly perfect measurements you may be destroying an important link to the human factor.

This brings us to another word related to *modus, manner*. Certainly one of the key definitions of the word *manner*, is that it is a character that makes an artist's or architect's work uniquely his/her own. This is the manner of the measure that the measurer requires for the human element. *Manner* comes from the Latin, "of the hand". It means kind, sort, nature or character of a thing. It is a characteristic or customary mode of acting, as in habit, usage or custom. Manner is the nature or normal behavior of a thing.[8]

Though the word *mode* is related directly to model and measure, I believe that it is most closely related to the word *manner*. A mode is a prevailing fashion or style of dress or behavior. It can be a musical arrangement or rhythmical scheme, *mode* relates to architecture by setting a mood, a temporary state of mind or feeling, or the manner in which the action or state expressed by a verb is viewed concerning functions such as factuality, possibility or command.[9]

Kant used the word modalitat, usually translated as modality, which meant the manner as actual, as possible, or as necessary - in which something existed.[10] Locke defined mode as the manner in which an idea is known. Mode to Spinoza was, "That which exists in and through, something other than itself."[11]

The model is the mode in which the manner is measured. The instrument for that measure is human and therefore imprecise. Architects have learned that the imprecision in their model machines is necessary because that is human.

The word *model*, also relates to *modest* through the Latin *modus*. *Modest* means having a limited and not exaggerated estimate of one's ability or worth; or lacking in vanity or conceit, or not bold or self-assertive. It can mean free from exaggeration or overstatement. Modest can mean reasonable or moderate. Modest can mean something that observes conventional standards of proper dress and behavior or limited in size or amount. Modest means not in excess. In its archaic form *modest* means to exercise control over or to act as a mediator or to be in the middle. This is quite similar to the word *moderate*, which means characterized by an avoidance of extremes of behavior.[12] The modest measure reflects the mode.

The reflection of our current thoughts and experiences from the small copy model is a measure of modernity. *Modern*, which comes to us from *modus*, means something that reflects the manner of today. The measure of architecture has always been related to its manner. Without manner, we have no idea of what we are measuring. This is how we gain understanding of the manner of a thing. This is also why, as society changes, so does our definition of manner change. In other words the model is our modest mode in which the manner is measured. This is how we define the measures that are essential to our technology.

NOTES

1. "Measure", *Encyclopaedia Americana*, (Danbury, Conn., Encyclopaedia Americana, 1982), XVIII, p. 585.
2. "Measurement, Principles and Insturments Of", *Encyclopaedia Britannica* (Chicago, Illinois, Encyclopaedia Britannica, 1974), XI, p. 728.
3. "Measure", p. 584.
4. "Measurement, Principles and Instruments Of", p. 728.
5. K. G. Hulten, *The Machine as Seen at the End of the Mechanical Age*, (New York, New York; Museum of Modern Art, 1968), p. 7.
6. "Model", *Webster's Third New International Dictionary*, (Springfield, Mass., C.G. Merriam Co., 1967), II, p. 1451.
7. Johannes Fabricius, *Alchemy* (paraphrased), (Copenhagen, Denmark, Rosenkilde and Bragges, 1976), p. 97.
8. "Manner", *Webster's Third New International Dictionary*, p. 1376.
9. "Mode", *Webster's II, New Riverside University Dictionary*, (Boston, Mass., Houghton Mifflin Co., 1984), p. 761.
10. Peter A. Angeles, *Dictionary of Philosophy*, (New York, New York, Barnes and Noble, 1981), p. 177.
11. Ibid., p. 177.
12. "Modes", Webster's II, p. 761.

CHAPTER 13

A Monument to the End of Modernity: Implications of Gianni Vattimo's Discourse on Architecture

GEVORK HARTOONIAN
Spring Garden College

In "The End of Modernity,"[1] Gianni Vattimo brings Martin Heidegger and Friedrich Nietzsche together, to establish the traits of a "post-modern philosophy." Heidegger's thought on metaphysics is blended with Nietzscheian nihilism in order to break the impasse of the postmodern condition. Vattimo's emphasis on the criticality of the work of art and the place he assigns to this subject relates his discourse to the tradition of German thought which conceives of the work of art as the last bastion of resistance against the will to power. Thus, he creates a distance between himself and Jurgen Habermas while bringing other figures of the Frankfurt School back to the fore. Drawing on the philosophies of Theodor Adorno, Ernest Bloch and Walter Benjamin, Vattimo foregrounds metaphysics and humanism, and points out their dependency on the nihilism of technology. Vattimo carries out his argument around and within the idea of the "weak thought" as a project, in Heideggerian sense of the term, where Being and the world come together.

The following pages focus mainly on Vattimo's development of Heidegger's conclusive assertion that the essence of technology is not technological. Vattimo sees in the nihilism of technology humanism's dependency on Western metaphysics. "Technology is a threat to metaphysics and to humanism in appearance alone, for it is in the very nature of technology that the defining traits of metaphysics and humanism--which both had previously kept hidden from view--should be brought out into the open."[2] My concluding remarks will study the implication of Vattimo's observation as it relates to architecture.

The idea of "weak thought" implies a state of subjectivity that one must pass through before arrives at the healing process. "Weak thought" is somewhat like the sick person who not only has to admit the existence and strength of the sickness but must live with it. Vattimo challenges self-conscious subjectivity, which for a long time has been considered the referential center of clarity in Western humanism. Vattimo also criticizes modern subjectivity which, thanks to its critical vision, recognizes the cause of sickness and plots a project to overcome it. In the context of the socio-cultural and political experience of the last decades, Vattimo proposes the idea of "weak thought" as an opportunity to heal the self who witnesses the bankrupting of ideology and the frustration of the bourgeois state by its own problematics. In opposition to the metaphysical idea of overcoming, Vattimo suggests Heidegger's concept of Verwindung: "an overcoming which is in reality a recognition of belonging, a healing of an illness, and an assumption of responsibility."[3]

In the world of medicine, "healing" has different connotations. A physician cures the patient by defeating the cause of sickness in stages. When necessary, surgery and transplantation are the last resort as an aggressive act of overcoming. Yet, it is the main concern of the psychoanalyst to heal the patient by modifying and readjusting the self to the unpleasant given conditions of life. "One of the earliest homages paid to psychoanalysis speaks of healing through consciousness. The phrase is exact," claims Paul Ricoeur, "if one means thereby that analysis wishes to substitute for an immediate and dissimulating consciousness a mediate consciousness taught by the reality principle."[4] Confronting the nihilism of technology and its impact on humanism, Vattimo's concept of healing recalls certain traits of Freudian therapy. This analogy could be generalized to include post-Hegelian thought, wherein Hegelian dialectics is questioned and the relation to the past is resumed from the scope of recollection.

A major object of Freudian healing is to neutralize the subject. A radical version of this is defined by Michel Foucault as the death of the man or the author. Yet, Foucault proposes that instead of just repeating an empty slogan that heralds the death of author and God, "we should await the fluid function released by this disappearance."[5] In response, Vattimo reactivates the dynamic implication of Nietzsche's view of the death of God--the situation in which "man rolls from the center toward X"--and unfolds the thematics of a post-modern subjectivity. I will come back to the idea of recollection as healing and modification of the subject in architecture shortly, but what is of interest here is the practical dimension of Vattimo's discourse, the "assumption of responsibility.''

Adorno has painted a grim picture of the culture industry: its regulated and systematic nature, its technological nihilism, and finally, the drive to desecrate historically accumulated values. Against this background, Adorno envisions hibernation as a strategic tactic for intellectuals, and the detachment of the work of art from its social context as a means of salvation. However, even Adorno's negative dialects does not help him veil the humanistic aspects of his prescription from Vattimo's position. Vattimo is also critical of the Deluzian simulacra and the Derridian textualism. Deconstructivists disintegrate metaphysical dualities, yet sustain the long-lived duality of subject and object. Vattimo's post-modern subject, on the other hand, accepts the nihilism of technology and engages in active reconstruction of Being in the ''setting-into-work of truth.''

The idea of technological nihilism is not a new subject. Nineteenth-century technology functioned in economic realms, transforming the conventional means of production. Machines, materials and labor were influenced by scientific and technical innovations. The ''organism of production'' of different cultural artifacts became subject to technological change. The depth of this technological infusion depended upon the topological place of an artifact in the pyramid of the overall organization of production. One can recall the importance of transportation in the years following the industrial revolution and its impact on the formal and conceptual aspects of the design of bridges. Through progress, technology has expanded its territory of domination from the technical to the cultural. Mass production has metamorphosized into mass culture.[6] Giovanna Borradori's observation is apt: ''Technology in fact has come to occupy a destinal horizon, since it no longer represents a variable of economic development but is established as the destiny, both congenital and irremediable, of the Western metaphysical discourse.''[7] Vattimo locates the nihilism of technology along the horizon of the project of the historical avant-garde. From that standpoint, he beholds the decline of art. ''The poetics of the avant-garde reject the limitations which philosophy, especially of the neo-Kantian and neo idealist sort, had previously imposed upon art.'' Vattimo continues that, ''avant-garde art refuses to be considered as a place of non-theoretical and non-practical experience, and instead claims to be the model for a privileged mode of knowledge of the real, a moment of subversion of the individual and society, and thus an instrument of true social and political action.''[8] The historical processes that encouraged the development of mass culture and mechanization to impact works of art, as discussed by Walter Benjamin, has convinced Vattimo to dispense with any attribute of authenticity or revolutionary function for art. Yet, he does not resign himself to the idea of the death of art. Vattimo's thought surpasses the critical discourse on art and the prevailing eclecticism of postmodernity. Without proposing a priori conditions, he suggests an understanding of art work from the point of view of ''weak thought.'' In fact, the post-modern subjectivity in favor of which Vattimo argues implies a ''project of historical cultural disarticulation of the sign.''[9]

Disarticulation of the sign, i.e., ''de-sign'', a phrase framed by Borradori, does not take place along a textual level. Rather, it appears in the ''striving relationship between setting forth and setting up,'' discussed by Heidegger.[10] Heidegger believed that a work of art differs from object-being when it becomes a work-being; that is, when art stands in relation to a historical world. The temporality of the work of art opens up a world in which ''all things gain their lingering and hastening, their remoteness and nearness, their scope and limits.''[11] Heidegger's concern for things can be read as a desire to modify the subjective ambitions of the artist. This prediliction recalls the notion of healing and the resignation of the self for a setting-into-work of truth.'' Yet the setting-up is not confined to the abstract realm of objective or subjective constructs. According to Heidegger, the work's work-being consists in the setting-forth, too, i.e., its making. In this instance, the concept of making is critical to an understanding of the truth content of the work of art, in order to discern an artifact from art. Heidegger argues that production of a work if art differs from fabrication of artifacts in that the usefulness of the artifact causes the material to disappear. In contrast, in a Greek temple, for example, ''The rock comes to bear and rest and so first becomes rock; metal comes to glitter and shimmer, colors to glow, tones to sing, the word to speak.''[12] Basing his argument on Heidegger's observation, Vattimo concludes that:

> All the difficulties that aesthetic philosophy encounter in accounting for the experience of the decline of art, distracted perception, and mass culture, derive from the fact that it continues to think in terms of the work as a necessarily eternal form, and, at a deeper level, in terms of Being as permanence, grandeur, and force. The decline of art is instead an aspect of the more general situation of the end of metaphysics, in which thought is called upon to perform a Verwindung of metaphysics, in all the various senses of the term. . .[13]

One can draw two conclusions from Vattimo's discourse on the decline of art. First, by disclosing the dependency of humanism on the nihilism of technology, Vattimo sheds some light on the experience of the historical avant-garde and the latter's influence on contemporary theories of architecture. I am thinking of Manfredo Tafuri's discourse on ''the project of history.'' Tafuri holds that the modern movement after the eighteenth century is followed by a gap that exists between avant-garde ideology and the translation into technique of that ideology.[14] At this juncture, I would also suggest that Vattimo goes beyond Peter Burger's insightful proposition that post-avant-garde art has turned art into an institution. Yet, Burger's conclusions about the historical avant-garde and its influence on the present work of art remains ambiguous.[15] Second, attention must be given to the scope of possibilities that the "weak thought" opens for registering new possibilities of meaning for architecture. The import of this last point is relevant to Vattimo's short and dense piece on ornament/monument.

Once again, plumbing Heidegger's thinking on the importance of spatiality for architecture, Vattimo radicalizes the question of the "distinction between decoration as surplus and what is proper to the thing and to the work." Nevertheless, Vattimo's major reference is Hans-Georg Gadamer. Discussing the differences between sign and symbol, Gadamer asserts that it is critical for a sign to attract attention to itself and to re-present the thing that is not present.[16] Gadamer also maintains that architecure "not only embraces all the decorative aspects of the shaping space, including ornament, but is itself decorative in nature."[17] I would argue that what is by nature decorative in architecture is the tectonic; the art of construction of purposeful space. The function of the tectonic is somewhat like the joint; to draw the viewer's attention to itself, to satisfy his/her taste, and then to direct attention away from itself to the greater whole in which the context of life is expressed. In this field of consideration, the idea of monument disarticulates its conventional meaning. Monument no longer implies a building which institutionalizes the foundation of the will to power. Instead, it is a flash of truth which recollects the fourfold of earth, sky, divinities and mortals. Monument is an ornament per se, a joint which does not cover a structural defeat. It inaugurates the conflict between the setting-up and setting-forth of the work.

Finally, I would like to bring your attention to the work of two contemporary archtiects who differed in matters of aesthetics, but whose architecture shares a common interest. With the change in the essence of technology, both Mies van der Rohe and Louis Kahn opened an architectural discourse in which the idea of the joint is formative in two senses. On one level, their work presents the conventional meaning of the joint as a device to bring different parts of a detail together. On another level, however, Kahn and Mies impart a metaphorical dimension to the joint. Both architects perceive architecture as a joint standing midway between tradition and civilization. Their discourse on the joint transcends the distance between building and signification into a constructed form conceived with existential depth. Numerical drawings by Mies depict a human figure within a space cleared of any figural dimension. The void maintains its meaning not in its non-ornamental surfaces, but by anchoring tectonic to the solitude of modern man. Kahn encloses this Miesian void and imparts an archaic existance to it. Both Kahn in Dacca and Mies in Berlin magnify the joint to the size of the building itself. Hence, the idea of monument, which for Vattimo, "is not a function of subjective self-reference. It is primarily--perhaps even from the point of view of cultural anthropology--a funerary monument built to bear the traces and the memory of someone across time, but for others."[18]

Compressing the temporal factor between us and "others" would weaken the subjective intentionalities of the self. It would also give things a chance to speak for themselves. In this way, architecture would speak, not by hiding a structural defect behind an ornament, but by incorporating one with the other. We think of the tectonic in the space where construction and signification traverse a middle ground. We think and DE-SIGN in this place of intimacy as does Heidegger's potter[19] who makes a jug not by thinking of its sides and bottom, or of the materiality of his clay. Instead, he shapes the void which gathers itself together for the purpose of containing. The void is empty; however, it holds something more. And it is precisely this surplus, Bloch notes, "that forms and maintains the substratum of the cultural heritage, the memory that is present not only in the early period but more so during the full day of a society, even partly in the twilight of its decline."[20]

NOTES

1. Gianni Vattimo, *The End of Modernity*, (Baltimore, Johns Hopkins University Press, 1988).
2. *Ibid*, p. 40.
3. *Ibid.*
4. Paul Ricoeur, *Freud and Philosophy: An Essay on Interpretation*, (New Haven: Yale University Press, 1970), p. 35. Ricoeur discloses the three figures responsible for demystifying hermeneutics--Marx, Nietzche, and Freud--who set up the rude discipline of necessity and thus dispense with the grace of the imagination. VAttimo, on the other hand, drawing on Heidegger's thought, touches certain aspects of what Ricoeur terms the mytho-poetic core of imagination. In fact, Vattimo bridges the gap between the two schools of interpretation, that is, the "suspicion," and the "recollecting," as defined by Ricoeur.
5. Michel Foucault, "What is an Author," *Language, Conter Memory, Practice*, (New York: Cornell University Press, 1977), p. 120.
6. Vattimo, *Op. Cit.*, p. 55.
7. Giovanna Borradori, *Recoding Metaphysics*, edited, G. Borradori, (Evanston: Northwestern University Press, 1988), p. 17.
8. Vattimo, *Op. Cit.*, p. 53.
9. Borradori, *Op. Cit.*, p. 5.
10. Martin Heidegger, *Poetry, Language, Thought*, (New York: Harper & Row Publishers, 1971), p. 49.
11. *Ibid*, p. 45.
12. *Ibid.*
13. Vattimo, *Op. Cit.*, p. 64.
14. Manfredo Tafuri, *The Sphere and Labyrinth*, (Cambridge: The MIT Press, 1987), pp. 1-21.
15. Peter Burger, *Theory of Avant-Garde*, (Minneapolis: University of Minnesota Press, 1984). In particular, see Jochen Schulte-Sass's Introduction.
16. Vattimo, *Op. Cit.*, p. 87.
17. *Ibid.*, p. 140.
18. *Ibid.*, p. 73.
19. Heidegger, *Op. Cit.*, p. 169.
20. Ernest Bloch, *The Utopian Function of Art and Literature*, (Cambridge: The MIT Press, 1988), p. 118.

CHAPTER 14

Invisible/Visible Technology

DAVID EVAN GLASSER
University of South Florida

DEUS EX MACHINA

> If we free ourselves from the view that there is a single legitimate sensibility by which the uniqueness of our time can be revealed, we make history a repository of meanings relevant to the present. For the rejection of historicism also liberates us from the belief that whatever was meaningful in past ages in meaningful only to those ages and to no others, least of all our own.[1]

Historical events appear to have differing rates of evolution and density of effect. According to George Kubler, for instance, historical time can be characterized in terms of categorical varieties, in the same way as the speed of gravitational fields will vary with mass.[2] Following the cosmic analogy, it is here suggested that the first decade of our century represented a period in which a number of crucial technological theories became compacted and formed a sort of intellectual black hole whose polemic density served to obscure a great number of opposing and potentially valid alternative theories of construction.[3] Although the quantity of built work accomplished by the Futurists was slight their passionate support of the technological society was so exigent that their radical views became a constituent part of the Modernist program at the expense of the French rationalist position exemplified by Rondolet, Guadet, and Choisy. For Choisy, in particular, architectural construction represented the embodiment of enduring, non-arbitrary, principles which were non-temporal and ideologically ahistorical. The linkage of the Foundation Manifesto of Marinetti and the Futurists to the French rationalist position, described by Reyner Banham[4], contains some paradoxical aspects. For one thing, the *rigoristi* and rationalists assumed that embryonic aspects of useful technology were subsumed in historical styles. For another, they envisioned a modern architecture which would represent a compilation of the past efforts of the ancients, rather than one which would require its deconstruction and dissolution. The Futurists, on the other hand, insisted on the establishment of a *tabula rasa* and the wilful sublimation of time honored technique.

THE CLOAK OF INVISIBILITY

Talking of the relation between Form and Function, Eliel Saarinen observed that, 'the problem of function -''form follows function''-is an intrinsic, necessary, and plainly self-explanatory phenomenon in life, art included'.[5] He went on to note that the issue was so transparent as to be beyond mentioning. It was, in other words, so much present in the minds of designers that it needed no special attention. Over time, the invisible nature of functionalism has altered to the extent that many practitioners question its validity as a prime form determinant in building design. The question of technology has not, in my view, undergone the same scrutiny and alteration as has functionalist theory. The progressive teleology of technology forecast by Marinetti-a future architecture of concrete, steel, and glass-has become a ubiquitous reality.

Reading the Manifesto now, the agitated polemics employed to suppress traditional techniques and forms seem remarkably quaint. The effects of the technological revolution unleashed by the Modernists were, however, less quaint and largely destructive of the positions outlined by their enunciated program. The call for the use of new materials was undoubtedly based on a genuine desire for tectonic authenticity. Traditional construction methods, and masonry in particular, were eschewed as having been too closely associated with archaic bourgeois styles. Like the DNA genetic mechanism, the new techniques were to function as carriers of avant-garde architectural personality and character. The possibility of mutation of their technological ideologies, as a consequence of capitalist intervention, appears not to have been considered.[6] In this respect, Tafuri's observations on the operation of ideological models undergoing transformation within the cycle of production is apt:

> In this task the work of pure reason must not be divorced from social ends: the innovating models must correspond simultaneously to the need of given moments, both for the restructuring of the production cycle and for the distribution of merchandise.[7]

It was the hope of the Utopian Modernists to find a mature correspondence between the means and ends of architectural construction which would transcend time and style. In this respect, it was envisioned that the role of technology would assume the cloak of invisibility in relation to design, in the same way as Saarinen had characterized functionalism. This accorded with the positions of Choisy and Viollet-le-Duc as well, whose preoccupation with Gothic construction was for its pre-eminent logic and not for its stylistic attributes.

A visible alternative to traditional technique at first, concrete and steel construction rapidly supplanted existing technology and managed within a few decades to assume the optimal global consequences envisioned by the Futurists and Le Corbusier.[8] In the process, the role of technology has moved from one of original visibility to ubiquitous invisibility to the current state of ambiguity which has stimulated vigorous discussion at conferences such as this. Machine production was to have provided the symbolic role of craft and perfection and establish the neutral grounds whereby the formal and spatial aspects of architecture would be primarily manifest. It was envisioned as a liberating and transparent setting for the establishment of an architecture with implicit meaning. Instead, what has occurred is the formation of a veiling, rather than revealing instrumentality.

TECHNOLOGY IN THE EMERGING CITY

The concealing nature of modern technology is nowhere more evident than in rapidly developing areas of the nation, such as Los Angeles and Tampa, where the free play of capitalist development can take place in an environment with few constraints. The combination of untrammeled speculation in urban land, banking regulations with respect to limited mortgage duration, and the bottom line propensities of the development community have conspired to produce a typology of scenographic architecture which has become a universal part of the visual landscape. In Florida, the environment with which I am most recently familiar, the pattern of development in both the private and public sectors follows along well-established and predictable lines. Initial proposals are made with respect to site coverage, massing, and architectural format. Subsequent analysis is undertaken to determine cost parameters and decisions are subsequently made with respect to structure and enclosure systems, usually without regard conceptual or spatial intentions. In many cases, contract documents are described in sufficiently flexible terms to permit contractors to make substantial alterations to building appearance in the interest of economy.[9]

The dispiriting effect of this process has been to reinforce the separation of design intention and system determination to the point that building concepts are usually selected on the basis of their inherent ability to accommodate a wide range of technological choices. This, in turn, has created an intellectual environment in which strong allegiance to concepts dependent upon intimate relationships between design and construction are discouraged. The result has been the creation of a building typology unforeseen by the early modernists: neutral volumes designed to accept a range of external treatments without respect to function or meaning.[10]

The successful partnership which has developed between the offices of Venturi, Rauch and Scott-Brown and the Payette Company, is a case in point. The Lewis Thomas laboratories at Princeton represent a paradigmatic example of a globalizing tendency. The Payette firm was contracted to prepare complete drawings for a research laboratory, leaving the outer 4" of the building to be determined by others. The exterior wall sections are drawn with a dotted line indicating finishes and wall details by others, in this case by Venturi and his partners. All the structural support conditions and exterior openings were established by Payette. Venturi's entire effort was directed to the selection of brick, determination of sill, jamb, and head conditions, etc. No alterations to the basic lab package was permitted. This division of responsibility and purpose was so well received by the clients, due in large part to budgetary and time controls, that the joint venture has been engaged to undertake at least five additional research lab projects. This partnership, however, represents the optimum example of this emerging prototype. The Payette firm has a substantial reputation for excellent and conscientious attention to technical detail. Venturi, whatever individual opinion might be with respect to his artistic style, is a widely recognized and premiated architect. In the majority case, however, neither the technical nor creative excellence provided by the Venturi/Payette association is present. The typical firm in Florida, for instance, is content to permit economic circumstances and/or construction exigencies to dictate building appearance; a position unlikely to be acceptable to a strong-minded designer like Venturi.

One of the factors clearly not understood by the Futurists was the impact of economic determinism on the building process.[11] This reductionist position, coupled with the uncritical belief in the teleological ends of technological progress, has created a situation in which the means of construction have become highly visible, with respect to their instrumental presence, and invisible with respect to their original role as carriers of meaning. A primary casualty in the development of contingent architecture has been the city. Certainly, in the case of Tampa, the expedient nature of building has served to establish an urban environment in which few residents feel particular allegiance. The visible disdain for individual building has created a city, invisible to most of its inhabitants, who are unaware if, or where, a city center exists.

THE RE-ESTABLISHMENT OF TECTONIC AUTHORITY

Florida has launched an ambitious legislative program, probably one of the most far-reaching in the nation, with respect to growth management. The regulations now in place deal primarily with the question of concurrency, that is, the development of a logical balance between civic and private investment in infrastructure and the amount of permitted development. The full impact of this program has not yet been felt, since it has only recently been put into effect. Not yet fully addressed in the legislation is the question concerning technology and its relation to the built environment. However, factors relating to weathering, climate and ecology are increasingly becoming important issues in the minds of legislative bodies. Environmental Impact studies have become a major industry in Florida, and in many cases years are required for their successful completion. The reality of severe hurricanes and substantial termite damage to timber structures, has produced a stiffening of building restrictions, which offers the promise of more substantial construction in the future.

The larger issue with respect to tectonic meaning is a problematic one in a democratic society, in which there is great reluctance to accept dictated limitations on private activities. There are, however, several promising tendencies present in Tampa, which could be extrapolated in terms of meaningful strategies to accomplish an architecture with some degree of tectonic significance. Tampa has recently adopted the formation of a Design Review Board with some supporting legislative muscle. More important, one of the area's largest developers, the Good Gulfstream Company, controlling almost 4,000 acres of North Tampa, has established an internal design review board with provisions for a highly restricted architectural design vocabulary. The University of South Florida, with the assistance of our program, is in the process of developing similar guidelines for landscaping and site treatment. These measures represent, however, instrumental means of review, and do not guarantee tectonic authenticity in the sense originally intended by the Futurists. What I foresee is an evolutionary process of densification in which the city operates as a palimpsest for successive waves of development, each more compact and more substantially built than the last. In this regard, the nature and placement of the infrastructure becomes the most significant factor in the development of both building and city.[12] This optimistic position allows for the gradual transformation of buildings over time and argues for an incremental re-establishment of tectonic authority as the society and city matures.

NOTES

1. Macrae-Gibson, Gavin, *The Secret Life of Buildings,* Cambridge, Mass., MIT Press, 1988, p.xv.
2. Kubler, George, *The Shape of Time,* New Haven, Yale University Press, 1962, pp. 84-85. In the chapter entitled, "Fast and Slow Happening", Kubler explains the impact of the mass of resources and technology on differing societies, observing that industrial nations are likely to experience accelerated change as a consequence of their concentrated wealth and technology.
3. See Hawking, Stephen W., *A Brief History of Time*, New York, Bantam Books, 1988, for an elegant description of the formation of black holes and the creation of densities so great that all light is gravitationally captured.
4. Banham, Reyner, *Theory and Design in the First Machine Age,* Cambridge, Mass., MIT Press, Second Edition, 1982, pp. 23-34.
5. Saarinen, Eliel, *The Searchfor Form in Art and Architecture*, Dover Publications, New York, pp. 216-224.
6. See Tafuri, Manfredo, *Architecture and Utopia - Design and Capitalist Development,* trans. Barbara Luigia La Penta, Cambridge, Mass, MIT Press, 1976, pp. 65-67. A convincing argument is advanced with respect to the tendency of avant-garde movements to be essentially removed from the explicit implementation of propositions. "Its [intellectual work] objective, however, it always to get out of productive work and stand before it as its *critical conscience*".
7. Tafuri, p.67.
8. Frampton, Kenneth, "Towards a Critical Regionalism:Six Points for an Architecture of Resistance" in *The Anti-Aesthetic*, Hal Foster, ed. , Pt. Townsend, Washington, 1983, pp. 16-30.
9. See Glasser, David Evan, "Curtains for the Wall" in the proceedings of the *Symposium on Architecture and ACSA Technology Conference, '89*, published by the Office of Building Research, School of Architecture, LSU, ACSA, and the Louisiana Solar Design Association, pp. 256,257. The article describes a major building at the University of South Florida whose technology was determined exclusively by economic and expedient exigencies.
10. See Herdeg, Klaus, *The Decorated Diagram*, Cambridge, Mass., MIT Press, 1985, for a discussion of the factors which has contributed to the architectural community's willingness to separate issues in architectural design.
11. Brolin, Brent, *The Failure of Modern Architecture*, New York, Van Nostrand, 1976, p. 16. The elimination all that was unnecessary in practical terms accorded with nineteenth century utilitarian ideals. This position formed the basis for the Protestant Ethic belief in the validity of cost-benefit analysis of all production, in which architecture, regrettably, has become subsumed.
12. Glasser, David Evan, "Disappearing Act: The Case for Transitional Construction" in the proceedings of the *Symposium on Architecture and ACSA Technology Conference, '89*, published by the Office of Building Research, School of Architecture, LSU, ACSA, and the Louisiana Solar Design Association, pp. 215,216. The case is made for accepting the temporal nature of construction in rapid growth areas and making adequate provision for consolidation and improvement over time.

CHAPTER 15

An Interpretation of Urban High Tech: Its Essence and Existence

NADIA M. ALHASANI
University of Pennsylvania

Similar to Aristotle, Avicenna, the eastern philosopher, was engaged in the notion of Being and the wish for a special science, metaphysics. For him, the idea of Being is acquired by experience, initiated by intuition, and eventually becoming necessary. Thus, Being is first possible, since it is initiated upon, it is then caused by an external force that transforms it into *existence* and into a necessary being.

Avicenna's distinction between the possible and the necessary in Beings is a distinction between potentiality and actuality. Potential Beings, whether absolute or operative, passive or active, are the beginning. Possibilities come into *existence* through an external force which causes them to become necessities. That is, the beginning of *existence* is its *essence*, once it is caused it comes into *existence*. This action holds true when applied to man's creations and inventions -- as opposed to discoveries -- a case in point is high tech. Its knowledge is a possibility that transforms itself into a necessity caused by man's intellect.

What is high tech? In architecture, it has been referred to as a style, a label, an approach, and even a formal language, but what remains a fact is that so-called high tech is an ambiguous term that even architectural technologists find difficulty in defining or setting boundaries for. In our profession, technology is frequently referred to the disciplines encompassing Computer-Aided-Design, Environmental Controls, Solar Energy, and to a lesser extent, to Construction, Structure, and the Building Industry. It does not include the actual design or composition of buildings. Therefore, one might commence with an investigation into its *essence* and *existence*, and attempt a schema to comprehend logically its standing in contemporary cities.

Society hails the *essence* of high tech in its urban context. High tech is readily adopted and adapted in its new surroundings. Such *essence* is exemplified through its hardware, in systems of communications, environmental controls, transportation, etc. Society is aware of it, moreover, accepts it as an artery that sustains its survival. Such technics as telephones, elevators, and trains are of the recent past; computers, escalators, and airplanes are technics of the present; all are undisputedly natural extensions of the hardware of a contemporary society. A skyscraper, automatically and implicitly, accommodates such state-of-the-art technics in its HVAC systems, vertical circulation, and telecommunication networks. Moreover, our consumers are prepared for tomorrow's technics, reflected in the audio-visual telephones and moving corridors and side-walks (the latter already being introduced extensively in numerous airport terminals around the world). This is evidence that points to the availability and acceptance of high tech in our societies, but always seen through the eyes of the scientist and engineer rather than through the eyes of the artist and architect. We are all enjoying the high tech technics as they facilitate life and enhance our performance.

Where does high tech architecture position itself amongst this high tech context? That it is present is evident in the last two decades more than in the past. The Italian Futurists and Russian Constructivists of the early century, the Archigram and some Modernists of the mid-century, shyly exhibited their inclinations toward high tech, both in their thoughts and unexecuted images. Since the mid-seventies, there appears to be a rising resurgence, in some of our practicing colleagues, who courageously and, in most cases, single-handedly, continue to produce what they believe should be, and is, appropriate architecture for a technological context. While their producers do not label them so, their *high tech architecture* has always been, and continues to be, a subject of debate and controversy, both in the professional and non-professional media.

Society rejects the *existence* of high tech in its urban environment. The *existence* of high tech is widely misunderstood, and its applications are very misleading. Dwellers of our cities are increasingly misjudging urban high tech; this is further provoked by a sense of incoherent recognition by those claiming supremacy and unanimity. Rather than assist in clearing the increasingly vague notions and public uncertainties, they are becoming instrumental in reinforcing this sense of ambiguity.

Contemporary materials, techniques, and technology might be necessary to sustain today's society, but they must remain implicit, discreet, and anonymous. Neither should an office building resemble a factory, nor should a house resemble a machine. Ironically, high tech architecture appears to be "appropriate" for such building types as stadiums, factories, and transportation buildings (airports, railway stations, various terminals, etc.), and might be extended to include any modern building type that is associated with progressive technology. It is the traditional building types, such as houses and offices, and sites that encompass historic landmarks that are considered by the society at large a restricted area in which high tech architecture must not to be present. Thus, high tech architects find it increasingly difficult to practice and design for city centers; as Charles Jencks notes: "Committed to continual invention, they are usually led to non-contextual buildings and one-upmanship, the over-expression of systems, structure and process, where these are inappropriate."

For example, in 1977, when the team of Rogers and Piano unveiled their design for the *Centre Pompidou*, a public outburst was heard; not only in Paris, but in many other cities, condemning the thoughtless and tasteless structure. Society was awaiting the disassembly of the scaffolding that never came down even after the building's inauguration. More than ten years later, it is now a Parisian landmark, and a french milestone representing their 20th century culture and progress. What evoked the change in perception is the society's comprehension of the building's essence and its crucial relativity to its *existence*.

Avicenna's formula is that "thought brings about the generality in forms," and that holds true in Charles Jencks's review of high tech. He views the following as the basic six essential rules of high tech which are brought together in all its built-text: 1. *Inside-Out:* The services and structure are usually exposed on the exterior of its building and exhibited as ornament to the viewer. 2. *Celebration of Process:* The building explicitly reflects its processes of production and displays its constructional logic both in its structure and services, revealing its joints and connecting details, materials and elements. 3. *Transparency, Layering, and Movement:* The aesthetical characteristics of high tech buildings are manifested in the use of transparent and translucent materials, the layering of structural elements, service pipes and ducts, and the emphasis on circulation elements (stairs, escalators, and elevators). 4. *Bright, Flat Coloring:* From the colors of an oil refinery, boiler room, and a sports car, red, yellow, blue, and green were borrowed, eventually transforming the color-coding to the "Silver Aesthetic", with the application of a multi-array of shades of grey, the colors of the space shuttle and the future. 5. *A Lightweight Filigree of Tensile Members:* With the application of thin steel cross-brace in most high tech buildings, it has been labeled as the "Doric Column" of high tech, visually symbolizing its order. 6. *Optimistic Confidence in a Scientific Culture:* High tech practitioners are applying a personal preference for a possible future vision rather than an actual presence. That is, they choose to address futuristic promises through their application of this approach to materials, colors, and modes of production (whether manufacturing, fabrication, assembly, or finish); not the expected emphasis on proportion, form, and compositional principles.

These six characteristics are represented in all high tech buildings, accordingly they constitute its *essence* for *existence*, since it is only those characteristics that may change in a Being that do not belong to its *essence*. Yet, this is naive, indeed an over-simplification of the *essence* of high tech; and it is only part of what brings high tech into *existence*.

Where does the difference lay between the *essence* and *existence* of high tech? Borrowing Avicenna's argument, the created being receives *existence* in its *essence*, whereas the *essence* of the uncreated Being is being itself. In other words, while *essence* is intrinsic in the notion of being, *existence* is based on this *essence*. In architecture, the *essence* of high tech is a *technological presence* based on factual knowledge, their extended possibilities and limitations; all are tangible in conception. The *existence* of high tech is a *philosophical presence* that evolves from its *essence*; yet is an intangible entity in reality. The former conveys assurance and advancement, the latter provokes contention and opposition. Accordingly, it is not surprising that the *existence* of high tech architecture becomes a recipient of condemnation and a point of argumentation and controversy. Such rules fail to provide us with what constitutes the *essence* of high tech and what makes its *existence*. Moreover, it charts a path of confusion that only contributes to the already existing ambiguity and loss of independence of high tech.

High tech architecture, particularly when applying its six rules referred to earlier, becomes almost a mode of projecting an image that is not by any means restricted to the 70s and 80s. The coupling of Joseph Paxton's Crystal Palace - 1854 with Richard Roger's Lloyd's Bank - 1986, Charles Eames's own house - 1949 with Michael Hopkins's house - 1976, and Pierre Chareau's Maison de Verre - 1932 with Nicholas Grimshaw's Digital's office building - 1982, are examples that reflect a trend that spreads out in its time span. Yet in spite of its longevity, the gaps observed in both its theoretical discourses and practical applications stand evidence for an approach that is lacking a frame of work and a point of reference. While their architects are genuinely seeking a true expression of the twentieth century spirit that can be reflected on and integrated in their buildings, they lack the tools of application and processes of production. Their visions are *incomplete projects* that are awaiting completion.

Contemporary high tech architectural practice is "presenting the image of quality and sophistication" rather than "raising the real quality and sophistication of building technology." Rather than seek new avenues for building, we continue to adopt those concepts of the past, aiming at new expressions. We are attempting an *existence* without an *essence*. Moreover, the building industry has not matured in order to contend with high tech; in spite of those incidents where high tech architects succeeded in creating a "high tech craft'' that tailors for their particular specifications. A case in point is Norman Foster's successful attempt to formalize the architect's relationship with the product manufacturer in the Hongkong Bank. But such an application is rare practice.

In discussing high tech and the city, Colin Davies wrote: If the city is the embodiment of tradition, permanence, continuity, and history then High Tech is an anti-urban style.'' High tech implies modernity rather than tradition, mobility rather than permanence, revolution rather than continuity, and the city's future rather than its history. Yet even so, one cannot but notice the shift of such prominent high tech practitioners, such as Foster and Rogers, who are demonstrating a diminishing interest with the *tangible* aspects of high tech architecture, and an inclination towards the more *intangible* aspects of the relationships between man and space, building and city. This is exhibited in Foster's design for a *Mediatheque* in the center of *Nimes*, France, in which he contents with the application of concrete and local stone, rather than bright colored steel; and Roger's schema for the revitalization of London's South Bank, where a more rigorous solution is introduced to reinforce public spaces rather than its hardware. It appears that the ``God Fathers'' of high tech are slowly and silently retreating from their once progressive and aggressive approach of introducing us to what might have been the architecture of the ``technological age.''

These subtle but crucial changes point towards a crisis in which technologists, in the field of architecture, are unable to find an operable definition and comprehensive interpretation of what lies beyond the facade of contemporary high tech architecture. Technology has, yet again, moved forward leaving architecture lagging behind. Architectural technologists always searched the aerospace industry for inspiration and imaging, yet that no longer holds possible. There has been an abrupt halt in this analogous relationship that is leading to the decline of high tech practice in architecture. As Davies continues to write: ``Architectural scholiasts of the future, wishing to pin down the precise date of the death of the High Tech style, might well choose January 28th 1986, the day the Challenger space craft blew up in front of the watching millions. The cause of the tragedy, we now know, was the failure of a Neoprene gasket.'' Consequently, we no longer hold an image of a being, an *essence*; we no longer seek a reality in beings, an *existence*; and we no longer are unable to transform an *essence* of being into an *existence*. That is, the process of creating high tech architecture can no longer hold valid.

Subsequently, high tech is lacking a self agenda that might lead it to establishing an individual identity for architectural high tech to come into being and exist in its own right. It lacks its own model that brings it forth as a separate entity independent of other high tech beings. And last but not least, it lacks a solid direction that sets its own program of life that challenges its process of transformation from a *possibility* into a *necessity*.

In conclusion, Avicenna's thesis on the idea of being is a comprehensive system that establishes a complete schema for any logical discussion regarding the general notion of creation. In order to attempt such notion, one is first confronted with an idea, a possibility, and therefore, an *essence*. Once it is caused by an external force, it is transformed into a reality, a necessity, and ultimately, an *existence*. This realization holds true for high tech architecture, being itself the product of a process of creation.

That is, when first considering an idea, it is initially, abstract and vague; by transforming it into a reality, it becomes defined and identifiable. As a variety of these transformations is created, we eventually identify dominant and respective characters that are relate back to the original idea. It is then that a being obtains an identity. For example, the idea of a space shuttle begins as a vague possibility that seeks to exist. In applying our knowledge of science and technology to implement this idea, we are creating a definite object. Eventually, with numerous similar objects present, the initial idea is no longer abstract; and its *essence* and *existence* is not a mystery or a cause for controversial debate.

In order to originate an identity for high tech architecture, the boundaries of its *technological presence* must be identified, defined, and established thus achieving its *essence*. This will instinctively induce a possibility for an *existence* through a caused force, be it man, society, or nature; sequentially, the *existence* of high tech is brought forth through its *philosophical presence*, eventually becoming a necessity. Thus the confirmation of a high tech *essence* and *existence*.

Establishing a link between the *essence* and *existence* of high tech architecture is beyond this initiative, and is considered yet another journey into the unknown. Nevertheless, when Francis Bacon wrote in his preface to *The Elements of the Common Law*: ``I hold every man a debtor to his profession,'' we must acknowledge that we are not to be the exception to the rule.

REFERENCES

Afnan, Sohail M. *Avicenna: His Life and Works*. London: George Allen & Unwin Ltd., 1958.

Davies, Colin. *High Tech Architecture*. New York: Rizzoli International Publications, Inc., 1988.

Goichon's, A. M. *La Philosophie D'Avicenne et son Influence en Europe Medievale*. Translated by M. S. Khan. Delhi: Motilal Bandarsidass, 1959.

Jencks, Charles. ``The Battle of High-Tech: Great Buildings with Great Faults,'' in *Architectural Design* 58 (November/December 1988): 18-39.

``Town and Technology,'' in *Architectural Review* 186 (October 1989): Entire Issue.

CHAPTER16

The Act of Making

MICHAEL BOROWSKI
University of New Mexico

THE POETICS OF CONSTRUCTION: A NON TECHNICAL NOTE

> *It isn't what he says that counts as a work of art, it's what he makes, with such intensity of perception that it lives with an intrinsic movement of its own to verify its authenticity.* --William Carlos Williams, introduction to *The Wedge*, 1944

The act of making is a basic condition of our being. A measure of our lives is insistently connected with this activity. One of the first proofs of our existence is the discovery that we can make things. I can clearly recall, as a child, seeing the horrified look on my mother's face as the result of the mess I had made.

If one thinks of the Greek root, *architekton*, meaning ''chief builder'', one comes to the sense of architect as a maker of things. This definition also suggests that one of architecture's distinctive characteristics is that it is an activity of making. Architecture is literally an activity of human being. It is this fact that enables architecture to become a revelation of the human condition that can project the possibility of life and beauty into the world.

When I speak of the act of making, I am thinking of the genesis of architectural form, that is, how form comes into being. Architectural form is affected by many particular demands; function, client, program, economics, site, technology, etc. There seems no doubt that there are many senses of possibility in architecture.

I am interested in how architectural form and meaning might emerge directly from the act of making. I believe that the *making* of a building may provide architecture with its most interesting and significant possibility of meaning. Louis Kahn wrote, ''Architecture comes from the making of a room.''

A building is a made thing, however inspired. No architect can afford to ignore this basic aspect of one's practice. Because the act of construction is intimate with the design process, it is necessary to disclose a methodology of design that is more sensitive to the basic activity of architecture, and less dependent upon assumed senses of taste, style and fashion. This preoccupation with how a building is made proposes the building to be the evidence of its own activity, with the act of construction becoming the subject matter. With the elevation of the act of construction to the level of content itself, new possibilities of architectural form and meaning are introduced which would otherwise be inaccessible.

I am interested in architectural form that is intimate with, and in fact is, the issue of its own nature. It is my own belief that the nature of architecture is to be found in the act of making and that the specific instance of the building becomes the declaration of that nature. Creativity is the intelligent ability of the architect to discover and reveal that nature.

Meaning expressed by the architectural language of how the building is made is a specific and exact meaning, that cannot exist in any other material or form. This stance suggests that architectural meaning and the craft of building cannot be separated. It also suggests that working within the limitations and constraints of materials and methods of construction is a basis for discovering and articulating architectural ideas.

Of course, the act of construction is an aspect of architecture, and acquaintance with the nature of its condition is most useful. However, it cannot be over-emphasized that craft is only a means of expressing an idea. The quality of the idea is what is significant. Technical ability is no distinction, it is a necessity.

By the very nature of its making, the work of architecture holds up the actuality of the idea, and allows its occasion in the world. Technical ability gives one the possibility of being able to follow an idea without blunting or disfiguring this act of imagination. I would like to see a more precise and constant attention paid to the nature of materials and methods, in order to avoid an imprecise and clumsy approximation of real architectural ideas.

I very much agree with Louis Kahn when he says, ''Form emerges out of a system of construction.'' I take one sense of his meaning to be that form grows out of the way in which it is made. In other words, the discovery of form is intimate with the literal activity of building itself. In much of his work, Kahn calls attention to and emphasizes the making aspect of architecture, and places it in a critical role in the form-making process.

I believe that buildings produced by the imposition of preconceived ideas, not discovered and growing out of the act of construction, are a representation of something that quickly loses its wonder and mystery. Architectural meaning that represents known facts and ideas, such as through the application of symbolic elements and historical references, unrelated to the act of making, merely skates on the form's surface as a kind of secondary meaning which can be described, explained, and then used up. Architecture's primary meaning does not exhaust itself so easily. Architecture is not referential or at least not importantly so. A building affects us by a more important fact; it's self-existence, without reference to any other thing outside its own nature. I remember Michael McKinnell's insistence on "deriving the appearance of a building from its construction, as opposed to constructing an appearance." I have always understood this to imply a distinction between architecture and architecture as signboard. I am interested in materials and methods of construction as fact, not symbols. Symbols obstruct the immediacy of architecture's direct experience on us. The way a building is made can carry the content as well as anything "said" through symbolic content.

Architects do not build, they draw. Drawing is the process that architects use in organizing mass and space into a structure which coheres to inform the user with a recognition of its order. Drawing is the creative act, the moment of insight. Drawing is the process through which architectural ideas are discovered and expressed. One is an architect while engaged in the activity of drawing. In the act of drawing one is in the immediacy of one's own content, that place deep within, which the architect has been given to make present and actual for others. Drawing is the touch of that place and measures the order of that place.

I am taking drawing here to imply many things, such as, architectural sketches, diagrams, models, working drawings, photographs, etc. In looking up the definition of the word "drawing" in the dictionary (*Webster's New World Dictionary*), I am pleased with the range and extent of its possible meanings, "1) the act of one that draws; specif., the art of representing something by lines made on a surface with a pencil, pen, etc., 2) a picture, design, sketch, etc. thus made, 3) a lottery." (Perhaps, this third definition refers to John Cage's mechanism of composition called "chance operations".) In addition, the word "draw" has among many other definitions the following, "to breathe in; inspiration; to bring forth; to pull out to its fullest extent; to attract; charm; entice; to arrange in order; to compose (a document) in proper form." Architectural drawings can incorporate all the potentialities of these meanings.

The act of construction, being intimately connected with the fact of drawing, must inform the drawing process. Like a musical score which tells how a work is to be performed, the architectural drawing indicates how a building is to be made. The architect transforms materials into architecture as sounds are made into music by the composer. Louis Kahn wrote, "Open before us is the architect's plan. Next to it is a sheet of music. The architect fleetingly reads his composition as a structure of elements and spaces in their light."

The making of architecture is a matter of thinking. "Don't draw a line unless you think about it," admonishes the job captain. In that way there is nothing mindless about the procedure. Drawing becomes a system of thought, drawing in the delight of thought as a possibility of form.

Louis Kahn also wrote, "Architecture is the thoughtful making of spaces." Architecture can have the density and complexity of pure thought. The building becomes the manifestation of the architect's thoughts in built-form and the realization of the possibilities of imagination. Contemporary buildings are thin and cold because we think less and less into them.

THE MEASURE OF AN ORDER

> *The Architect, by his arrangement of forms, realizes an order which is a pure creation of his spirit; by forms and shapes he affects our senses to an acute degree and provokes plastic emotions; by the relationships which he creates he wakes profound echoes in us, he gives us the measure of an order...* Le Corbusier,
> *Towards A New Architecture*, 1927

Architecture is building charged with meaning. One of architecture's special attributes is its ability to communicate experiences and ideas through form. Architecture is the active transformation of the architect's thoughts and feelings into a coherent form. The creative stimulus for a building comes from the architect's content, that place where experiences, thoughts, and feelings lie deep within.

It is the responsibility of the architect to create meaningful form. One aspect of architectural meaning is found in the order that holds material together in a relationship. This order can express the architect's underlying thoughts and feelings. The more concretely and vividly they are articulated the better the architecture.

Space and mass are the raw materials of architectural form. The architect arranges them into a coherent and lucid order, and makes something come to life that has not existed before. Order is the direct evidence of the architect's engagement with the possibilities that space and mass offer. Space and mass are the medium for an idea only by reason of the order that is applied. The architect does not give meaning, but in the act of making, works through an awareness of meaning.

Order must not force space and mass into preconceived patterns but must allow them to reveal the truth of their *own* nature without any opposition. Architecture is a *made place* where space and mass can truly gather in an information of each other and participate in a relationship. Relations are more important than the actual material. Meaning is achieved by the way in which materials are put together and it is the specific instance of the relationship which has relevance. One must look not only at the quality of the materials used, but more importantly at the quality of the thought process used in the arrangement of the materials.

Architectural design is a process of discovery. Significant architectural meaning comes about through formal invention, and not by the use of preconceived notions of forms borrowed from others. When architecture becomes the filling out of forms with stylistic and decorative devices, the result is a sense of form that is extrinsic to the creative act. This leads to a superficial view of form that denies architecture's essential nature.

The very definition of the word "make" implies a preconceived order called type; for example, "a foreign *make* of car." Type is a sense of form as convention and conformity. Right there is the trouble, when typology is used in the production of architectural form. Even if type is thought of as a frame within which change can occur, there is the likely possibility that the frame will confine and restrict meaning. In addition, because type exists with historical and cultural meaning, there is the danger of it easily becoming used in a sentimental and nostalgic manner. Therefore, it is necessary to find a methodology for the use of type that moves it from a rigidity of accumulated habits of order and brings it to an intensity found in the creative process.

It is of extreme importance that architecture transcend utilitarian needs. A building that merely solves functional requirements does not reach the realm of architecture. Louis Sullivan's dictum, "Form Follows Function" has been misunderstood by many modern architects. Sullivan's functionalism did not mean merely the programmatic accommodations and utilitarian requirement of the building. Sullivan wrote in his book entitled *Kindergarten Chats*, "... in a state of nature the form exists because of the function, and this something behind the form is neither more nor less than a manifestation of what you call the infinite creative spirit..." And elsewhere in the same book, he wrote, "The pressure, we call Function: the resultant, Form." In other words, form grows out of the condition that calls the building into being. Form is inextricable from the force which brings it into being.

Architecture does not deal just with the rational mind but must also appeal to the emotions with a direct impression, flashing through regions where the intellect can only grope. Architecture makes visible the invisible. It has that power of revelation. Architecture must somehow be a revelation, no matter how modest that transformation be. Perhaps even more to the point is a wonderful poem by the American poet Robert Duncan. In his book, *The Opening of the Field*, the first poem begins:

OFTEN I AM PERMITTED TO RETURN TO A MEADOW

as if it were a scene made-up by the mind,
that is not mine, but is a made place,

that is mine, it is so near to the heart,
an eternal pasture folded in all thought
so that there is a hall therein

that is a made place, created by light
wherefrom the shadows that are forms fall.

Wherefrom fall all architectures I am...

CHAPTER 17

Ronchamp: Structure as Symbol - Symbol as Structure

ROBERT L. COOMBS
Texas Tech University

RONCHAMP HISTORY

There are local traditions in Ronchamp that a Roman temple had existed on the site of Notre-Dame-du-Haut, and in the fourth century A.D. a sanctuary had been erected there to the Virgin Mary. A chapel of this dedication existed on the site in 1269; further, it was a place of pilgrimage and of miraculous cures.[1]

The medieval church was destroyed by fire in 1913. Rebuilt again, it was destroyed in 1944 by German artillery attacking French forces dug in on this spur of the Vosge mountains. After World War II, a number of people in Ronchamp wanted to rebuild the medieval church of Notre-Dame-du-Haut, but that proved too expensive. Thus, the search for an architect to design a new chapel began.

Canon Ledeur, Secretary of the Commission of Sacred Art of the diocese of Besancon strongly supported the choice of Corbusier as architect for the new Notre-Dame-du-Haut. Father Pierre Marie Alain Couturier, co-director of the magazine, *L'art Sacre* probably was the deciding factor in Corbusier's decision to accept the Ronchamp commission. Father Couturier had been Corbusier's friend for some years, and gave Corbusier his support in this endeavor, as well as La Tourette.

Corbusier treasured memories of his youthful journey to the monastery and church of the Virgin Mary on Mount Athos (Hagion-Oros, Chalcidium) in Greece where he spent three weeks in 1911.[2] And Corbusier confirms his fascination for Mount Athos in *Modular I*.[3] Corbusier was disillusioned with modern industrial society after two world wars, the holocaust and the atomic bomb. Moreover, he would be designing a sanctuary of the Virgin Mary in the region where he was born. He began designing Notre-Dame-du-Haut in 1950; permission to build was given in 1951; construction began in 1953; and the chapel was completed in 1955.

RONCHAMP: LES CARNETS DE LA RECHERCHE PATIENTE

This slim volume was published by Corbusier in 1956 as an apologia for Ronchamp, a response to criticism by the architectural community. Beyond a defense, Corbusier seems to have conceived of the book as a key to an elaborate game of symbolic meanings, geometries and proportional harmonies at Ronchamp.[4]

In his dedication letter to the Bishop of Bescancon, Corbusier stresses: "...the drama of Christianity has taken possession of the place from this time onwards." A chapel dedicated to the Virgin Mary required him to fuse the drama of Christ with that of Mary. Corbusier's greatest concern was the miraculous image of the Virgin Mary and its role in the chapel; he needed to know as much as possible so that he could site the image most effectively for the Virgin's great feast days of August 15 and September 8. Francois Mathey recalled the important role played by Canon Ledeur who made regular visits to Le Corbusier's atelier in Paris where he spent many hours explaining the theological functions of the Church and especially the spiritual role of the Virgin Mary in the Roman Catholic tradition to the architect. Moreover, he had to seek correspondences between Christian theology and Pythagorean traditions which played so important a role in his architecture. He would do this through sacred geometry in which numbers generate multiple symbolic readings of shapes and forms.

Apparitions of the Virgin Mary and Marian miraculous image sanctuaries have a long history in Western Europe.[5] As Jung stressed, the Marian phenomenon was populist in origin.[6] Before the nineteenth century, the Virgin Mary's messages were personal in nature, relating to the peasants who experienced Her apparition. With the coming of the Industrial Revolution, Her words were directed to the whole of humankind. And they were words of warnings. Certainly Corbusier was made aware of the Virgin Mary's warnings in the modern era by Canon Ledeur.

In *The Sun Her Mantle*, John Beevers stresses the importance of two texts in the post-World War II period: "Revelations'': ''and now, in heaven, a great portent appeared, a woman that wore the sun for her mantel, with the moon under her feet, and the crown of stars above her head''; and Pope Pius XII's encyclical *Evangeli Praecones* of 1951: ''The human race is today involved with the supreme crisis, which will end in its salvation by Christ, or in its destruction.''[7]

And so many did in Europe after World War II, Corbusier must have felt strongly that he was living in an apocalyptic age. Thus, Mary's role as the Mother of God, Mediatrix and Intercessoress in a time of great danger became an inspiration for Corbusier's design of Notre-Dame-du-Haut. Corbusier's focus on Apocalyptic imagery for the east wall of Ronchamp is not unique. It was a popular theme in French art after World War II.[8]

In *Ronchamp* Corbusier begins the book with a frontispiece which is a simplification of the processional door's imagery, encapsulating the main themes of Notre-Dame-du-Haut.

First, the proportions of the door seem to conform to his Modular. Within this ideal geometry, Corbusier places the iconography of the Annunciation: the hands of the Angel of the Annunciation and of the Virgin Mary, when the Virgin Mary becomes the Mother of God: ''And the word was made flesh.'' In many Medieval and Renaissance representations of the Annunciation, rays of divine light are fused with the angel's words: ''Hail Mary full of Grace, the Lord is with Thee.'' This mystical fusion of light and sound probably was Corbusier's inspiration to use natural light to symbolize divine light and translate sound into harmonic proportions in Ronchamp.

According to Corbusier, the composition of the door's front imagery is based on the pentagon, which is the symbol of life and was used in many Gothic rose window mandalas.[9] According to Corbusier: ''I was telephoning--the photograph of the redos by Boulbon was in front of me upside down. The pentagon hit me in the eyes...'' The retable of Boulbon depicts Christ Scourged which Corbusier reduces to the pentagram/pentagon/cross inscribed in a circle. He extracts from it a series of dualities which are Marian in their symbolism, but heavily tinged with Pythagorean implications.

The reverse side of the door concludes Corbusier's interpretation of the Marian iconography. Here, the expanding spiral of the Modular/Fibonnaci series with the hand reaching heavenward probably symbolizes the Virgin Mary's Assumption. This ray surging upward is a primary motif in the plan and section of Ronchamp.

At the great processional entrance, Corbusier also displays the mathematical keys as solid blocks. One, standing vertically to the right of the door, is the corner stone of the chapel. If it is composed on the square roots of 2, 3 and 5, this cornerstone transverses two worlds, the world of the body and the world of the spirit.''[10] Above the door is another block which appears to levitate. This probably represents complete spiritual evolution: existence on the divine plane, symbolized by the square root of 5 which Lawlor chooses to call the 'Christic Principle.' ''This opens the way for the family of relationships called the Golden Proportion...generates a set of symbols which were used by the Platonic philosophers as a support for the ideal of divine or universal love. Each of these: processional door imagery, the cornerstone(s) and Panel Exercise in the Modular above the door Corbusier will develop into the forms, spaces and proportions of Ronchamp.

RONCHAMP: SYMBOLIC COMPOSITION

1) The west end of Notre-Dame-du-Haut begins with the seminal event in the Virgin Mary's life; the Annunciation. 2) The church's interior is an architectural procession or promenade beneath Her Assumption. 3) This culminates in the east wall with the image of the Madonna as the Queen of Heaven/Woman of the Apocalypse.

On p. 27 of *Ronchamp*, Corbusier says, ''The key is light/ and light illuminates shapes/ and shapes have an emotional power,'' he is speaking of mystical/physical light. The two light towers at the chapel's west end begin Corbusier's mystery drama--the Annunciation. On page 95 of *Ronchamp* the caption is 'Light Flows Down'; this is Corbusier's conception of the light towers as mystical/physical light sources at the Annunciation. His interest in light descending from a hidden source can be traced to Corbusier's sketches of the Seraphium of Hadrian's Villa at Tivoli. The tower's 'ear' shape in plan strongly hints that Corbusier was depicting the Annunciation architecturally. Richard A. Moore interprets the ear motif alchemically ''as sound sublimated into light, the reverse process of the *Acoustique Plastique*, which turned light phenomenon of perception into the more concrete one of sound.''[11] This is identical to the Annunciation. Moreover, these chapels are linked to the main altar at the east end by the cross incised in the floor.

And Corbusier is explicit about the role of the cross: ''the consecration of the host is performed on the altar under the sign of the cross placed on the tabernacle dominating the axis which commands the architectural arrangement of the building.'' The arms of the cross link the Annunciation light towers, while the body divides the chapel laterally and points to the altar in the sanctuary. His use of the cross inscribed on the floor grid reflects imagery of Christ implied in the plans of many Medieval churches.[12]

However, the towers possess another Marian iconography. They probably incorporate imagery from the Litany of the Blessed Virgin, where Mary is called Tower of David, Tower of Ivory. This is a symbol of Mary as the refuge in time of danger and protection against evil. Thus, the towers at the west end affirm Mary as the Protrectress of humankind, as well as dramatize the Annunciation.

The other tower on the north helps mark the secondary entrance on that side of the chapel, but it remains to be defined iconographically other than as completing the obvious Trinity concept.

DIVINE MATHEMATICS

Corbusier writes in *Ronchamp*: "A project difficult, meticulous, primitive, made strongly by the resources bought into play but sensitive and informed by all embracing mathematics which is the creator of that space which cannot be described by words." Of course, Ronchamp is based on his Modular, which he says "is everywhere" and derived from Pythagorean mathematics.

Corbusier followed Medieval architects -- as Male points out: "The Middle Ages never doubted that numbers are endowed with some occult power. This doctrine came from the Fathers of the Church who inherited it from those Neo-Platonic schools in which the genius of Pythagoras lived again..."[13]

In Sacred Geometry the source numbers are 1, 2, 3, 4, 5. One is the number of unity, represented by the square: Unity (1). "The perfect symbol of God, can become multiplicity and diversity through division into 2, Duality." As Lawlor points out, "Thus the extreme, essential polarity of the universe, Unity and Multiplicity, is perfectly represented and observable in the simple drawing of the square and its diagonal: the square root of 2... Transformation is accomplished through the square root of 2: the Generative; the square root of 3: the Formative; the square root of 5, the Regenerative, and its related function of Phi, the Golden Mean."[14] Corbusier was fascinated by the Golden Mean which has complex association both in nature and the occult.[15]

The panels above the south processional door prepare the pilgrim for the panel exercise on the floor extending from the west end with its light towers through the chapel and out to encompass the exterior altar. The Modular is played out in the "Panel Exercise" on the floor. It unifies the duality of the chapel's interior and exterior. And it acts as a geometric counterpoint to the more fluid organic forms of the chapel which are ultimately generated by this system.

DIVINE LIGHT MADE TANGIBLE: THE RAY AS SPACE AND STRUCTURE

In Christian iconography, light rays symbolize divine power, wisdom and human revelation. Usually, these rays descend from a single point.[16] This can be read as coming from the eye of God -- the divine Architect. In Ronchamp, divine light generates space and form. Corbusier conceptualized the ray motif as an expression of "a diminishing series of right-angle triangles similar to the first confirming the principle of the diminishing series Phi, the Golden Mean."[17] He relates it to the human eye, and dwells on its ability to bring all into "perfect harmony". The slope of the floor and ceiling mimic the light ray motif from the rear of the chapel to the sanctuary, with its altar and the image of the Madonna. Further, the slope and angle of the pyramidal south wall reflects his "diminishing series of right-angle triangles."

Corbusier plays most elaborately on the duality of sunlight and divine light in the south wall. The number of embrasures: 25 (25 is 5 x 5) is the ideal Pythagorean number of regeneration. The windows are set in 4 (the number of unity) vertical bays which are each divided horizontally into 3 compartments. Three times 4 = 12, the Zodiac stars in the crown of the Queen of Heaven/Woman of the Apocalypse, etc. The individual windows of the south wall appear to have been composed according to a harmonic proportional system.[18]

The most dramatic instance of light as divine intervention is the crack between the south wall and the roof. This crack of light has 4 glass panes in each of its sections. The major rhythm of supports is 3, and this division can represent the Trinity of father, mother and son, or the Holy Trinity. The minor 4 rhythm of the panes is the Great Mother number: the square.

Corbusier does not stress the north wall by showing it in section in *Ronchamp* as he does the south wall. In the axonometric on page 93 he indicates 9 embrasures in the sanctuary. Of course, the number 9 plays on 3 symbolism. Moore interprets the north wall as the rear of the building with the south as the front. He sees it as an imitation of the northern, or summer, zodiac sign of Cancer, the crab.[19]

Corbusier prominently displays a photograph of a shell he found on a Long Island beach when he visited the USA -- the source for the roof of Notre-Dame-du-Haut.[20] He notes: "the shell will rest on these columns but it will not touch the wall. A horizontal crack of light 10 cm. wide will amaze." The roof appears to miraculously rise and hover over the south wall. This levitation can be read as dualities relating to Corbusier's earlier work and his now overt mysticism. He 'raised the roof' for symbolic reasons related to the crab shell.

According to Ad de Vries, the crab is a "symbol of death: a. related to the Summer-solstice and the death of the Sun-hero through Cancer (Cancer: the House of the Moon)..."[21] Thus the crab is associated with death and the moon. The moon is a primary Marian symbol. From various angles the roof can be read as referring to the moon. While Moore sees this in alchemical terms, I believe its overt meaning relates to Marian iconography.[22]

But if the crab and here, the crab shell, is a symbol of death, what does its levitation mean? Most probably, the Virgin Mary's Assumption -- Her bodily triumph over death. As J.E. Cirlot points out "Our Lady is depicted above the moon, thereby denoting that eternity is above the mutable and transitory.[23]

Even Corbusier's choice of seven great beams for the roof has symbolic significance. As Lesser quotes from E. Male: "Seven -- composed of Four, the number of the body, and of Three, the number of the Soul -- is pre-eminently the number of humanity and expresses the union of man's double nature."[24] In Marian iconography this symbolism is echoed in Her seven joys and seven sorrows.

The sanctuary's east wall, is the liturgical and symbolic

climax of Ronchamp. The wall swells inward to emphasize the force of divine light surrounding the image of the Madonna, echoing "The Sun Her Mantle" of Revelations. The image is set in a rectangular embrasure-window in the upper right side of the east wall behind the altar. Surrounding it are 12 smaller pin-point windows which confirm that this is the Queen of Heaven/Woman of the Apocalypse. When pilgrims hear Mass outside on feast days, they face west. In Gothic cathedrals, the west facade usually is given over in part to the iconography of the Last Judgement. Thus at Ronchamp, the Madonna's image plays the role of Intercessoress at the Last Judgement in the open air chapel.

CONCLUSION

Externally, Ronchamp is an enigmatic, largely closed sculptural monument similar to an ancient Greek temple where religious ceremonies are enacted outside of it on feast days. Internally, it is an architectural promenade/procession through the Marian mysteries. As pilgrims move from the semi-darkness of the west end to the light of the east end, they witness the three great events of the Virgin Mary's life: Annunciation, Assumption, and finally, Her triumph as Queen of Heaven/Woman of the Apocalypse.

Through symbolic number systems, Corbusier followed Medieval architects' beliefs in the virtue of numbers endowed with some occult power in which the genius of Pythagoras lived again. Thus, in his fusion of Marian iconography and Pythagorean number systems, Corbusier obviously saw himself as continuing the great French master-mason and architect traditions of the Middle Ages in Ronchamp.

CODA

That permission to build Ronchamp was given in 1951, construction began in 1953, and chapel was completed in 1955 proves Corbusier and destiny conspired to play the Pythagorean game with time as well.

NOTES

1. Daniele Pauly, *Ronchamp; Lecture d' une Architecture*, Paris: editions Ophrys, 1980, p. 22.
2. Le Corbusier, *Le Voyage d'Orient*, Paris: Forces Vivres, 1966, p. 141.
3. Le Corbusier, *Modular I & II*, Cambridge, MA: Harvard University Press, 1980.
4. Le Corbusier, *Ronchamp: Les Carnets de la Recherche Patiente*, New York: The Chapel at Ronchamp, 1957, p. 25.
5. Mary Lee Nolan and Sidney Nolan, *Christian Pilgrimage in Modern Western Europe*, Chapel Hill & London: 1989.
6. C.G. Jung, *Psychology and Religion: West and East*, trans., R.F.C. Hull, Bollingen Series XX, Princeton: Princeton University Press, 1976, p. 312.
7. John Beevers, *The Sun Her Mantle*, Westminster, MD: The Newman Press, c. 1954.
8. *New Catholic Encyclopedia*, Vol. I, p. 663.
9. Robert Lawlor, *Sacred Geometry; Philosophy and Practice*, London: Thames and Hudson, 1982, p. 32ff.
10. Lawlor, p. 31ff.
11. Richard A. Moore, "Alchemical and Mythical Themes on the Poem of the Right Angle 1947-1965," *Oppositions* 19/20, Winter/Spring, 1980, p. 126.
12. George Lesser, *Gothic Cathedrals and Sacred Geometry*, London: Alec Tiranti, 1957, Vol. I, pp. 147-8.
13. Lesser, p. 144.
14. Lawlor, pp. 31, 35.
15. Le Corbusier, *Modular II*, p. 18ff.
16. Ad de Vries, *Dictionary of Symbols and Imagery*, Amsterdam: North-Holland Publishing Company, 1984, p. 475.
17. *Modular I*, p. 64.
18. I am indebted to Erik Mar Johnson who brought this to my attention.
19. Moore, p. 128.
20. Le Corbusier, *Ronchamp: Les Carnets de la Recherche Patiente*, pp. 89, 94.
21. de Vries, p. 114.
22. Moore, p. 126.
23. J.E. Cirlot, *A Dictionary of Symbols*, Second Edition, trans., Jack Sage, New York: Philosophical Library, 1971, p. 216.
24. Lesser, p. 144.

CHAPTER 18

Kahn's Details at Salk

DANIEL S. FRIEDMAN
University of Pennsylvania

"...Architecture has limits--and when we touch the invisible walls of the limits, then we know more about what is contained in them." --Louis I. Kahn

This essay speculates on certain details of Kahn's Salk Institute for Biological Studies at La Jolla (1959-1966). My discussion is a reconnaissance of the relation between detail and partition, taken as analogous units of expression within the total order of the building. The details of the studies are chosen to demonstrate a proportional unity of relation among parts, which manifest the operation of number, outline, and position[1] in Kahn's project. Moreover, the studies can be shown to embody an ethical or practical disposition, which serves as the mediative realm in the universe of the building. This paper will test Vittorio Gregotti's claim that Kahn managed "to pierce the wall of functionalism from the inside and to glimpse from the outside, through his own methods, the form of the historical container which defines it." In this way, Gregotti continues, "the principles of modern architecture are projected outside the historical contingencies and...outside any idea of history in terms of dialectic or conflict."[2] It is precisely in the manifold operations that delimit 'outside' and 'inside' that Kahn's details at Salk may yield some insight into its uncommon unities. I ask to what extent Kahn's details demonstrate both material and textual joinings in order to locate the threshold to a study of his drawings.

EQUIPMENT. Design that conceals structure has no place in Kahn's order of architecture: "I believe," he says, "that in architecture, as in all the arts, the artist instinctively respects the traces which show how a thing has been made."[3] This is the mentality that governs the design of the joint in Kahn's constructions. In the joint resides both the record of a building's making and the source of its meaning. For Kahn the joint becomes the locus of appropriateness. Ornament is therefore "a recognition that a joint is ceremonious."[4] To draw ornament out of the joints of construction is to order the building and equip it, to make it sufficient for habitation. Thus in Kahn's oeuvre, the meaning of ornament spreads toward its root, which suggests "increase, abundance, becoming in greater degree": the ornamented body is "made more in being."[5]

ADORNMENT. What begins to emerge at the Salk laboratories in La Jolla is a mature ornamental order that draws its form from the particularities of the project. Kahn situated the building on the basis of neither an overriding rationality nor 'method' nor ideology, but rather in relation to the the project's physical and intellectual locality. As is well-known, Kahn's first loyalty is always to the Question, e.g. What does the brick want to be? or How am I doing, Wonder? or, eyeing the pyramids, Why anything? Kahn is allergic to rote positivism. He positions himself against the "peril of the 'objectification' of the human being," against a narrow empiricism content to reduce certain "intractable mysteries" to a "*this* is only *that*." Borrowing Gabriel Marcel's phrase, Kahn defends "the integrity of the real."[6] Though Kahn's office produced impeccable construction documents in keeping with contemporary practices, he relies on few if any conventional or prescriptive 'graphic standards' in the architecture at Salk. Detail for detail, the building is invented anew, conjured up out of the ground of the problem.

SITE. The building draws expression from a swelling of local (or topical) conditions that inhabit the moment of the project; the most significant of these circumstances converge at the end of 1959. One might first consider, for instance, Kahn's experience with the Richards Medical Laboratories in Philadelphia, which was rife with difficulty and conflicting audience response--architectural historians and critics celebrated it as a modern manifesto (prompting the Museum of Modern Art to make it the subject of its first single-building exhibition), while many of the building's occupants and medical academicians decried its insensitivity to the realities of scientific research. One might also consider the contemporaneous debate over the modern antinomy between science and art, typified by C. P. Snow in his essay "The Two Cultures," which was published in

1959. Not least importantly, one might also consider the extraordinary rapport between Kahn and Jonas Salk, inventor of the killed-virus poliomyletis vaccine and a scientist whose philosophical inclinations are unabashedly humanist and integrative.

AUSPICES. First in Philadelphia, then in La Jolla, architect-philosopher and scientist-philosopher came together over the problem of the creation of a new interdisciplinary institution from which Salk could mount an ''assault on the unreasonableness of life.''[7] With Kahn's help Salk augured a site from among those offered him by the city of San Diego, one that is ''not just any land or merely fine land but the most beautiful coastal cliff property left in La Jolla.''[8] It sits atop a bluff on the Torry Pines mesa, four hundred feet above the ocean beach, roughly U-shaped. Its two arms--a fat one and a thin one (which is skewed and wears a thumbless mitt)--point west to the Pacific, embracing a deep ravine. Dr. Salk likened the site's vivid geomorphic features to ''cerebral convolutions.''[9]

NUMBER. At play in Kahn's project at Salk is the number three, the pre-eminent number of architecture and ''the number of our space.''[10] Foremost in this game of three at Salk is its master plan, which (though incomplete) consists of three discrete, necessary, and indissoluble components: the laboratories, the meeting place, and housing for fellows. Between 1960 and 1962, Kahn developed three schematic designs for the Institute. Construction began on the laboratory component in June 1962 (and though the ''as-built'' construction documents are dated 23 July 1965, Kahn in fact did not resolve the design of the central court until August, 1967). Here is a brief description of the laboratory plan, reading transversely through each building's six layers of function, heading from the outside in: vertical circulation (laboratory stair towers, spaced by sunken courts), horizontal circulation (covered exterior walkway), the laboratory, horizontal circulation (covered exterior walkway), vertical circulation (the study wing stair towers, spaced by sunken courts), the studies, the central court, and so on, mirror-wise, to the opposite hand. To reiterate, the laboratory complex is composed of two nearly identical three-story buildings, symmetrically reflected about a central court, which comprises the middle of each building's two primary elements--thus on either side of the center line of the court, each building has three distinct parts: court, studies, and laboratories. The studies are situated between the court and the laboratories and thus become their 'middle term', while the court remains the middle term between the north and south laboratory buildings, and thus constitutes them into a single reflexive compound.

POSITION. Kahn's spatial composition is an ingenious and compact system of interlocking volumes. Three ''laboratories for biology'' are served by three interspersed one-story-high ''laboratories for pipes,'' full-height horizontal chases for which cantilever out over the exterior walkways, providing them with cover. Look at the building in section (again, transversely): one entire laboratory level and its attendant plenum are set below grade, which is established by the level of the court. Kahn then sets the base of the study wings (which form the 'arcade') on the same plane as the court and deftly alternates laboratory and study levels, to wit: lower level labs are served on both sides by sunken gardens (which admit ample light), ground level labs are served by the court arcade, and upper level labs are served by an exterior portico. The upper portico level is sandwiched between the first and second level of studies. Studies are thus aligned with the story-high ''laboratories for pipes,'' a disposition that enhances a sense of separation between the space of research and the space of contemplation; moreover, it retains the position of the studies as a 'middle term'.

OUTLINE. Salk has no façade, no entry in the conventional sense: arrival is a matter of reaching the middle. 'Wall' filters out of complex depths in the margins of the central court--this is not one, but an assembly of common buildings, as though Kahn flipped the cortile of the monastery at Galluzo. Salk is made out of poured-in-place concrete and finished with wood, glass, travertine, and wrought iron. Non-load-bearing wood panels, which incorporate fenestration, are set between expressed floor levels in both the administrative and library wings and in the studies. The north and south walls of the laboratories (240 feet long) are full-height sheets of quarter-inch plate-glass set between columns in stainless steel frames. Travertine, Kahn's gift to the sky, covers the floor of the central court and lower gardens, both of which are furnished with travertine seating. In the sunken courts, between the stair towers, dry-set brick pavers are framed by crossed travertine bands. Simplewrought iron railings line the porticos and taller wrought iron fences and gates secure east and west openings to the court.

FABBRICA. At Salk Kahn wrestles with the perfectability of concrete. Every sketch and specification desires to bring it into agreement with the form work, the builders, and the climate. Several types of California concrete were blended with pozzolan and other admixtures to impart a more volcanic color to the finish.[11] Plywood panels, coated with polyurethane to ensure the consistency of color between section and surface, were selected for their complexion, durability, economy, and sheet size. Care accumulates at edges. Impressions of construction--pour joints, hydrotatic bleed lines, control joints, all lines revealing the seams of form work, and tie-rod holes (later plugged with lead)--constitute the composition of exterior surfaces. Kahn insists on the expression of material essence and how a thing is made. His agent, Fred Langford, project architect for concrete production at Salk, vigorously protected these intentions. He enumerated to the builders the purpose of each component of the form work and specified the exact character of each of the several types of joints and seams, which were variously designed to reflect correct relation to the temperament of the wall (its structural, thermal, and constructional reality). Langford attacked even the smallest suggestion of insouciance on the part of the builder (to Langford this was a matter of religion): "We must make the concrete in this building say 'I am expressive of the hands and forms that hold me in place until I could grasp the inner steel and gain the strength and power that I now possess; that I must possess to...span the laboratories in a single leap, to lift the studies to the grand view of the sea, and still be friendly enough to touch with human hands.'"[12]

UPRIGHTNESS. Representation and function merge in the construction of the studies. Images out of which Kahn coaxed this composition reside in a symphyseal 'idea-column', which conflates his interpretation of the monastic arcade, the ruins of Paestum, modern steel and reinforced concrete technology--the sum, in fact, of columnar expression. Kahn's famous dictum "the wall parted and the column became" seems to point to Wittkower's discussion of Alberti's notion of the column as ornament, in consideration of which Wittkower notes Alberti's assertion that "'a row of columns is indeed nothing but a wall, open and discontinued in several places.'"[13] In his fidelity to the unalterable essence of building--"a column is to me darkness and light, darkness and light, darkness and light"--Kahn works back toward the precondition of the column , through *temenos* and the spacings of structure (spent light), in order to locate ground on which to reconstitute the column in the changed terms of modernity, though retaining its virtue as "principal ornament."[14]

HOLLOWNESS. Kahn's idea-column inheres the image of hollowness, in which we find his purest union of representation and function. He wants to invent a modern column that embodies the essence of its classical progenitor, the solidity and breadth of which expressed its obligation to load. Modern material technology and engineering disencumbered the antique column of its burden and requisite mass. So the body of the modern column for Kahn becomes a habitable space, which he variously fills with light, circulation, and use. In the studies, we see it operate in the arrangement of the standing column-walls, which suggest the enclosure of rooms, but also uprightness, which conjoins ethical and bodily posture, revealed not so much in surfaces as in hollows (in the virtual body of the walls). The construction and representation of the studies manifest Kahn's mediation between material and intellect. Kahn said: "I want to give the wall a consciousness."[15]

PHYSIOGNOMY. In the configuration of studies, Kahn turns two column-walls out forty-five degrees to make paired triangular bays, small rooms inside larger rooms. Salk had asked Kahn for studies that were "free from distraction...for both the photophilic and photophobic" occupant.[16] Kahn responds with three sliding window components--the window sash, the screen, and louvered shutters (each with three vertical rows of operable, horizontal slats). Built into the panel is a pocket that houses the sliding components when they are not in use (between fully open and fully closed, the permutations of use are infinite). The exterior face of the panel is finished in teak millwork, with thin vertical tongue and groove slats separated into five bands by horizontal drips. The interior side is finished in oak. A change of plane on the exterior side of the court-facing panel reveals a vertical edge between the window and pocket components, which enunciates their difference (a limit)--here again a sliding or nesting action is suggested, representing that one is housed by the other (relation in operation).

THRESHOLD. Kahn takes an extra slice of sun into the studies through narrow floor-to-ceiling slots on either side of each panel. These he fills with glass, such that the wood panel is joined to the the concrete wall by a strip of light. It is precisely at the site of this juncture between glass and wood that Kahn unites the outer skin of teak with the inner skin of oak, setting the glass into the press of a common half-lap joint on one end, and directly into the concrete on the other. Here in this three-material detail, at the distinction between inside and out (between light and dark, between court and lab, between God's workshop and *homo faber*), resides the triad expressed in the Albertian canon as *finitio*, *lineamenta*, and *partitio*. Through Kahn's ternary magic these relations constitute a fractal dimensionality, wherein (within the whole) self-same qualities inhabit each part of each part of each part (and so on ad infinitum): "...the world is divine: it is a large god, image of a God even larger."[17] It can be said of the project at Salk that lines and walls, in the words of Claudio Sgarbi,

> ...are not a neutral element of separation. The form and the figure come to rest together not within or without the *lineamenta* , but rather in the *lineamenta* themselves. Any partition, any delimitation whatsoever, precisely because it is *diffinitio*, a definition, generates a homogenous, symmetrical space on both sides of the line that one could continue to divide; how might one explain differently the fact that ensembles of little houses (*minima domocilia*) constitute themselves in a single house? The Latin term *consquiesciere* (to rest peacefully together) seems to appropriately complete the Albertian discourse: the partition, be it social or architectural, is not the creation an internal or external tension, but rather of a profusion of tranquility: tending in a direction, to be sure, but at-tending to the liminal field of the partition, where lines and angles come together.[18]

Kahn likewise says that "the social structure and the physical structure is not on one side or the other....physical structure and social structure is all in this threshold, at no point is it anywhere else, really...."[19]

RAGIONE. To reiterate on the triadic operation of the project: it is possible to interpret the three parts--laboratories, studies, and central court--as analogues for three realms of knowledge.[20] The central court, Kahn's "facade to the sky," cleaves to the Pacific horizon and points toward the divine; it can be taken as the realm of the invariant, which suggests theoretical knowledge. The studies, which Kahn calls rooms of oak table and carpet, provide scientists with a place to reflect on "the best thing to do"; they constitute a realm of right conduct and suggest practical (or ethical) knowledge, which is embedded in custom and habits. The studies subordinate the laboratories, which Kahn calls rooms of stainless steel and clean air, in which scientists implement their hypotheses and undertake physical experiments. Here in the labs, the only concern is with the right choice of means for pre-given ends and purposes. The labs therefore constitute the realm of the changeable, suggesting technical knowledge. These three distinctions open onto the epistemological ground of the Vitruvian triad, in which grace can be aligned with theory, utility with practice (taken as ethical action), and strength with technology.

MEZZO. In the spirit of these analogies, I would like to adumbrate another reading of the studies. The design and construction of the studies at the Salk Institute first of all constitute a 'correction' or 'setting right' of errors at the Richards Medical Laboratories, where the plan of the labs derived from Kahn's earlier metaphor of laboratory-as-studio. That image yielded an integrated lab/office space, which met with serious discontent and criticism on the part of Richards' occupants, who accused Kahn of romanticizing scientific research. Separation of lab and study was therefore essential at Salk, as the earlier schemes demonstrate. In the resulting construction, the study wings evolve into a line of columns, hollow and habitable, a liminal field that stands between Kahn's space of the not-yet and his space of has-always-been. The studies "go between" the court and the laboratory, between the theoretical (*thea*, "showing," and *theo*, "god") and the technical (*tekhne*, "art" or "skill"). In this middle position, the studies inhere the mediative aspect of practical or ethical knowing, which is the domain of Hermes (the go-between) and therefore of interpretation and hermeneutical work--the studies house activities that mediate between divine and human worlds, between theory and know-how. To translate this distinction into Kahn's rhetoric (which I take to be the kind of artful speech that "gives effectiveness to truth"[21]), the studies are situated between the *measurable* and the *unmeasurable*, terms with which Kahn underscored the essential intentions of the project at Salk.[22] By this contradistinction, Kahn meant that numerical magnitudes cannot be the ground of the essence of spaces and locations, which is how Heidegger put it.

DIBOUTADES. The evolution of the details of the studies are well-documented in Kahn's autograph drawings, sketches that generated the development of construction details by his forces in the Philadelphia and La Jolla offices.[23] Kahn's personal drawings for the project tend to be reflective, exploratory, iterative, and ambiguous. Kahn is well-known for his eager charcoal stick: the majority of drawings he makes in his explorations of the final design of the laboratory studies at Salk--there are nearly fifty--are executed in charcoal on yellow tracing paper, most of it twelve inches wide, presumably consumed at an impressive rate. Kahn's delineations feature thick, strong, often short and over-stroked lines, quickly-worked, *felt* --his physical and intellectual engagement with the image is apparent in the abundance of smears and streaks that more often than not obscure the legibility of the detail under scrutiny. Charcoal resists erasure, thus the urge to correct passes through Kahn's fingertips, which register the aim of his criticism and doubt in the testimony of smudges. Distinctions between lines are often kneaded into a dark cloud: in Kahn's drawing, heaviness becomes lightness as forms become clear. Kahn's charcoal leaves a spray of dust in the wake of an idea's trajectory, a record of motor intensity that settles on the surface of the paper like an aura.

CLEARING. Kahn's project at Salk does not look better on paper. Draftsmen probably avoid charcoal: charcoal does not make a good line. Its mark is uneven, of irregular weight and density, and does not reproduce well in diazo. It is difficult to trace a charcoal drawing because the charcoal is too imprecise. Worse, charcoal is disinclined to remain on the surface of the paper (graphite or even negro lead is more coöperative). Kahn's thick charcoal lines are the first expression of the building's *lineamenta*, lines and angles that constitute a limit, "that limit which is a field (a place within which there is space and time)."[24] Kahn traces the form in his head, not the form under his trace. His lines are precisely inexact: he is thinking the question of concrete, bringing the reality of the material into consonance with the desire of the form. The product of this union is *lineamenta*:

> 'The whole business of building,' [Alberti] says, 'consists of structure and lineamenta, and the whole power and purpose of lineamenta is that an absolute, straight manner be used for the adjustment and joining of lines and corners into which the facade of the building is inserted and framed .' Lineamenta thus assign distribution and number throughout the building....Hence lineamenta ['a sure and constant record, conceived in the mind, expressed in lines and angles' Alberti says], though comparable to idéae, have greater primacy. They transcend and pre-exist the material building, which is checked against them....They are the intermediary between the unique universality of Idea and the repeated local imagery of the material world.[25]

Kahn's drawings have long since jettisoned any residue of self. They transmit only unimpeded will, which readily seizes on the properties of material being worked in the mind's hand, pouring out of the end of the charcoal into forms of building.

FINITIO. Kahn says that "if we were to train ourselves to draw as to build, from the bottom up...stopping our pencil to make a mark at the joint of pouring or erecting, ornament would grow out of our love...."[26] "Wherever the limit occurs, precisely there," Sgarbi tells us, "design...will always intervene. These liminal places are justly called joints....Clearly only one who knows how to attend to the limit (the field where only lines and angles exist), only one who reaches a perfect partition will have nothing to add or to take away. To add nothing, to take away nothing, means knowing how to dwell (reside) in the *lineamenta* themselves, not beyond them, not beside them."[27] Kahn says: "A great building must begin with the unmeasurable, go through the measurable means when it is being designed, and in the end must be unmeasurable."[28]

NOTES

1. L. B. Alberti, *On the Art of Building in Ten Books*, trans. Joseph Rykwert et al. (Cambridge, MA: The MIT Press, 1988), Bk. IX, Chap. 5, 302. Others have translated this Albertian triad as "number," "finishing," and "collocation": see M. Frascari, "The Tell-the-Tale Detail," *VIA* 7 (1984), 23-37; and Claudio Sgarbi, et al., "Speculation on De-sign and Finitio ," *VIA* 9 (1988), 162-165.
2. V. Gregotti, "Modern Connection," trans. Eva Korytko, *Rassegna* 21 (March 1985), 4; see Richard Saul Wurman, *What Will Be Has Always Been: The Words of Louis I. Kahn* (New York: Accesspress, Ltd. and Rizzoli, 1986). 125.
3. Wurman, 178; Gregotti, 4.
4. Wurman, 17.
5. A. K. Coomaraswamy, "Ornament," in *Coomaraswamy 1: Selected Papers, Traditional Art and Symbolism* , edited by Roger Lipsey, Bollingen Series LXXXIX (Princeton: Princeton University Press, 1977), 241-44.
6. Walter J. Lowe, "Introduction," in Paul Ricouer, *Fallible Man*, translated by Charles A. Kelbley (New York: Fordham University Press, 1986), viii.
7. Pamphlet, "Let Us Build a Laboratory of Life: A Statement by Basil O'Connor, President, The National Foundation," La Jolla, CA: Salk Institute for Biological Studies, n.d., p. 7, "Salk Institute Booklets," Box LIK 108, Louis I. Kahn Collection, University of Pennsylvania and Pennsylvania Historical and Museum Commission (hereafter cited as Kahn Collection).
8. Mary Huntington Hall, "Gift from the Sea," *San Diego* (February 1962), 41.
9. Esther McCoy, "Dr. Salk Talks About His Institute," *Architectural Forum* (December 1967), 29; Kahn described the site in the first two paragraphs of a program abstract he wrote in June, 1961, after the completion of the second phase of schematic design: "...From the presence of the uninterrupted sky, the sea and the horizon, the clear and dramatic configuration of weather-beaten land spare of foliage, the buildings and their gardens must find their position in deference to Nature....The buildings are to serve the science of Biology and men as men aware of their total being. This spatial environment which finds a place for men in the arts and letters and men in this particular science is a place where Question is always present" (from "Abstract of Program for the Institute of Biology at Torrey Pines, La Jolla, San Diego," n.d. "Salk Program Notes June 19," File Box 27, Kahn Collection).
10. Claude Bragdon, "An Architecture of Changeless Change" [from *The Beautiful Necessity*, 1922], reprinted in *Parabola*, Triad (Winter 1989), 39; this issue of *Parabola* treats the diverse manifestations of the triadic structure in myth and religion, such as in this quote from Anatolius: "The triad, the first odd number, is called perfect by some, because it is the first number to signify the totality--beginning, middle, and end....Triangles both reflect and are the first substantiation of being plane; and there are three kinds of triangle--equilateral, isosceles and scalene. Moreover, there are three rectilinear angles--acute, obtuse, and right. And there are three parts of time. Among the virtues, they likened it to moderation: for it is commensurability between excess and deficiency...." in "Trinities, Above and Below" [reprinted from *The Theology of Arithmetic: On the Mystical, Mathematical and Cosmological Symbolism of the First Ten Numbers*, translated by Robin Waterfield (Grand Rapids, MI: Phanes Press/Kairos Books, 1988)], *Ibid.*, 79; and no less in these lines from Lao-tzu: "The Tao begot one./One begot two./Two begot three./ And three begot the ten thousand things...," [reprinted from Tao Te Ching , translated by Gai-fu Feng and Jane English (New York: Vintage Books, 1989)], *Ibid.*, 80.
11. "Laboratory 1: Procession of massive forms," *Architectural Forum* (May 1965), 44.
12. Letter, Fred Langford to Greer Ferver (Ferver & Dorland), "Re: Design of form work for concrete, 5 April 1963, cc: Dr. Salk, Mr. Kahn, and Mr. Conn, Box LIK 89, "Salk--Dr. August Komendant," Kahn Collection.
13. Rudolf Wittkower, *Architectural Principles in the Age of Humanism* (New York: W.W. Norton & Company, 1971), 33-34; see also Alberti, translated by Joseph Rykwert et al. (1988), Bk. I, ch. 10, p. 25 (since Wittkower's English quotations are from an edition of the Leoni translation of 1726 edited by Joseph Rykwert in 1955).
14. Alberti, trans. Rykwert, 25.
15. Wurman, 127; cf. "Consciousness is not a given but a task" [Paul Ricouer, "Consciousness and Unconscious," translated by Willis Domingo, in *The Conflict of Interpretations*, Northwestern University Studies in Phenomenology and Existential Philosophy, ed. James M. Edie (Evanston, IL: Northwestern University Press, 1974), 108; quoted in Lowe, xiv].
16. Jonas E. Salk, typewritten draft, 26 July 19??, "Study Program," Box LIK 27, Kahn Collection; this draft corresponds to typewritten statement, "Design Program for Studies," received by Kahn's office 9 August 1962, "Salk Project--Dr. Jonas E. Salk Correspondence April 1960-June 1963," Box LIK 107, Kahn Collection.
17. Sgarbi, note 21 (citing Alberti's *minima domicilia* , the little houses of which the big house is composed), p. 162 : "...This Platonic or Aristotelian metaphorical synecdoche (it is important to take into account the relation between metaphor and analogy, since both of them create similitude between separable things...) has also been used by Andrea Palladio: 'As the city is not other than a certain large house and, on the contrary, the house a small city' [translation by A. M. Borys]...; consider also the Palladian passage where the cosimilarity between the 'large temple' ('the beautiful machine which is the world'), and the 'small temples' (which we

make) is emphasized...; ''Also the world is divine: it is a large god, image of a God even larger' (our translation) from the Italian translation of Francis Yate's English translation of a passage in Guiilio Camillo (*L'Idea di Teatri*), who is quoting Marsillo Ficino (*Corpus Hermeticum XII: Sull' intelletto comune*), who is interpreting/translating Greek writings supposedly by Hermes or Mercurius Trismegistus (Greek name, meaning Thrice-Greatest, applied to the Egyptian god Throth as the reputed author of the Hermetic writings, who was identified by Greeks with their god Hermes); see Francis A. Yates, *The Art of Memory* (London: Routledge & Kegan Paul, Ltd., 1966)...''

18. Ibid., 164.
19. Wurman, 50.
20. I am indebted to Dr. David Leatherbarrow for his elegant exegesis on this constellation of terms; many of these phrases are his, though he is in no way to be blamed for my abuse of them here; see also Hans George Gadamer, *The Idea of the Good in Platonic-Aristotelian Philosophy*, translated by P.Chistopher Smith (New Haven: Yale University Press, 1986), 159-178.
21. A. K. Coomaraswamy, ''A Figure of Speech or a Figure of Thought,'' in *Coomaraswamy 1: Selected Papers, Traditional Art and Symbolism*, edited by Roger Lipsey, Bollingen Series LXXXIX (Princeton: Princeton University Press, 1977), 14.
22. Kahn said that his client, Dr. Salk, ''wanted to be able to invite Picasso to the laboratory. He felt that the belief which makes a painter paint must be constantly felt by the scientist so that he never forgets, in his measurable work, that the unmeasurable desires, somehow has come together...''; Kahn noted elsewhere that the meeting place would be ''laid out in a manner which would suit the unmeasurable qualities--and the laboratories were dedicated entirely to measurable qualities. The contrast was between law, which is unchangeable, and rule...which is changeable...'' (quoted in Wurman, 23 and 77; see also 216); Kahn also said ''I only wish that the first really worthwhile discovery of science would be that it recognizes that the unmeasurable...is what they're really fighting to understand, and that the measurable is only a servant of the unmeasurable; that everything that man makes must be fundamentally unmeasurable...'' [quoted in Alexandra Tyng, *Beginnings* (New York: John WIley & Sons, 1984), 172-73; see also 71-72 and 175-77].
23. See drawings 540.51 through 540.118 in Alexander Tzonis, General Editor, *The Louis I. Kahn Archive: Personal Drawings*--The Completely Illustrated Catalogue of the Drawings in the Louis I. Kahn Collection, University of Pennsylvania and Pennsylvania Historical and Museum Commission , The Garland Architectural Archives (New York: Garland Publishing, Inc. 1987), Vol. 2, Buildings and Projects 1959-1961, 62-86.
24 Sgarbi, 165 and (155).
25. G. L. Hersey, *Pythagorean Palaces* (Ithaca: Cornell University Press, 1976), 65-66.
26. Wurman, 125
27. Sgarbi, 156.
28. Wurman, 89.

CHAPTER 19

The Crisis of the Construction Pattern Book

KENT KEEGAN AND GIL SNYDER
University of Wisconsin-Milwaukee

ABSTRACT: *RES COGITANS* AND *RES EXTENSA*

The division of labor has been a driving force in shaping technology throughout architectural history. That rupture of the building process has been abetted by an increasing sophistication in our level of mechanization. Lewis Mumford argues that contemporary society is "a society based on the worship of the machine". What was once mined, shaped, extruded and installed by hand has been replaced by machine products. The art of building is undergoing major transformation. The distancing of the craftsman from the material, due to the influence of the machine, has produced a building/construction industry dependent upon new forms of communication: the pattern book and its progeny. The "pattern book" guides to construction technology provide a curious dilemma for the modern condition. While purporting to represent the synthesis of modern knowledge about construction technology, they in fact reinforce its secularization within the practice of architecture.

This article examines the decline of holistic and poetic thinking by investigating the evolution of the professional "pattern book", and the impact of its "standard detail". The gradual shift from individual responsibility to that of a delegated collective made up of architect, constructor and manufacturer suggests the need for an alternative form of pattern books that can address the technological imperative and sustain the process of productive reasoning.

"BARBARISM" AND THE PRE-MODERN PATTERN BOOK

According to Giambattista Vico, the eighteenth century philosopher and professor of Latin Eloquence at the University of Naples, the cycles of human history can be divided into three ages.[1] The first and last are periods of barbarism, the middle a period of heroes. Although not contemporary with Vico's cycles, the transformation of the role of the pattern book can be seen developing in three distinct periods. Within each of these periods we see changing definition of the roles of the architect, the constructor and the manufacturer, and their relationship to the construction pattern book.

The history of construction is best characterized by man's continuous struggle with physical material and the translation of this material into built form. The regional availability of construction materials influenced, if not entirely dictating, the outcome of buildings. The vision of spatial form (e.g. church, hospital, palace, etc.) and its construction were united by the constructor, in a manner that produced structures of undeniable beauty and directness of intent. Whether shaped by hand or hammer, those monuments represented a fusion between intent and realization, a particular quality no longer prevalent within our contemporary technocracy. The evidence suggest that our ability to comprehend the whole vision is eroded.

As a consequence of regional building and the need to record empirical discoveries, the codification of design and construction processes arose in both descriptive and analytical modes: the means of conveying design intent was an inherent part of the construction process. Evidence can be found as early as the Sumerian era to support this unity of building and designer. "As-built" drawings and three-dimensional models, based on Cartesian coordinate systems have been discovered throughout the Mesopotamia, Tigris and Euphrates river valleys. The Egyptians described their construction processes with a high degree of accuracy, relying on a geometric perfection of angles, proportions, and measurements carved in bas-relief on their structures, from the Pyramid complex at Giza to the great temple of Abu-Simbel in upper Egypt.

From empirical recording to careful observation and rationalization of the past, the pattern book emerged. The Roman architect/historian Vitruvius undertook to organize, in a series of ten books on architecture, the principles, methods of construction, materials, and proportions of Greek architecture and its influence on the state of Roman architecture during the time of Caesar Augustus.[2] The text is both descriptive and analytical in its nature, carefully explicating for contemporary interpretation the layers of meaning in construction and design. Whether laying out the Greco-

Roman theatre or the analemma (sundial), he dictates a comprehensive and consistent set of building standards. The clear statement of those standards represented a major breakthrough in establishing an approach to design grounded in graphic representation and description of materials, their limitations, means of assembly, and a variety of construction techniques.

The writings of Vitruvius provided a critical model for the emergence of the pattern book and the organization of building design and construction. Alberti, Serlio, Palladio, Inigo Jones, Philibert de L'Orme and Thomas Jefferson, for example, emulated the *Ten Books* when generating their own pattern book interpretations to codify their principles and theories of architecture. As it developed during this stage, the pattern book format was characterized by the continued use of orthogonal graphic representation coupled with technically accurate descriptions and interpretive annotations of materials, design and construction methods. These were interlaced with historical perceptions, suggesting an expanded vocabulary of architectural elements. These pattern books represented, in the fullness of their textual commentary and graphic depiction, the aristocratic, semi-feudal, humanisitc and agrarian order. Their success lay in the ability to create a unified order, "an order whose language was poetically amenable, whose structures were total and capacious, and whose forms were impressive in their apparent permanence and rootedness".[3] Once again the unity between meanings made and the art and process of building was allowed by a conscious reinterpretation of the past as a source of cultural guidance.

RUPTURE: *ANIMAL LABORENS* AND *HOMO FABER*

> *"... the elevation of labouring was preceded by certain developments of the modern age and which , indeed, arose almost automatically from the very nature of the events that ushered it in. What changed the mentality of 'homo faber' was the central position of the concept of process in modernity. As far as 'homo faber' was concerned, the modern shift emphasis from 'what' to 'how', from the thing itself to its fabrication was by no means an unmixed blessing. It deprived man as a maker and builder of those fixed and permanent standards of measurement which, prior to the modern age, have always served him as guides for his doing and criteria for his judgement."* - Hannah Arendt .[4]

By the early nineteenth century, the culturally transparent pattern book reflected the prevailing sentiment to systematize the principles of design and construction to accommodate the emerging industrial method and its success through division of labor. During this shift away from craftsmanship, which had implied a unity of architect, constructor and manufacturer, a major explosion in the art of building occurred - the generation of the "standard detail". Scientism became the new ideology invoking an exaggerated trust in the efficacy of the methods and principles of building design, fabrication and construction. The creation of disembodied construction pieces, each dictating their own spatial and technical requirements, as Konrad Wachsmann has noted, establishing the standard detail as a series of modular orders.[5] The shift in emphasis was from the 'what' or unity of meaning and instrumentality which had characterized the pattern book to this point, to the 'how', the manufacturer's standard detail, a modular fragment of the building viewed a in a two dimensional graphic representation. It became the new symbol for the building professions: disconnected from form, structure, material and aesthetics, the standard detail became the thread that linked the architect, the constructor, and the manufacturer.

HEROES IN CRISIS: LOCATING TECHNOLOGY AFTER THE GREAT DIVIDE

> *"Severed from tradition, intellectually excluding imagination and all that is beyond mathematical logic and positive reason, obsessed with maximum efficiency and minimum effort as primary, exclusive values and confused about the nature of symbol; the modern architect after Durand has struggled even to define his position as a professional. The present situation is still hostile to the essential role of architecture as a primary form of reconciliation: the architect is made to respond as either 'engineer' or 'decorator' under the pressures of a technological world view."* - Carlos Perez Gomez .[6]

Pattern books as they currently exist confirm this separation of the structure of rational thought from the poetic component of mystical thought .[7] They do this, with the series of standard details, by creating a false sense of objectivism about the instruments of making and encouraging the disintegration of the designing and building process into fragments controlled by individual manufacturers. Pattern books address only pieces, never related to a whole. The use of the pattern book reduces the architect's approach to the process of construction to a passive, abstract composition around combining and joining of pre-determined details .[8] The impetus to approach the generation of details as a "method of productive reasoning", as Marco Frascari suggests, is turned over to the manufacturer.

There is no evidence to indicate that the pattern books contribute, in practice, to a higher standard of building, an argument which is continually trotted out to support them. Speaking about architecture in the early 1970's, Jean Prouve said, "A representative of the aircraft industry has said that if airplanes were put into production in the manner of buildings, they would not fly".[9] In fact they reinforce failure, both technically and culturally. They increase the role definition and subsequent distance between the architect, constructor and manufacturer. As a result each one strives to eschew responsibility to avoid liability for any aspects of the process. This has led to inadequate, mismanaged, uneconomical and poorly built structures.

Based on recent findings, the architectural design profession is undergoing dramatic changes. Changes being shaped by an acceleration of social and technological factors (liability insurance and computers, etc.) The current state of the "art of building" suggests that economic constraints have a far greater impact on formal design considerations than at any time in the evolution of the profession. The denigration of the art of building has been pushed one step further by the logarithmic escalation of building failures and the resultant financial awards to injured parties. Liability insurance, once considered a reasonable and realistic part of a job cost, has sky-rocketed beyond the capabilities of many architectural practices and construction companies.

Yet, the manufacturer continues to dictate forms of construction and technology. The manufacturer's technical data sheet, has become the new "drafting room companion". The manufacturer, like Vitruvius, has published the equivalent of the "Twelve Books on Architecture", to organize the principles, methods of construction, specifications (product or performance), and material standards details of the new state of the art. Sweet's Catalogue, as published by McGraw-Hill, is one form of expression the new pattern book has taken. Within this setting, the manufacturer is capable of affecting the final product by controlling the economic, cultural and technical conditions under which the structure is fabricated, assembled, and constructed. Phillipe Starck, a French designer, remarked recently about the effect of the pattern book mentality on practice in the United States, "Here, I build less at ease, because of the American system of construction, which forces you to arrive at a very standardized method. It is the architecture of catalogs... We can't make magic anymore in America" .[10]

The role of the constructor, once an integral part of the triumvirate, has been transformed into that of a a broker mediating between the "designed part" as drawing by the architect and the "catalog part" detailed by the manufacturer. The contractor accomplishes that mediation by negotiating the price, performance and longevity of a building through translation of a series of construction documents prepared by the architect into built form. The success of the constructor's performance hinges on the authenticity of the construction drawings which, in their graphic format, are often confusing, misleading and at times, faulty. Because the architect has embraced the authority of the pattern book part, itself a generic distillation of the building process without reference to time and place, a substantial dichotomy arises between the interpretation of the construction drawings of the architect and the constructor's normative construction practice based on specific reference to time and place. The building, conceived as a kit of parts, requires that each part be assembled according to this "generic" form of logic. Trapped in the web of liability, the contractor finds unacceptable the risk of building from the architect's rendering of the standard detail parts. Turning directly to the manufacturer for the interpretation and translation of the generic details originally derived from the pattern book, the constructor is simply following the lead already established by the profession.

RETURN TO BARBARISM: LOSS OF FAITH, LOSS OF MEANING

> *"The brute fact of a relationship between the internal composition of an artwork and its references is not in itself sufficient to make a metaphor either compelling, sublime or profound. The relationship must be of a particular kind, possessing certain properties and intentionalities which more intimately relate the structure or tectonics of the work to the meanings made... But here we encounter several formidable problems. For one aim of an artwork, as E.H. Gombrich has shown, is to make its own material structure pass quickly over into the meanings made."* - John Whiteman .[11]

The new technology, supports the contention that the manufactured part is central to the design process. Whatever the formal design principles are that generate architectural invention, however varied and esoteric, their translation into built form currently relies less on the architect's ability to imbue design with its full representative potential through the exercise of detailing, than it does on the architect's ability to make a selection of pre-determined materials, assemblies and parts from the pattern book to satisfy functional criterion .[12] The distancing of the builder from the manufacturer, has succeeded in 150 years in neutralizing the design professions to such an extent that the "shop drawing" has become the final authority in the translation to the built form. The "shop drawing" has become the standard on which everyone depends. When the architect's "approved" stamp appears on the shop drawing, it represents the transfer of authority to the manufacturer. The manufacturer or assembly fabricator has translated the building into its final form. The contractor and architect, dependent on the "new design", look to the manufacturer for the authenticated image, an image found within the manufacturer's product literature. Any potential convergence between function and representation is lost.

Given the exponential explosion of technological information confronting the design profession, the need for reliable data about materials and assemblies becomes increasingly evident. Technology, to paraphrase George Santayana, "which had in his early years seemed like a family of absolute monarches - sovereign axioms, immutable laws - was very shortly transformed into a 'democracy' of theories elected for a short term of office." [13] The pattern book has emerged as central figure in the building construction industry to represent the "democracy" of standard details. With its apparent success has come the arid approach to detailing which does not allow "certain properties and intentionalities to relate the tectonics of the work to the meanings made". In the hands of the design professional it has become a constant companion, an imperative, a map to which one refers for direction and disembodied inspiration. In the hands of the constructor, it has become a resource on which the assemblage of the kit of manufactured parts is totally dependent. In the hands of the manufacturer, its is the means through which the machine can dictate the final objective - a built form generated exclusively by technological constraints. What was once implied, has now become evident: the designer has been allowed to design within the aesthetic and technical limits dictated by the manufacturer.

CONCLUSION

It is a time of full mechanization with still newer developments occurring on a daily basis whose technical complexity and cultural effect cannot be fully anticipated. Uncontestedly, the computer and its programs which permit the architect to draw, to specify and to verify, as well as communicate, have had a major impact on the design profession. Computer aided design continues to transform our conception of design and detail drawings to the extent that manufacturer's details can now be incorporated directly into the design via the telephone. The electronically transmitted detail is the final connection between machines. The designer sits in front of the display terminal and marvels at the dexterity of the machine - the tool has achieved the status of designer replacing the human component.

There is no doubt that the pattern book, as it is now constituted, clouds, rather than reveals the role of the detail in building. Architects would appear to have surrendered to manufacturer's their role as makers of meaning and champions of productive reasoning in the face of the burden of technological change and the crisis of meaning. The education of the new design professional suggests the need to reformulate the pattern book to accommodate a technique which Vico described as the unity of the ''poetic component of mystical thought with the structure of rational thought'',[14] creating ''an architecture which embodies in itself the narration of the sequence of the symbolic and practical uses of its parts''.[15]

NOTES

1. Marco Frascari, ''The *Particolareggiamento* in the Narration of Architecture'' in *Journal of Architectural Education*, Volume 43, Number 1, (Fall 1989), p. 8.
2. Vitruvius, *The Ten Books of Architecture* (New York: Dover Publications, Inc., 1983).
3. Richard Sheppard, ''The Crisis of Language'' in Malcolm Bradbury and James McFarlane, eds., *Modernism* (New York: Penguin Books, 1986), p. 325.
4. Hannah Arendt, *The Human Condition* (New York: Anchor Books, 1959), p. 280.
5. Konrad Wachsmann, *The Turning Point of Building: Structure and Design* (New York: Reinhold Publishing Corporation, 1961), pp. 55 ff.
6. Carlos Perez Gomez, ''The Potential of Architecture as Art'', *Architectural Design*, Numbers 7-8, (1982), p. 55.
7. See Marc Angelil, ''Technique and the Metaphysics of Science: The Rational-Irrational Element of Science-Technology within the Making of Architecture'' in *The Harvard Architecture Review*, Number 7, (1989).
8. Marco Frascari, op. cit., p. 8.
9. Jean Prouve, *Jean Prouve* (New York: Praeger Publishing Corporation, 1971).
10. Karen Stein, ''The World According to Starck'' in *Architectural Record*, (Mid-September, 1987), p.102.
11. John Whiteman, ''Still Movement: E.E. Cummings and Louis Kahn'' in *Midgard: Journal of Architectural Theory and Criticism*, Volume 1, Number 1, (1987), p. 16.
12. Marco Frascari, op. cit., p. 6.
13. James McFarlane, ''The Mind of Modernism'' in Malcolm Bradbury and James McFarlane, eds., *Modernism* (New York: Penguin Books, 1986), p. 80.
14. Marc Angelil, op. cit., p. 75.
15. Marco Frascari, op. cit., p. 5.

CHAPTER 20

Chicago-Los Angeles: The Concrete Connection

KATHRYN A. SMITH
Southern California Institute of Architecture

The two most important material advances in the twentieth century are steel and reinforced concrete. While steel is synonymous with the neutral frame of the commercial architecture of the Chicago School, concrete is a plastic material, readily transformed into a myriad of structures and forms, which cannot be solely identified with any one designer or movement. Although all four architects who experimented with concrete in Southern California between 1900 and 1930 -- Irving Gill, Frank Lloyd Wright, R.M. Schindler and Lloyd Wright -- lived and trained in Chicago early in their careers, each turned away from the steel frame in favor of an exploration of various structural methods in concrete construction. Their achievements, although individual, are linked and result from their common origins in the stimulating and innovative atmosphere of Chicago before and after the turn of the century.

As contemporaries, both Frank Lloyd Wright and Gill had apprenticed in the office of Adler and Sullivan during the most creative period of that firm's output, overlapping for the years 1890 to 1892, when Gill departed for California. Growing up in Chicago as the child of one of its leading architects, Lloyd Wright was surrounded by the landmarks of the Chicago School during the formative years of his youth. Although he was never employed in a commerical Chicago firm, his father's Studio was directly connected to the family home, and there can be no doubt that Lloyd experienced first hand the lessons that his European contemporaries would only know from the Wasmuth portfolio, which he helped to prepare. One of these was the Viennese R.M. Schindler who arrived in Chicago in 1914 to work in the office of Ottenheimer, Stern and Reichert. Henry A. Ottenheimer, the chief partner of the firm, had also received his training in the Adler and Sullivan office. After completing his three year contract, Schindler joined Frank Lloyd Wright's office in 1918 where working drawings were in preparation for the Imperial Hotel in Tokyo, Japan.

There was extensive experimentation and invention in concrete technology taking place throughout the United States at the turn of the century. Frank Lloyd Wright was the first among this group of architects to begin to adapt this new

R.M. Schindler for Frank Lloyd Wright, The Monolith Home, 1919.

technology to his architectural practice. His first executed concrete building was the poured-in-place Unity Temple, 1904-06, followed by the design for a monolithic concrete dwelling, the "Fireproof House for $5000," first published in 1907. Gill began using the material as early as 1908 and in 1909 completed three cast concrete structures, a church and two school buildings. A connection between Wright and Gill was reestabilshed in 1912 when Lloyd Wright joined Gill's San Diego office. He was there until 1915 a period that includes Gill's adaptation of a technique for tilt-up walls in the Banning House, the Women's Club and the Community House. Frank Lloyd Wright visited Lloyd Wright at least once while he was with Gill, and perhaps more, as he made more frequent trips to California on his way to Japan for work on the Imperial Hotel.

Wright's work between 1918 and 1921 in Japan and California draws in first Schindler and then Lloyd Wright. Schindler began by working on the drawings for the Imperial Hotel, a structure which was designed to withstand earthquakes. The problem was further complicated by the unique soils conditions of the site which was located on a landfill that had once been a part of Tokyo Bay. The structure, which was designed and engineered in Chicago, but redesigned on-site as conditions necessitated, consisted of a reinforced concrete frame resting on a foundation of concrete piles. Wright employed two systems for constructing the concrete structure. One was the usual process of using wood formwork. The other was to build the finish materials first, custom-made brick and local lava stone, and to use the double shell of the exterior and interior walls as the formwork, thus creating a monolithic structure. The latter system was used to build the outer walls and most of the columns, the former for beams and slabs. Wright's method, however, prolonged building because pouring could not begin until the stone was carved and the brick and stone walls, built in increments, had hardened. The construction time which doubled from two to four years kept Wright pre-occupied and away from his local practice longer than he anticipated.

Schindler, in Wright's Chicago office, took over more responsibilities than were customary including the design for several jobs, most of which were minor. However, a larger commission for a residential development in Racine, Wisconsin was brought into the office in 1919 by a former Prairie House client, Thomas P. Hardy. All evidence points to Schindler as the designer for what was labelled a "Workingmen's Colony of Concrete Monolith Houses," a project that bears comparison with LeCorbusier's "Quartier Moderne" at Pessac for Henri Fruges between 1924-1926. The surviving drawings indicate there were three schemes for the "Worker's House." The preliminary drawings were drawn in July, 1919. The working drawings followed in the same month and were revised by Wright in September, 1919 during his three month return visit from Japan. Schindler drew a new set of working drawings in April, 1920. Although Wright made minor, but significant changes, primarily adding more pattern thereby softening the austere abstraction of Schindler's composition, the essential ideas prevailed through all versions.

The major theme of the building is the use of one material for all elements -- cast concrete used throughout on the exterior and interior for floors, walls and roof. Although an influence from Wright's work is evident, especially the planar compositions such as Unity Temple, Coonley Playhouse, and the Bach House, Schindler's European background can be detected in the uncompromising juxtaposition of horizontal and vertical planes and vertical strip windows. It is in this project that a floor to ceiling corner of glass first appears as two inward projecting windows in the living room.

Wright's prolonged absence in Japan also affected the construction of the residence in Hollywood known as "Hollyhock House" for Aline Barnsdall. In late 1919, Lloyd Wright went to Los Angeles to supervise construction and when difficulties arose, Schindler followed in late 1920 to take over. Although the materials were hollow tile, wood and plaster, the silhouette, as Wright later wrote, typified a concrete building. It was because of the Barnsdall commission that both Wrights returned to Los Angeles where they would renew acquaintance with Gill and where Frank Lloyd Wright and Schindler would continue their adaptations in concrete technology. Through Lloyd Wright, in 1921, Schindler met Gill, now located in Los Angeles. A few months later, Schindler encouraged his wife's friends, Clyde and Marian Chace, to move to Los Angeles to work with Gill. Clyde Chace, trained as an engineer, came to do drafting, estimating and contracting and began work on the Horatio West Courts, a poured-in-place structure in Santa Monica.

With Wright still in Japan and work on the Barnsdall jobs halted, Schindler designed his own studio-residence as a duplex with Clyde Chace in late 1921. Adapting Gill's system, Schindler employed what he called "slab-tilt" construction conforming to his aesthetic of modular vertical slabs. The dwelling was built in 1922 with Chace as contractor using a small crew. Chace borrowed some concrete equipment from Gill, who visited the site at least once, one block from his last major building, the Dodge House of 1916. Simultaneously, Lloyd Wright was at work on the Henry Bollman House in Hollywood where he introduced concrete blocks as an ornamental band along the balcony to contrast with the flat planar walls. The concrete blocks were not structural but were tied to the balcony with steel rods.

When Wright returned to the United States for good in 1923, he moved to Los Angeles. Utilizing concrete blocks also, Wright invented a structural system which he called the "textile block" system. Based on the module of a 16 inch square, Wright used concrete for interior and exterior walls. This was the most productive year for designs in concrete for this group of architects. Although Gill had almost retired, Wright designed four buildings and six projects in "textile block," while both Lloyd Wright and Schindler built large commissions in slip-form construction, the Oasis Hotel in Palm Springs by the former and the Pueblo Ribera Courts in La Jolla by the latter.

Although Wright left Los Angeles in 1924, he continued to use the "textile block" system for residences throughout his life, with an interruption between 1932 and 1947 when he switched to wood in the Usonian Houses. Many landmarks of his second major career, beginning in 1936, are notable for the use of concrete, not the least of which are "Fallingwater" and the Guggenheim Museum. Lloyd Wright employed concrete blocks throughout the 1920s, but never as a complete structural system. Schindler continued to use concrete, most dramatically in the five concrete frames of the Lovell Beach House; but by the end of the 1920s, his use of concrete had ceased.

How can we explain the fact that for several years in the early teens and twenties, Southern California was the most innovative center for architecture in the United States and that the majority of this work was in reinforced concrete? In fact, this achievement resulted from the efforts of four architects who shared a common background and were linked in direct and indirect ways. All four had trained or worked in Chicago immediately preceding their move to Southern California. Three of the four had trained in a Chicago firm that was noted for using the steel frame in commerical architecture. All four had turned away from the steel frame in favor of concrete. The most obvious explanation is that none of these architects had a commerical practice; indeed, their predilection was decidedly residential or residential in scale. However, although this simple answer appears to suffice, a closer examination of each architect's work reveals formal and symbolic preferences that explain the choice of concrete over steel. All four architects compose in enveloping, sliding or intersecting planes juxtaposed with voids, transparent bands of glass or ornament. Gill's mature style in the Dodge House or La Jolla Women's Club consists of a reduction of the wall plane to a flat surface punctuated by deep openings for windows, doors or archways. Wright's development throughout the decade of the Prairie House was consistently devoted to an expressive space in the Willitts, Martin, and Robie Houses, for example, and his invention of the "textile block" system was a search for a solution that would integrate structure and form. Lloyd Wright, combining influences from both Wright and Gill, juxtaposed the unadorned planar wall with strong sculptural ornament in buildings such as the Sowden and Derby Houses. Schindler's interest in an abstract space defined by sliding planes, as seen in the "Monolith House" and his own Studio-Residence, synthesized his European background and the influence from Wright.

Even these formal criteria do not fully explain the choice of concrete. These same results could be accomplished in other materials, primarily wood frame and plaster, and were, as Wright's "Hollyhock House," most of Lloyd Wright's work, and Schindler's buildings after 1930 testify. These architects, however, had inherited from their Chicago training, and for Schindler, from Vienna as well, an inclination for technology and a moral committment to a modernity associateed with industrial methods and materials. The paradox which presents itself is that, although this body of work is recognized for its technological experimentation, a theme that was consistently promoted by the architects themselves, it was as much dedicated to traditional tectonic ideals as it was influenced by modernist ambitions. Thus, for all the standardization of units and the allusions to prefabrication, the architectural inferences are to traditional buildings; that is say, they refer to the masonry architecture of pre-industrial American cultures. For Gill, it was to the early California Mission buildings of Spanish settlement; for Schindler, to the dwellings of the Pueblo Indians of the Southwest; for the Wrights, to the Mayan monuments of Pre-Columbian Mexico. While the degree of abstraction which all these projects present is the key factor in the design, the tactile quality of light-reflecting, solid earth walls is recalled in Gill's Bishops School, Schindler's Studio-Residence, Frank Lloyd Wright's Ennis House, and Lloyd Wright's Sowden House. Unlike the steel frame of the Chicago School office building, concrete contained a dual symbolism; at once the material of a technological society poised on the brink of progressive future, and at the same time, a plastic substance that could be manipulated to evoke the strength and solidity of a traditional architecture that these four architects sought to preserve.

REFERENCES

Gebhard, David. *Lloyd Wright, Architect: 20th Century Architecture in an Organic Exhibition.* Santa Barbara, CA.: Art Galleries, University of California, 1971.

McCoy, Esther. *Five California Architects.* New York: Reinhold, 1960.

Smith, Kathryn. "Frank Lloyd Wright, Hollyhock House, and Olive Hill, 1914-1924," *Journal of the Society of Architectural Historians*, XXXVIII, no. 1 (March, 1979): 15-33.

______, "Frank Lloyd Wright and the Imperial Hotel: A Postscript," *The Art Bulletin*, LXVII, no. 2 (June, 1985): 296-310.

______. *R.M. Schindler House, 1921-22.* West Hollywood, CA.: Friends of the Schindler House, 1987.

______, "Frank Lloyd Wright's Unknown Imperial Hotel Annex," *SD: Space Design* 286 (July 1988): 77-80.

CHAPTER 21

The Poetics of Thermal Technology

JOSEPH B. ODOERFER
University of Detroit

INTRODUCTION

The suggestion that the technology of heating and cooling buildings may have an aesthetic dimension is sometimes met with skepticism from even the most open minded of practitioners. This skepticism appears to be based in part on the belief that technology, as a direct application of science, is quantitative in method rather than qualitative, and therefore is incapable of possessing a poetics. Technology, however, is distinct from science in the process of its application. It combines the abstract quantitative methods of science with concrete qualitative judgments.[1] I would argue further that when technology is applied to an art it ultimately shares in and influences that art's aesthetic dimension.

Among those who agree that thermal technology has an aesthetic dimension, two quite different positions can be identified. The most commonly accepted of these will be referred to as the vision theory. It defines the relationship between thermal technology and aesthetic experience as occurring in visual perception, and it focuses on the compositional implications of the implements of thermal control. The second position, which will be referred to as the holistic theory, argues that aesthetic experience occurs not only in visual perception, but in all forms of sense experience, including thermal sensation itself. The holistic theory focuses on the design of thermal experience and its relationship to other forms of sense perception. The objective of this paper is to provide a sound basis for evaluating these theories by attempting to reveal their underlying assumptions and implications. Contemporary writings will be examined and synthesized to arrive at a coherent and comprehensive understanding of each theory and the ideas on which it is based. Where appropriate the philosophical and historical roots of the idea itself will be traced in order to evaluate each theory in the broadest context possible.

THE VISION THEORY

It is probably best to begin this process with the vision theory since it has been the traditional approach to architectural aesthetics.[2] The central premise of the vision theory is that the aesthetic dimension in architecture is limited to the sense of sight (and its interaction with the mind). The other senses such as, hearing, smell, or thermal sensation make no contribution to this aesthetic experience and, in fact, can diminish the pleasure by interfering with mental concentration. These aspects of the theory are described by Le Corbusier in *Towards a New Architecture* where he writes:

> Architecture is a plastic thing. I mean by "plastic" what is seen and measured by the eyes. Obviously, if the roof were to fall in, if the central heating did not work, if the walls cracked, the joys of architecture would be greatly diminished; the same thing might be said of a gentleman who listened to a symphony sitting on a pin-cushion or in a bad draught.[3]

As Le Corbusier's comments imply, the aesthetic task, in the vision theory, with respect to thermal technology is twofold. Since architecture is classified as "what is seen" the visual impact of mechanical equipment must be taken into consideration. Generally, this task is addressed in one of two ways; equipment is either concealed from view or it is treated as a plastic element and integrated into the building's formal composition. The second task is to eliminate any distracting thermal sensations, such as drafts, which might interfere with the aesthetic experience.

Prior to the industrial revolution, both tasks were the responsibility of the architect. In the nineteenth century, however, the current split between architectural and mechanical services began to take place. The newly formed profession of heating and ventilating engineers assumed responsibility for what must have been perceived as a scientific or quantitative task, that of temperature control. The architect retained responsibility for the qualitative or aesthetic task of controlling the building's visual appearance. The new technologies of central heating and mechanical ventilation, the complexity of which necessitated the split, also provided the architect with tremendous freedom in accomplishing this aesthetic task.[4] Mechanical ventilation allowed lower ceiling heights and greater building depths than its predecessor, the operable window, while central heating facilitated the use of complex free-flowing arrangements of interior space, the open plan, and the extensive use of glass to create visual interpenetration of interior and exterior space.[5] While architects explored the visual implications of new thermal technologies, the engineering profession attempted to quantify thermal experience through objective comfort standards and "thermally neutral"[6] environments. This approach led to a more radical implementation of the vision theory where non-aesthetic forms of sense experience are categorically rather than qualitatively, eliminated. Thus, pleasant as well as unpleasant sensations are neutralized. As a result, modern building environments have moved toward a more distilled form of architectural experience, which depends increasingly on visual perception. Since experience in modern urbanized environments is largely architectural, this description is characteristic of modern society as well as building.

To determine the implications of this phenomenon it is necessary to have a clearer understanding of the nature of vision-based aesthetic experience. Traditionally, this experience has been defined as a form of intellectual pleasure[7] (which is ironic since the word aesthetic is derived from the Greek verb aesthanome which means "to feel"). Intellectual pleasures have been distinguished from merely sensuous pleasures in that they require thought as a necessary part of their enjoyment, whereas sensuous pleasures are not dependent on thought.[8] For example, while warming my feet on the floor of a Frank Lloyd Wright house, I may think of the radiant floor slab as a metaphor for the earth and its nurturing and life sustaining qualities and this line of thought may be in itself pleasurable, but it is not necessary to think these thoughts to enjoy the sensation of having my feet warmed. Therefore, thermal sensation is a sensuous rather than an intellectual pleasure. If, however, I examine the same floor with my eyes noticing that it is flush with the exterior grade and that it has a warm red-brown color, I may experience the same thoughts concerning its metaphorical relationship to the earth, but in this instance, without these thoughts there is no enjoyment. Thus, the pleasure is dependent on the thought and is, therefore, an intellectual pleasure. It is a very subtle distinction, the point of which seems to be to distill intellectual experience from bodily enjoyment.

This notion of solely intellectual aesthetic experience poses no problem for arts like painting or sculpture which are self-contained experiences distinct from everyday life. In architecture, however, aesthetic experience is submerged in the context of everyday existence. In urban environments it often constitutes a major portion of total experience. For this reason, a fragmentary experience, which addresses the mind and not the body runs the risk of dehumanizing rather than enriching life.

HOLISTIC THEORY

The holistic theory can be understood as the product of a reaction to this failure of the vision theory to address the unique problems of architectural experience as a domain of lived experience. Despite the long history of vision theory this reaction appears to begin in the twentieth-century. The reasons for this late response, most likely, relate to the restructuring of the building profession after the industrial revolution and the more strictly visual approach architects have taken to design since that restructuring.

The holistic theory contended that in architecture all of the senses, not simply the sense of sight, must be engaged aesthetically. It argues that architecture, as an inhabited environment, is distinct from the other arts. James Marston Fitch writes:

> Analogies between architecture and the other forms of art are very common in esthetic literature. Obviously, architecture shares many formal characteristics with them. Like a painting or a sculpture, like a ballet or a symphony, a building may be analyzed from the point of view of proportion, balance, rhythm, color, texture, and so on. But such analogies will be misleading unless we constantly bear in mind that our experiential relationship with architecture is fundamentally of a different order from that of the other arts. With architecture, we are *submerged* in the experience, whereas the relationship between us and a painting or a symphony is much more one of simple *exposure*.[9]

Fitch argues that because of this broader experiential context the aesthetic dimension in architecture cannot be confined to the sense of sight, but must address a "multidimensional totality." He writes that, "[r]ecognition of this fact is crucial for esthetic theory, above all for architectural esthetics. Far from being narrowly based upon any single sense of perception like vision our response to a building derives from our body's *total* response to and perception of the environmental conditions which that building affords."[10] Thus, rather than diminishing aesthetic experience, the other senses contribute to and complete it. This argument is also made by Lisa Heschong in *Thermal Delight in Architecture*, where she writes:

> Since each sense contributes a slightly different perception of the world, the more senses involved in a particular experience, the fuller, the rounder, the experience becomes. If sight allows for a three-dimensional world, then each other sense contributes at least one, if not more, additional dimensions. The most vivid, most powerful experiences are those involving all of the senses at once.[11]

The contribution which thermal sensation makes to architectural experience is to provide immediacy to the experience, locating it in space and time. This sense of immediacy is derived from the fact that "thermal nerve endings are heat-flow sensors, not temperature sensors."[12] They provide information about what is directly happening to the body, thus creating a milieu for other more differentiated sense experience. This contribution and the interaction of thermal sensation with the other senses can be illustrated in the fireplace, which engages nearly all the senses, and thus provides an example par excellence of holistic thermal technology. The captivating visual experience of the open flame has been well documented by Gaston Bachelard.[13] This visual experience, however, is enriched by the crackling and hissing sounds of burning logs with their accompanying scent, as well as the pleasurable sensation of warmth provided. This thermal experience provides a profound sense of reality to these other forms of sense experience. The other senses also contribute to the thermal experience. The warm colors and constant movement of the flames give an impression of warmth and a visual focus to the experience, reinforcing the centrality created by radiating heat and light. The low pitched and reverberant sounds of wood burning deep within a masonry shell also conveys warmth and the smoky smells recall other fires and the memory of other experiences of gathering around a hearth.

Although the fireplace offers an example of a holistic approach to thermal technology, the proponents of the holistic theory do not advocate its revival. Rather, what they do propose is that the same qualitative approach to thermal technology which existed in architectural practice prior to the industrial revolution be revived. In this sense, although it is a new theory, it is an old practice, a practice that slowly disappeared as the vision theory was applied more rigorously to architecture.

As a theory of architectural aesthetics, the holistic theory is more revolutionary, recognizing a fundamentally different form of aesthetic experience than the distilled intellectual pleasure of the vision theory. The holistic theory attempts to unite pleasurable bodily experiences, which are derived from simply using the senses, with intellectual pleasure, by directing the aesthetic experience to a poetic understanding of one's relationship to the material world. This explains why increasing the number of senses involved enriches the experience; knowledge is increased and verified as more forms of sense perception are included, resulting in a more complete understanding of this relationship. In so doing, aesthetic experience is more fully integrated into everyday experience.

In conclusion, the holistic theory avoids the duality of aesthetic and ordinary experience, which poses an uncomfortable contradiction for architectural experience, where the two must inevitably be united. It also provides a framework for addressing what the vision theory has failed to acknowledge, namely, that architecture, as the domain of human existence, must embrace the totality of what it is to be a human being; a totality which includes bodily as well as intellectual experience. Therefore, it is a holistic poetics of thermal technology that holds the greatest potential for enriching architectural experience.

NOTES

1. John M. Staudenmaier, *Technology's Storyteller: Reweaving the Human Fabric*, (Cambridge: MIT Press, 1985), pp. 95-103.
2. Richard Neutra, *Survival Through Design*, (New York: Oxford University Press, 1969), pp. 138-139.
3. Le Corbusier, *Towards a New Architecture*, trans. Frederick Etchells, (New York: Holt, Reinhart and Winston. 1985), p. 199.
4. Robert Bruegmann and Donald Prowler, "Architecture Confronts Environmental Technology: An Historical Perspective," *Energy Conservation Through Building Design*, ed. Donald Watson (New York: McGraw Hill, 1979), p. 29.
5. Reyner Banham, *The Architecture of the Well-tempered Environment*, (Chicago: The University of Chicago Press, 1969), p. 86.
6. P. O. Fanger, "Thermal Comfort in Indoor Environments," in *Thermal Analysis - Human Comfort - Indoor Environments*, ed. B. W. Mangum and J. E. Hill, (National Bureau of Standards Special Publication; 491, 1977). p. 4.
7. Roger Scruton, *The Aesthetics of Architecture*, (New Jersey: Princeton University Press, 1979), p. 71.
8. Ibid., p. 72-74.
9. James Marston Fitch, *American Building and The Forces That Shape It*, 2nd Edition. (Boston: Houghton Mifflin Company, 1972), pp. 2-3.
10. Ibid., p. 2.
11. Lisa Heschong, *Thermal Delight in Architecture*, (Cambridge: The MIT Press, 1982), p. 29.
12. Ibid., p. 19.
13. Gaston Bachelard, *The Psychanalysis of Fire*, trans. Alan C. M. Ross, (Boston: Beacon Press, 1964), pp. 13-20.

CHAPTER 22

High-Rise Building Structure Types

WOLFGANG SCHUELLER
Virginia Polytechnic Institute and State University

The building shape and building function very much determine the nature of the support structure aside from the design attitude towards structure. Vertical structures range from massive building blocks to slender towers; they may occur as isolated objects within the urban fabric, or they may form urban megastructures. They encompass types from simple symmetrical to complex asymmetrical forms, from boxes to terraced buildings, and from ordinary bearing wall, skeleton, and core construction to bridge buildings, cellular clusters, suspension buildings, tubes, superframes, and the new breed of compound hybrid skyscraper forms. From an appearance point of view, buildings may disclose themselves as organisms by exposing how they were constructed, how they stand up, and how they function. These buildings may celebrate technology, experimentation, and innovation as art. On the other hand, buildings may represent sculptures or other formal objects that are inspired by symbolism, ornamentation, and the preservation of past values. In this case, the building image is controlled by external considerations as may be expressed by complex spatial geometry, massing, and imposed surface composition, where the facade wall forms an independent decorative enclosure articulating values possibly reminiscent of the Art Deco Style. whatever the position of structure in architecture, the architect must understand structure in order, either to control it from a professional point of view or to articulate its spirit as an artist.

Structure makes enclosure ‘‘ that is, the spaces within a building ‘‘ possible; it gives support to the material. In addition, it acts as a spatial and dimensional organizer similar to the skeleton in the body with respect to the life-supporting systems. A building structure can be visualized as consisting of horizontal planes or floor framing and the supporting vertical planes of walls and/or frames. The horizontal planes tie the vertical planes together to achieve a box effect and a certain degree of compactness. It is quite obvious that a slender, tall tower building must be a compact, three-dimensional closed structure where the entire system acts a a unit. The tubular-, core interactive-, and staggered truss buildings are typical examples of three-dimensional structures. On the other hand, a massive building block only needs some stiff, stabilizing elements to give lateral support to the rest of the building. Here, the building structure represents an open system where, for instance, separate vertical planar structure parts such as solid walls, rigid frames, and braced frames are located at various places and form stand-alone systems that provide the lateral stability. Although buildings are three-dimensional, their support structures often can be treated from a behavioral point of view as an assembly of two-dimensional vertical planar elements in each major direction of the building. In other words, structures can usually be subdivided into a few simpler assemblies since structural elements are rarely placed randomly in plan.

Every building consists of the loadbearing structure and the non-loadbearing portion. The main loadbearing structure, in turn, is subdivided in the gravity structure, which carries only the gravity loads, and the lateral-force resisting structure, which supports gravity forces but also must provide stability to the building. The non-loadbearing structural building elements include wind bracing as well as the membranes and skins ‘‘ that is the curtains, ceilings, and partitions ‘‘ which cover the structure and subdivide space. The lateral-force resisting structure in a building tower may be concentrated entirely in the central core, for instance, when on optimal view and thus a light perimeter structure is desired. Conversely, rather than hiding the lateral-force resisting structure in the interior, it may be exposed and form the perimeter structure such as tubes. The most common high-rise structure types are identified in the following sections. They range from pure structure systems such as skeleton and wall construction and systems requiring transfer structures to composite systems and megastructures. As the buildings increase in height, different structure layouts are needed for reasons of efficiency (i.e., least weight). The sequence of the classification corresponds roughly to these efficiency considerations.

BEARING WALL STRUCTURES: The bearing wall was the primary support structure for high-rise buildings before the steel skeleton and the curtain wall were introduced in the 1880s in Chicago. The traditional, tall masonry buildings were massive gravity structures where the walls were perceived to act independently " their action was not seen as part of the entire three-dimensional building form. It was not until after World War II that engineered thin-walled masonry construction was introduced in Europe. Bearing wall construction is used mostly for building types that require frequent subdivision of space such as for residential application. The bearing walls may either be closely spaced e.g., 12 to 18 ft and directly define the rooms, or they may be spaced, for instance, 30 ft apart and use long-span floor systems that support the partition walls subdividing the space. Bearing wall buildings of 15 stories or more in brick, concrete block, precast large-panel concrete, or cast-in-place reinforced concrete are commonplace today; they have been built up to the 26-story range. The bearing wall principle is adaptable to a variety of building forms and layouts. Plan forms range from slab-type buildings and towers of various shapes to any combination. The wall arrangements can take many different forms, such as the cross-wall-, long-wall-, double cross-wall-, tubular-, cellular-, and radial systems. Naturally, there are an endless variety of hybrid systems possible by combining the cases above. The walls may be continuous in nature and in line with each other, or they may be staggered; they may intersect, or they may function as separate elements to form individual wall columns.

CORE STRUCTURES: Many multi-core buildings with their exposed service shafts have been influenced by the thinking of the Metabolists of the 1960s, who clearly separated the vertical circulation and the served spaces. According to Kenzo Tange, "Buildings grow like organisms in a metabolic way." Their urban clusters consisted of vertical service towers linked by multilevel bridges which, in turn, contained the cellular subdivisions. Other examples can be found in the hospital planning of the 1970s. The linear bearing wall structure works quite well for residential buildings where functions are fixed and energy supply can be easily distributed vertically. In contrast, office and commercial buildings require maximum flexibility in layout, calling for large open spaces subdivided by movable partitions. Here, the vertical circulation and the distribution of other services must be gathered and contained in shafts and then channeled horizontally at every floor level. These vertical cores may also act as lateral stabilizers for the building. There is an unlimited variety of possibilities related to the shape, number, arrangement, and location of cores. They range from single-core structures (core with cantilevered floor framing, core with massive base cantilever, core with large top and/or intermediate cantilevers, core with other structure systems) to multiple core structures.

BRIDGE STRUCTURES: The idea of the bridge structure was vitalized by the designers of the 1960s, who were concerned with large-scale urban architecture and wanted to separate the ground and services from social activities. These megastructures or urban structures were proposed by the Metabolists in Japan, Archigram in England, and designers such as Yona Friedman in France and Eckhard Schulze-Fielitz in Germany who used horizontal space-frame structures. The long span from vertical support to vertical support can be achieved through an endless number of possibilities as has been expressed in architecture. Closely related to the bridge concept is the core structure, where many of the buildings formed megaframes to support, in bridge-like fashion, secondary building packages. Similarly, several of the suspension structures are based on the bridge principle, as are supertall buildings that use megaframes or superdiagonals to gather the building weight to certain points for the purpose of stability. Space can be bridged by using one of the following structural concepts: Vierendeel trusses, trusses, arches, suspended arches, and wall beams.

SUSPENSION BUILDINGS: The application of the suspension principle to high-rise buildings rather than to roof structures is essentially a phenomenon of the late 1950s and 1960s, although experiments with the concept go back to the 1920s. The structuralists of this period discovered a wealth of new support structure systems in the search to minimize the material and to express antigravity, that is, the lightness of space and openess of the facade, allowing no visual obstruction with heavy structural members. The fact that hanging the floors on cables required only about one-sixth of the material compared to columns in compression, as in skeleton construction, provided a new challenge to the designers. In addition, this type of structure allowed a column-free space at the base. The tree-like buildings with a large central tower, from which giant arms are cantilevered at the top to support the tensile columns at their ends, are quite common today. From the support structures are suspended the floors or spatial units (e.g., capsules, entire building blocks) by using either vertical or diagonal tensile members. The typical suspension systems use the rigid core principle (single or multiple cores with outriggers or beams, megaframes, tree-like frames, etc.), the guyed mast principle, and the tensegrity or spacenet principle.

STAGGERED WALL-BEAM STRUCTURES: In this innovative structure system, developed in the mid 1960s by a team of architects and engineers at M.I.T., story-high wall-beams span the full width of the building on alternate floors of a given bay and are supported by columns along the exterior walls; there are no interior columns. The wall-beams are usually steel trusses but can also be pierced reinforced concrete members. The steel trusses are concealed within the room walls. In the interstitial system, wall beams are used at every other floor to allow for uninterrupted free flow in the floor space between, while in the staggered wall-beam system, the wall-beams are used at every floor level but arranged in a staggered fashion between adjacent floors. The arrangement of the story-high members depends on the layout of the functional units. One can visualize apartment units to be contained between the wall-beams and to be vertically stacked to resemble masonry bond patterns. As the unit sizes change, the spacing of the wall-beams may be adjusted or additional openings may be provided. The most common system of organization is the running bond or checkerboard pattern.

SKELETON STRUCTURES: When William Jenney, in the 10-story Home Insurance Building in Chicago (1885), used iron framing for the first time as the sole support structure carrying the masonry facade walls, the all-skeleton construction was born. The tradition of the Chicago Frame was revived after World War II when the skeleton again became a central theme of the modern movement in its search for merging technology and architecture. Famous landmarks became SOM's Lever House in New York (1952) and Mies van der Rohe's two 860-880 Lake Shore Drive Apartment Buildings (1951). These landmarks have been most influential to the subsequent generation of designers; they symbolized with their simplicity of expression the new spirit of structure and glass. Although the pure, boxy shapes of the 1960s are closely associated with skeleton construction, as derived from Miesian minimalism, other high-rise building skeletal forms, based on quite different design philosophies, have been built, e.g., the unusually hammer-shaped Velasca Tower in Milan, Italy (1957). Today, there seems to be no limit to the variety of building shapes '' the skeleton as an organizing element for this new generation of hybrid forms has been extensively experimented with. Odd-shaped towers, possibly with tapered frames, reflect the change of irregular plan forms with height '' skeleton buildings may be stepped at various floor levels where large set-back terraces may be fully landscaped. In the Lloyd's of London Building, the braced perimeter concrete frame is surrounded by six satellite service towers while the internal perimeter columns carry the elaborate central atrium structure. Kisho Kurokawa articulated the regularity of the three-dimensional grid and its adaptability to growth and change by constructing the Takara Beautillion for Osaka's Expo '70 from single six-pointed spatial cross units. The typical unit is made from twelve steel pipes bent into 90-degree angles and welded to steel plates; a unit measures about 22 ft. Facade framing ranges from long-span deep girder systems and Vierendell frames to perforated walls. The open, airy skeleton is contrasted with the framed tubular wall. Frames may be organized as continuous rigid frames, hinged frames, and any combination.

FLAT SLAB BUILDING STRUCTURES: Flat slab buildings,developed during the mid 1940s in New York, consist of horizontal planar concrete slabs directly supported on columns, thus eliminating the need for floor framing. This results in a minimum story height '' an obvious economic benefit that is especially advantageous for apartment buildings. Drop panels and/or column capitals are frequently used because of high shear concentrations around the columns. Slabs without drop panels are commonly called flat plates. The system is adaptable to an irregular support layout. From a behavioral point of view, flat slabs are highly complex structures. The intricacy of the force flow along an isotropic plate, in response to uniform gravity action, is reflected by the principal moment contours. Here, the main moments around the column support are negative and have circular and radial directions, while the positive field moments basically connect the columns linearly. The patterns remind us of organic structures, such as the branching grids of leaves, the delicate network of insect wings, radial spider webs, and the contour lines of conical tents, realizing a similar relationship between cable response and loading as well as the corresponding moment diagram. Pier Luigi Nervi, for the Gatti Wool Factory (1953) in Rome, Italy, actually followed the principal bending moments with the layout of the floor ribs. Centuries earlier, however, the late medieval master builders had already intuitively developed patterns for ribbed vaulting, predicting these tensile trajectories; the fan vaults of the Tudor period in England are a convincing example.

BRACED FRAME STRUCTURES: The concept of resisting lateral forces through bracing is the most common construction method '' it is applied to all types of buildings ranging from lowrise structures to skyskrapers. At a certain height, depending on the building proportions and the density of frame layout, the rigid frame structure becomes too ''mushy'' and may be uneconomical so that it must be stiffened by, for example, steel bracing or concrete shear walls. The architects Burnham and Root developed the concept of vertical shear wall (or the vertical truss principle) in the 20-story Masonic Temple Building (1892) in Chicago.

TRUSSED FRAME STRUCTURES: Trusses not only constitute support structures hidden within the building but also may be revealed on the exterior. One of the earliest examples of braced skeleton buildings is the Chocolate Factory at Noisiel-sur-Marne near Paris by Jules Saulnier (1872), where the walls consist of exposed trussed iron framework. This method of construction was surely inspired by trussed bridge construction as well as by the timber framing that first occurred in Europe during the Middle Ages. Here, each region developed its own distinct pattern of braced wall heavy timber framing with the space between the timber members infilled with masonry or other material mixtures. An early example of high-rise braced frame construction is Gustave Eiffel's interior braced iron skeleton for the 151-ft high Statue of Liberty (1886) in New York. He also designed the braced skeleton wrought iron structure of the Eiffel Tower (1889) in Paris, at almost 1000 ft, the tallest building of its time '' this first modern tower became a symbol for a new era with its daring lightness of construction. The elaborate tops of the skyscrapers of the early part of this century required complex bracing systems. For example, a high spire structure with a needle-like termination was designed to surmount the dome of the Chrysler Building (1930). Currently, the post-modern building tops with their spires and pinnacles revive ornamentation and the architectural styles of the past. Intricate braced frames are required for the various roof shapes such as pyramids, domes, spirals, and gabled, stepped, folded, or arched forms. These structural complexities are not only found in the roof spires but also in lobby entrances and atria of high-rise buildings. The basic bracing types for frames are single diagonal bracing, X-bracing, K-bracing, lattice bracing, eccentric bracing (single diagonal or rhombic pattern), knee-bracing, and combinations. When the diagonal members must be kinked for the placement of openings, then they must be stabilized by additional members.

SHEAR WALLS WITH OUTRIGGERS: At a certain height the braced frame will become uneconomical, particularly when the shear core is too slender to resist excessive drift. Here, the efficiency of the building structure can be greatly improved by using story-high or deeper outrigger arms that cantilever from the core at one or several levels and tie the perimeter structure to the core by either connecting directly to individual columns or to a belt truss. This interaction activates the participation of the perimeter columns as struts and ties, thus redistributing the stresses and eccentric loading. Pier Luigi Nervi applied the outrigger concept to the 47-story Place Victoria (1964) in Montreal, the first reinforced concrete building to utilize the principle.

TUBULAR STRUCTURES: The development of tubular structures is closely associated with SOM during the 1960s ‘‘ the Brunswick Building (1964) and the John Hancock Building (1968), both in Chicago, are famous early examples. Much credit must be given to the eminent structural engineer Fazlur Khan, a partner of SOM, who invented the concept in the search for optimizing structures with the use of computers. As the building increases in height in excess of roughly 60 stories, the slender interior core and the planar frames are no longer sufficient to effectively resist the lateral forces. Now the perimeter structure of the building must be activated to provide this task by behaving as a huge cantilever tube. Here, the outer shell may act as a three-dimensional hollow structure; that is, as a closed box beam, where the exterior walls are monolithically connected around the corners and internally braced by the rigid horizontal floor diaphragms. The concept evolved from the three-dimensional action of structure as found in nature and in the monocoque design of automobiles and aircraft. The dense column spacing and the deep spandrell beams also tend to equalize the gravity loads on all the exterior columns, similar to a bearing wall, thereby minimizing column sizes. In addition, the closed perimeter tube provides excellent torsional resistance. In the 1960s, the tublular concept revived the bearing wall for tall building construction, but in steel, concrete, and composite construction rather than in masonry. Now, window lights can be placed directly between the columns of the punched wall; hence the need for a separate curtain wall is eliminated. The pure tubular concepts include single perimeter tubes (punched, framed, or trussed walls), tube-in-tube, and bundled tubes. Modified tubes include interior braced tubes, partial tubes, and hybrid tubes.

COMPOSITE AND MIXED STEEL - CONCRETE BUILDINGS: The integral interaction of reinforced concrete and steel can be seen not only in the popular composite metal deck and floor framing systems but also on a much larger scale. It is not the composite action of the structure members ‘‘ the slabs, beams, and columns ‘‘ that are of interest here, but rather the combination or interaction of these members that are blended into a single structure system. Typical *composite building types*, which have developed over the last decade or so, are composite framed tubes, composite steel frames, composite panel-braced steel frames, composite interior core-braced systems, composite megaframes, and hybrid composite structures. Recently, *mixed steel-concrete buildings* have also become popular; the combining of major structure components of concrete, steel, or composite buildings is a relatively new development. For example, it may now be economical to place a steel building on top of a concrete building or vice versa; alternately, a central concrete core may be slip-formed to a predetermined height and then a steel frame built around it.

MEGASTRUCTURES: In this context, the term megastructure refers not to the visionary concepts of the 1960s expressing the comprehensive planning of a community or even an entire city, but solely to the support structure of a building. However, this megastructure is still formulated on the basic concept of a primary structure that supports and services secondary structures or smaller individual building blocks. In the early 1970s, Fazlur Khan of SOM proposed to replace the multicolumn concept by the *four massive corner column supporting superframe* by using supertransfer trusses at every 20 floors or so on both the exterior and interior of the building thereby allowing all the gravity loads to flow to the four supercolumns. The principle can be traced to Khan's studies of superframes for multiuse urban skyscrapers, with the John Hancock Center in Chicago representing the forerunner of this idea. The megastructures of today evolve out of structural efficiency in response to spatial requirements; in addition, computers now make it possible to understand the behavior of structures much better. In the current hybrid building forms with their many setbacks, as well as in slender building shapes, the material must be arranged to efficiently resist overturning.

HYBRID STRUCTURES: The current trend away from pure building forms towards hybrid solutions as expressed in geometry, material, structure layout, and building use, is apparent. In the search for more efficient structural solutions, especially for very tall buildings, a new generation of systems has developed with the aid of computers, which, in turn, have an exciting potential for architectural expression. These new structures do not necessarily follow the traditional classification of the previous sections. Now, the selection of a structure system as based on the primary variables of material and the type and location of structure is no longer a simple choice between a limited number of possibilities. Mathematical modeling with computers has made mixed construction possible,which may vary with building height, thus allowing nearly endless possibilities that one could not have imagined only a few years ago. The computer simulates the effectiveness of a support system so that the structure layout can be optimized and non-essential members can be eliminated to obtain the stiffest structure with a minimum amount of material. Naturally, other design considerations besides structure will have to be included, but the design concepts can be tested quickly and efficiently by the computer.

UNCONVENTIONAL BUILDING STRUCTURES: There are many other structure types than those covered in the previous classification. Some are experimental in nature, demonstrating fascinating new structural concepts, possibly motivated by more encompassing design philosophies. Quite often, these concepts relate to structures in nature or have evolved from biology in the search for innovative solutions. On the one hand, they may directly reflect the cell structures of plant organisms or the uniform repetitive order of crystals to inspire the structure of space frames and the packing of polyhedra. On the other hand, they may represent visionary schemes such as biogenetic models with self-generating environments where designs initiate processes, such as chemical reactions in seawater causing coral-like growths to enable a structure to build itself. Other solutions may derive their structure systems from the ''tensegrity'' principle, space frames, box construction, or pneumatics.

One may conclude that there is no limit to the creation of new structure systems and that imagination and ingenuity of designers knows no boundaries.

REFERENCES

Schueller, Wolfgang: *The Vertical Building Structure*. New York: Van Nostrand Reinhold, 1990.

CHAPTER 23

Building Heights and the Calculation of Early Skyscraper Frames

ELWIN C. ROBISON
Kent State University

Many factors influenced the height of office buildings in the late 19th and early 20th centuries. Speculative land values, desire for corporate image, and the development of mechanical system technologies were each important and necessary factors in creating the tall office building. However, more fundamental than these issues of economics, image, and utility was the problem of designing a frame to safely support these heavy and complex towers against gravity and wind loads. The earliest skyscrapers were limited in height partly due to the limitation of frame calculation methods, especially the calculation of wind loading. However, the development of the so-called cantilever method of analysis in the first decade of the 20th century removed structural requirements as a serious impediment to building height.

Many buildings constructed in the late 1800's and early 1900's had no provision for resisting lateral forces[1]--experience showed that the many interior walls and crude connections usually provided adequate lateral stability for buildings whose height did not greatly exceed their width. However, as economics and the desire for corporate recognition pushed tall, slender towers ever higher, designers could no longer rely on precedent, and great care had to be exercised in order to guarantee stability. One of the earliest forms of wind bracing was a vertical truss composed of X-braces strategically placed within the building's skeleton. These were typically placed adjacent to elevator shafts where they would not restrict the movement of space on each floor, but some vertical trusses had to be located out in the rentable floor areas which hampered designers in their arrangement of office suites. The X-braces were sometimes made two stories high so that a doorway could be squeezed in along the chord of the truss and between the X diagonals, but office plans were still severely hampered in their planning. Although an X-brace vertical truss is an efficient system for resisting lateral loads, it does not lend itself to efficient space utilization.

In order to avoid the difficulties encountered with continuous X-braces running vertically through the spaces, the portal arch framing system was developed in Chicago. This system uses vertical stacks of heavy iron arches, or portals, to resist lateral loads, first employed in an American office building by Corydon. T. Purdy on the Old Colony Building in Chicago, completed in 1894.[2] Similar systems employed knee braces, or deep wind girders. The open portals did not restrict the internal arrangement of spaces like the X-braces, although when constructed of heavy plate iron arches they did restrict head room somewhat. Unlike the vertical trusses which were easily calculated by simple statics,[3] stacks of portal arches were practically uncalculatable in the 1890's without making some gross simplifications, resulting in stresses considerably higher than actually present in the portals.

Whether composed of plate iron arches, knee braces, or deep girders, these portals were calculated in the same manner. They were considered as tables standing on top of one another, with a rigid (fixed) connection at the top of the leg, and a flexible (pinned) connection at the bottom. Lateral forces pushing on the portal tend to 'rack' it, or push the rectangular portal into a skewed parallelogram. In a portal with pinned connections at the bottom of the legs, the rigid upper corners keep the portal from deforming while the pinned connections keep the portal from sliding sideways. In a portal with a fixed connection at the bottom of the legs, the force resisting the deformation is distributed over two additional joints, reducing the stresses in the joints. Although engineers recognized that a rigid connection at the bottom of the portal would result in a stronger structure, designing such portals to include moment transfer from one story to the next through the bottom of the portal involved a difficult statically indeterminant calculation which was too time consuming to be practical in the 1890's. The form of these building portals was developed from bridge portals which keep bridge through trusses from being blown over by wind and vibration while maintaining an open carriageway for crossing vehicles. These wind bracing portals were calculated as if many bridge portals were piled one on top of the other, each with a flexible, or pinned, connection to the next lower portal.

Although some designers did rigidly connect the legs of

the portals to the next lower story, they were not able to properly model the transfer of internal bending force in these windbracing portals. As a result, the calculated bending stresses in the upper corners of the portals (which were not the actual forces) were 50% greater than they would be if full continuity of the frame from portal to portal were possible to calculate, resulting in escalating steel costs. Engineers also realized that they were not taking into account the total action of the portal arches, and must have felt some reluctance in putting too much reliance on a system only partly understood.[4] These factors, combined with other economic and social pressures resulted in a leveling off in skyscraper height at the turn of the century of just under 30 stories.

Many early skyscrapers after 1895 were designed with these portal arch frames (or knee brace portals, or deep girder portals) calculated without continuity from one story to the next. Good building practice called for the monitoring of built structures so that engineers had confidence in the safety of their admittedly crude calculations. However, when tall buildings began to be built by corporate clients in New York City as symbols of corporate wealth and power, the increased demands on the structural frames initially created difficulties for their designers. One of the tallest of these early corporate symbols, the Singer Building of 1908 did not use portal bracing, but instead relied on vertical trusses with X-braces. Apparently the open portals with their incomplete calculation method were not to be trusted for such a tall, slender structure. These X-wind braces forced the architect, Ernest Flagg, to create nearly solid corners in the tower, relieved only by small windows positioned between the diagonals of the trusses. The wind bracing system worked very well, but a heavy price was paid in terms light and air in the corners of the tower.

The first major step in reliably calculating a skyscraper frame without diagonals was made almost contemporaneous with their first use in tall office buildings. In 1893 J.B. Johnson published a solution for a bridge portal with fixed supports which assumes a point of contraflexure at the midpoint of the column.[5] In other words the column of a frame subjected to a lateral force with the columns rigidly fixed at top and bottom will deflect into a gentle S-curve. The point where the column starts to bend back in the opposite direction is called a point of contraflexure, and Johnson realized that by mathematic definition all internal moments, or bending forces, are zero at this point. By isolating the structure at this point of contraflexure, the computation of internal bending moments in the columns is eliminated, reducing the calculation of 6 unknowns and 3 equations of equilibrium to 4 unknowns and 3 equations of equilibrium. With the further assumption that the horizontal forces in each leg of the portal are equal (an accurate assumption when the portal is symmetrical) then the problem is reduced from 4 to 2 unknowns to be solved with the three equations of equilibrium, a statically determinate problem quickly calculated by hand. Doubtless others recognized that points of contraflexure have no internal bending moments. However J.B. Johnson's genius came in realizing that the point of contraflexure would always occur very close to the middle, and that by assuming this location ahead of time the calculation work load would be reduced from practically impossible to simply accomplished.

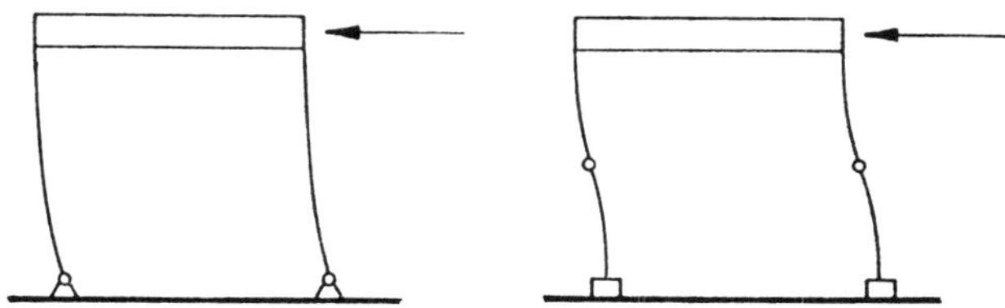

1. Portal with pinned (flexible) connections at base of legs on left, and portal with fixed (rigid) connections on right showing location of points of contraflexure at the midpoint of the legs.

The next step in developing an accurate method for designing skyscraper frames of open portals was to develop a procedure for analyzing multiple stacks of portal frames. The computational advantage of assuming points of contraflexure was quickly applied to skyscraper frames, but there seems to have been considerable difficulty in agreeing where the location of the points of contraflexure would occur in multiple bay frames, especially the points of contraflexure in the girders.[6] It took about ten years for engineers to come to an agreement about frame behavior sufficient to accept a general method of analysis. An early proposal was made to the American Society of Civil Engineers on November 1, 1905 by Ernst F. Jonson, and subsequently published in the Society's *Transactions*.[7] In his discussion Jonson isolated each story of the frame by assuming the location of the point of contraflexure, and then solved for the forces on each story by noting that the sideways deflection of all the columns must be the same because they are rigidly connected by floor girders. Using this equality, Jonson was able to write expressions for the moments at the connections in terms of three variables, which he was then able to solve using three equations of equilibrium. Other stories could be calculated by proportioning the values according to the total wind force to be resisted. Jonson's method was accurate, but a little difficult to apply in practice, both because it required the solution of three unknowns with three equations (not real difficult, but requiring a little calculation time), and because it required a clear understanding of the relationship between moment, slope, and deflection of the beams and columns.

Three years later A.C. Wilson published a method of frame analysis which was much simpler to apply, and quickly became the standard method for frame design.[8] Wilson's method, known as the cantilever method, is similar to Jonson's, except that instead of working with complicated deflection equations, Wilson assumed that the vertical forces in the columns would be proportional to their distance from the neutral axis of the building (an accurate assumption with a symmetrical, slender structure). The utility of this assumption is twofold. First, all of the values are given in terms of forces, and not in deflections or slopes, making the method conceptually easier to understand. Second, by assuming the distribution of the vertical forces, and by isolating each bay of the story by assuming a point of contraflexure at the midpoint of the girders, Wilson broke down the multiple bay frame into separately calculated single bays which were then added together, reducing the problem to two unknowns and three equations, resulting in a much quicker calculation. Perhaps most importantly, Wilson's method was easily organized into tabular form, which made the work easy to check, and made it so that with a few simple 'cookbook' instructions virtually anyone in the office could perform or check the calculation. Researchers checked the results of the cantilever method (and the similar portal method) against the 'exact' solution using slope-deflection and work-stress methods and reported stresses within 10% of actual values in most cases, considered very accurate by the prevailing standards.

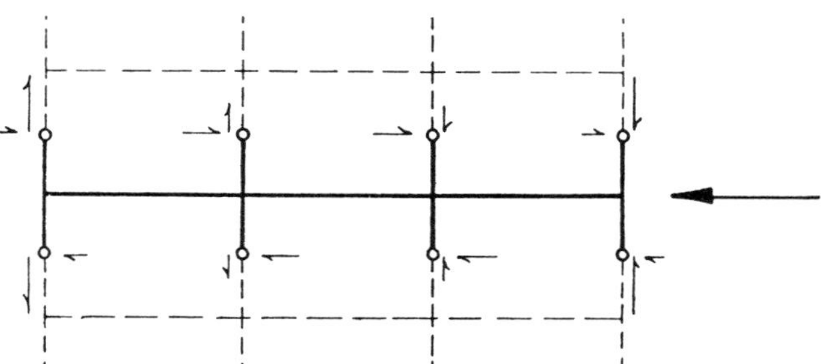

2. A single story of a multistory frame isolated according the cantilever method showing forces exerted by the isolated story on the remainder of the frame. Note that there is no moment (internal bending force) at the points of contraflexure where the story is isolated. Since all the vertical forces are proportioned according to their distance from the neutral axis (center line) of the building, the only unknowns are the horizontal forces at the bottom since the horizontal forces at the top were previously calculated by isolating the story above.

With this method, engineer's confidence in their ability to calculate the stresses in an open portal frame greatly increased, and structural calculations were no longer an impediment to building heights. The Woolworth, Equitable, Chrysler, and Empire State Buildings all were made possible by the development of this cantilever frame analysis method, and the similar variation of the portal frame analysis method. These analysis methods were accurate enough so that the height of skyscrapers was not limited by calculation methods. While difficulties in analyzing skyscraper frames contributed to a leveling off of the increases in building heights from 1890 to 1905, the removal of that impediment contributed to the tremendous explosion of skyscraper heights in the 1920's and 30's. These skyscrapers of the 3rd and 4th decades of the 20th century not only inform us as to the operations of corporate America and the economics of the day, but they also serve as graphic testimony to the improving structural calculation methods developed in the previous decades.

NOTES

1. See for example Henry H. Quimby, *ASCE Transactions* 28:221-52 (September 1892).
2. There are earlier examples of rigid-jointed frames. However, these earlier forms employed cast iron elements which are subject to catastrophic failure under concentrated moments. These systems avoided failure through the presence of other stiffening elements, or through tremendously heavy connections whose sheer size kept stresses in the cast iron elements relatively low. For example the London Crystal Palace used cross bracing to supplement the rigidity of the portals (which were not very rigid since the portal connections were tightened by oak wedges which would be crushed between the cast iron members under high lateral loads). The Home Insurance Building also had cast iron columns, with some rigidity provided by a hook detail, see Gerald R. Larson and Roula Mouroubellis Geraniotis, "Toward a Better Understanding of the Evolution of the Iron Skeleton Frame in Chicago," *Journal of the Society of Architectural Historians* 46:39-48 (March 1987). In this case lateral stability was probably due to interior partitions. In the case of the British Marine warehouses with open interiors stability was due to a combination of exterior walls and tremendously large columns and connections.
3. Although X-braces technically form a statically indeterminate system, when subjected to lateral loading the diagonal in compression is usually not considered because of buckling due to its slenderness. In systems employing tie rods or channel sections this simplification closely matches physical reality.
4. It was common practice to connect the portals together as rigidly as possible, even though the rigid connection was not calculatable. Note Dubois's stressing the importance of detailing joints properly to give rigidity to the frame without any indication as to how this might be calculated; see A.J. Dubois, *The Stresses in Framed Structures* (New York, 1897). This parallels the work on the Britannia Bridge where Stevenson fixed the sections of the tubular bridge into a continuous beam without flexible (pinned) supports even though he was unable to calculate the continuous beam. He knew, however, that the fixed beam was stronger, and calculated the bridge as if the connections were pinned knowing that he was adding to the factor of safety of the bridge.
5. J.B. Johnson, C.W. Bryan, and F.E. Turneaure, *The Theory and Practice of Modern Framed Structures* (New York, 1893) p. 267.
6. See Guy B. Waite, "Wind Bracing in High Buildings," *Transactions of the American Society of Civil Engineers* 33:190-234 (March 1894). See especially the discussion on p. 219.
7. Ernst F. Jonson, "The Theory of Frameworks with Rectangular Panels, and Its Application to Buildings Which Have to Resist Wind," *Transactions of the American Society of Civil Engineers*, paper 1012, pp. 413-29 (1905).
8. A.C. Wilson, "Wind Bracing with Knee Braces or Gusset Plates," *The Engineering Record* 58:272-74 (September 5, 1908).

CHAPTER 24

High-Rise Buildings: Firmness, Commodity, or Delight?

IVAN ZAKNIC
Lehigh University

The skyscraper as a building type has been dreamed of since the Tower of Babel, but it emerged into its own only in the 1870s, and today is an urban fact. Its height continued to grow, thanks to advances in technology and construction methods. Many studies have been made of the impact of tall buildings on the urban context: physical, cultural, psychological, social and economic.

Prognoses have even been made about the death of skyscrapers and other giant structures, as in James R. Chiles's essay in the Smithsonian about the life-span and death of these world wonders if they should be neglected or abandoned due to weather, rusting, acid rain or earthquakes.

Less attention has been paid to this type of building as it relates to its own integrity, a synthesis of its three most important aspects: structural, environmental, and aesthetic. But in fact, a successful integration of these three "envelopes" in the modern skyscraper is as indispensable as Vitruvian beauty, "rational integration of the proportions of all parts of the building in such a way that every part has its absolutely fixed size and shape, and nothing could be added or taken away without destroying the harmony of the whole." Each building depends on its own chosen systems, and a hybrid building is often the result.

The 1st envelope of this hybrid, which can be detached from the others, deals exclusively with the technology of its skeletal construction and resolves loads (including wind, earthquake, temperature and soil effects); the 2nd envelope deals with the complete mechanical systems (light and air, heating, cooling, plumbing, electrical wiring and conduits which give the building its vital flows, natural and artificial); the 3rd envelope, the skin, has little to do with cladding. It deals with form, the proportions of the building and its inevitable aesthetic expression.

Within the trinity "Firmness, Commodity, Delight" (defined by Sir Henry Wooton in 1600), the most difficult of the three to measure is the third, "delight." The reason why this purely aesthetic aspect is so difficult to define is that, in a good building, the aesthetic cannot be separated from the other two aspects -- which can, in fact, be analyzed, and even physically separated. Analytical processes are of great use in determining the structure (the "firmness") and the environmental comforts (the "commodity"), but the aesthetic aspect of the tall building cannot really be stripped off and measured, and therefore the very metaphor of an "envelope" could be somewhat misleading.

In practice, problems automatically arise from the preemptive presence of both structural and environmental envelopes, as well as often repetitive floor plans. Their disposition and shape might have an overriding effect on the aesthetic enclosure, and often limits the massing and facades. The enclosing envelope, mediating between the inside and the outside, however simplified or subordinated to other issues, is not often recognized as an important component in the organic integrity of the whole building. This was not always the case with very tall buildings, and here a small historical digression is in order.

Historically, very tall buildings were rare. They usually served not practical but culturally symbolic needs: the domes or spires of churches or mosques, tombs, and pyramids, axial points or obelisks. These tall structures often expressed a community's need for a spiritual and cultural identity. Such "pre-modern" high-rises were relatively few in number.

Then came the modern high-rise, a very different concept, largely a stacking of office space. It was first realized in the 1920s, but flourished in the 1960s. For a host of reasons including zoning, the design became reasonably standardized: a stacking-up of the same repetitive floor plan layout around a central service core, up to 50 stories high. The idea of the megastructure or "Ultra High-Rise Building" followed, a term introduced in the U.S. about 1970. These high-rise buildings can be towers such as the World Trade Center, John Hancock, or Sears; they can be slab-like (the U.N. in New York City) or cruciform-like (dreamed of by Le Corbusier in his Contemporary City of the 1920s), or ziggural-like as in the proposals of Paolo Soleri. But the true master and revolutionary of the modern high-rise remains Mies Van der Rohe, and not necessarily for championing the height or shape alone. Its greatest document, the Seagram's Building, is a medium-height tower.

In appreciating Miesian architecture, we should try to separate it from the crude glass boxes that mimic it and fail to observe its craft and proportions. Mies's dictum "Less is more" was paradoxically turned upside down to read "Less is a bore." Consequently a whole generation was to dismiss Mies or consider him the chief villain. His abstraction and universal values that transcended period and style could no longer fit changing fashions. "And what could be more non-bourgeois than an unadorned wide-flange beam?" wrote Tom Wolfe. Robert A. M. Stern argued that America stands for the individual against the universal, and that rational Miesian architecture has no roots in America. Did he forget that the skyscraper was invented in America, and the steel frame in Chicago? Mies gave harmonious and beautiful form to technology-based optimism, perhaps the strongest sentiment felt in America in the 1950s.

What we tend to forget about Mies is that the most pioneering aspect of his thought is not just universal space, or the beauty of a single detail, but his fascination with the aesthetic envelope, his inclination to make it primary, just as did the builders of the pyramids and the cathedrals. Mies's own ideas and first experiments with the aesthetic concerns f skyscrapers date from the early 1920s. In the two buildings Mies proposed for Friedrichstresse in 1921 and 1922, he changed from the crystalline, triangular forms of his 1921 plan to the "Glass Skyscraper" of 1922 to a curved plan. Admitting that the experiments might seem arbitrary, Mies explained that the curves were determined by three factors: 1) sufficient illumination of the interior (an environmental consideration); 2) the massing of the building as viewed from the street (an aesthetic consideration); and 3) the play of reflections on the glass (a pure delight!).

Mies was not alone with such priorities during these years. The early 20s was a period of economic inflation and visionary utopianism. Architects, poets and artists, especially in Europe, were producing expressionistic images more evocative than buildable. Bruno Taut's "Crystal Mountain" (1919) and Lionel Feininger's "Cathedral of Socialism" (1919) were the logical extensions of Taut's Glass Pavilion in Cologne (1914), where every possible wall was made of glass. It was the building material of the future; as the poet Paul Scheerbart put it, "It is not the crazy caprice of a poet that glass architecture will bring a new culture. It is a fact."

At the time, Mies also saw glass, and later steel and glass, as inherently poetic. As a pioneer, he did not have access to the technology that his imagination required; but in all things the aesthetic envelope was primary for him. The aesthetic was closely linked with the structural; as he observed, "Skyscrapers reveal their bold structural pattern during construction. When the outer walls are put in place, the structural system which is the basis of all artistic design is hidden by the chaos of meaningless and trivial forms," and that is why his skin solutions for the high-rise reflect a concern for all three envelopes. Mies believed that technology, fully realized, would "transcend" into architecture, but that such architecture would be highly subtle and specific, difficult to mass-produce. "Architecture depends on its time, it is the crystallization of its inner structure," he wrote in 1950. "That is why technology and architecture are so closely related."

Just as Mies was concerned to relate the aesthetic and structural envelopes, so Le Corbusier related the aesthetic and environmental. His brise-soleil invention went far beyond a simple shading device. It was conceived as a strong "plastic" element -- an environmentally sponsored means of architectural articulation -- according to Le Corbusier, an "organic or biological" necessity. The brise-soleil as he proposed to apply it to a skyscraper in Algier (1938-42) would be equivalent in size to a loggia, a traditional environmental element, here reintroduced into modern architecture. The brise-soleil might be applied as a regular and repetitive form in the major part of the facade, and its form would be elongated in front of the glass windows of the larger rooms. Like no one else, Le Corbusier was searching for an plastic-aesthetic solution to the skin of the building, where environmental and aesthetic envelopes are fused. The Algiers skyscraper design became a classic example of "phenomenal transparency" (Slutzky and Rowe).

Glass was eventually incorporated into experimentation with other materials such as steel and reinforced concrete. These materials provide maximum flexibility in the structural and aesthetic envelopes, but also an opportunity for a degree of concealment of the relationship between them. More importantly, glass and steel ceased to be "poetic" and began to be treated as prosaic, "practical" -- and reinforced concrete as a "brutalist" material. Problems were either solved piecemeal, with no larger vision of the whole, or the aesthetic envelope was mass-produced, as a facile slick surface, while the environmental was buried as equipment.

In his description of the Alcoa building in Pittsburgh (1955), Charles Jencks gives a good example of American virtuosity in advancing skyscraper technology: "The Alcoa building," he writes, "is the perfect expression of transcendental technique of the pragmatic school: light screens of aluminum only an eighth of an inch thick are strengthened by their shape, by triangular facets which cast a shimmering, dissolving light over the gigantic mass. The aluminum sheets were mass-produced, pierced in the center by a green-glass window, erected and sprayed on the inside for heat and comfort -- the whole process being the epitome of American logistics. The image is otherworldly" ("Modern Movements in Architecture", 1986, p. 200).

Jencks's description is not necessarily negative or ironic. But here we have all the least attractive aesthetic aspects of modern technology, which was to become the symbol of the corporate look: its mass production, repetitive "mathematical logic," and speed; the common denominator acting in a crude advertising appeal. What Mies had hoped would make us think poetically now makes us think commercially, or not think at all. The question is: how can we, under present conditions, re-introduce art into the aesthetic envelope without it disintegrating into a banality or a pastiche?

One architect who recently reintroduced steel and glass elegance into his building through the use of technology is Jean Nouvel, in his Arab World Institute in Paris -- which is not a high-rise at all but a curtain wall building. Its south facade is a technical triumph, where an Arabian screen composed of 113 panels of 27,000 light-sensitive diaphragms open and close like a camera lens, changing the shape of the facade. Its geometries recall the traditional mucharabieh screen. An electronically controlled sensor permits the desirable amount of daylight to enter. The technical and metaphorical tour de force of this wall unites into one the environmental, aesthetic, and symbolic envelopes.

Most designers are content with Sullivanesque tripartite subdivision: base, shaft, top. Seldom is an enlightened client, engineer and architect seeking a genuinely new model of a high-rise that, in addition to a successful integration of the three envelopes, answers another special demand, unique for each location and going beyond the needs of client and occupant: the context and spirit of the place. Some examples, such as Norman Foster's Hong Kong and Shanghai Bank, will not only become part of the architectural inventions of the second machine age, but will pass on as truly inspiring monuments for a secular age.

There seem to be at least two ways that architects are currently addressing this problem. We might argue about the positive or negative aspects of the "art" that is being "applied" to our buildings, but there is no doubt that something more artistic is being expected: the prosaic of eclecticism and the pragmatic of commercialism will no longer suffice.

One approach we might call "editing," or "changing dress." It often comes along with changes in the other envelopes. On January 11, 1990 the New York Times reported that "the 32-story former I.I.T. building on Park Avenue in New York City will be redesigned and substantially rebuilt." The building was built in the 1960s, and the primary tenant is now moving out. The owner will address the asbestos problem, but also plans to strip the building down to its steel structure, which in turn will be reconfigured to provide larger tower floors. The structural envelope will remain in place, the environmental envelope will be corrected, and the aesthetic envelope will be updated to be more in keeping with the prevailing style of the day.

What exactly this "updating" means can be seen by looking at some additional modernist buildings around the country that have fallen out of favor and are thus scheduled for a "face-lift." Bryan Tower, the first reflective Miesian glass building in Dallas (built very cheaply, $20 per sq. ft.), with a curtain wall all the way to the ground, will receive a base in stone veneer, and its pilotis will be exposed to give it a "human scale." As soon as S.O.M. finishes this job, it will apply the same techniques to three more modernist buildings in Houston, Dallas, and Denver.

Will modernist buildings for the most part disappear under the post-modernist "fashion veil," or under the pressure to remain attractive and competitive? The question is already becoming not only an aesthetic but a legal one as well. In Chicago, the 80-story Amoco building will be completely reclad because of the weakening of its one-and-a-quarter inch marble skin, a victim to harsh wind and climate, at a cost of $60 to 80 million. Parties have already begun to sue one another, although the original architect is dead and the original supplier of marble is out of business.

The most famous Chicago building for its innovative use of technology, John Hancock, is in an unusual "updating" predicament. Recently an atrium was proposed for its base. Some felt that the dreary hole of the sunken plaza should be filled in. A prime characteristic of the building is its honest, even proud display of diagonal reinforcements in the form of huge X braces displayed on the facades "to tell people it's a tall building," in the words of its designer Bruce Graham. For twenty years it has been an icon on the Chicago skyline, but its owner is now eager to have a multi-level shopping complex at its base, like all other buildings on Michigan Avenue. "Big John" is limited to a single Bonwit Teller shop. This would not do. So the Hancock Company hired an architectural firm specializing in shopping malls, after the original designer refused the commission.

The first proposal tried to echo the original cross bracing, but, as Paul Goldberger put it, this was seen "more like a vulgar parody than a case of genuine respect for the precedent" (NYT, Oct. 15/89). When the atrium was revealed to the public it became very controversial. Architects protested and wanted to protect the building's integrity. Angry residents feel that the addition "will deface their home." Originally the building was allowed to be built so tall because a zoning bonus was given in return for the open space provided at the base; legally, if the base is filled in, the city could insist on taking down a few floors from the top. At first, city zoning administrators approved the proposed atrium addition. Then the zoning board of appeals overturned the city's approval -- on the grounds that it would violate the zoning envelope that applied twenty years ago. The Hancock Mutual Life Insurance Company then filed a suit against the city of Chicago, seeking a reversal. It seems that we might soon expect law courts to decide the aesthetic and environmental impact issues of tall buildings.

In addition to "updating" modernist buildings and thus incurring aesthetic and legal difficulties, there is a another way architects are trying to restore a sense of poetic art to the high-rise building. And this is to begin straight off with the aesthetic envelope, and presume that the technology would be found to solve whatever problems might arise. Ricardo Bofill, in his recent book about himself, Espaces d'une Vie, speaks of his own attempts at building a "tower" in the USA. "If the people of Chicago proposed to me that I design them a tower," he wrote, "it is because they no longer want the International Style and such cold materials stuck up." Bofill claims that the image of his architecture seduces some people, and although his office has never built a skyscraper, he would never think of building one in Europe: "he couldn't think of towers except in the context that gave rise to them, the USA.''

In New York City, Bofill explained that he would introduce the proportional system right from the start (1:7 in this case, with 5 orders spread over 10 stories, which constitute the basic body of the building). In Chicago, where Bofill has a real commission, a 1:4 proportional system was chosen, and it will stylistically recapture other styles, from classicism to refined Baroque. So much for the Chicago formula. Bofill is remarkably versatile in his selection of prototypes for each location: in a competition project (which he lost) for the Communication Tower in Barcelona, Bofill was inspired by the off-shore platforms of the North Sea oil-drillers, whose engineers he considers the greatest Anglo-Saxon specialists.

In conclusion, we might pose the question of the future of the high-rise. However functionally inefficient, urbanistically inappropriate, and environmentally inhumane, the ultimate high-rise dream has not been abandoned. ''Firmness'' and ''commodity'' have perhaps been eroded. But the push to the sky, the struggle for impractical height, remains a ''delight'' that symbolizes human ambition and achievement. Even Frank Lloyd Wright, who believed passionately in the horizontal line and had written that ''the vertical is vertigo in human life,'' proposed in 1956 a ''Mile High Illinois,'' a building over 500 stories high (5,280 feet), holding a hundred thousand people, 15,000 cars and 100 helicopters, in Chicago, a city notorious for its high winds.

The ''Mile-High Building'' did not catch on, and the dream has been somewhat scaled down to half the size. Donald Trump, for example, unveiled in 1986 his proposal for Trump T.V. City by Helmut Jahn in New York City, with the world's tallest tower at the center (1,670 feet, surpassing Sears by 216 feet). A half-mile high skyscraper has been proposed for Chicago's North Loop by Stanley Roskow, a Chicago development firm: it would reach 210 stories, contain 800 condominiums and 2,400 hotel rooms in addition to office space, restaurants and a heliport. The city response here too was skeptical. In 1989 Cesar Pelli's design for the World's Tallest Building, a structure in the shape of a tapering obelisk, was unveiled (again to be built in Chicago). If built, it would surpass the Sears Tower, the world's current titleholder, by 355 feet. But the most deceptive fact about the proposal is that the building would contain only one-fourth the square-footage of the Sears. Unlike Trump's proposal, this one received a favorable reaction from City Hall as well as from the general population. Chicago seems to have an open mind and no limitations placed on any aspect of their skyscrapers.

The attempts at dealing with these three envelopes and the ''race toward the sky'' are nowhere more dramatic than in Japan, a country where land is in short supply, where earthquake damage to tall buildings is real, and where land prices are higher than the prices of buildings. There are, of course, conventional high-rise buildings and competitions -- such as the towers 1,000 meters high proposed by the Group Takenaka, a series of rings conceived as autonomous little villages in which 35,000 people would live and another 135,000 would come to work each day (Le Point, 28 August 1989). But more interesting and radical is a study begun last year by the Japanese Ministry of Commerce, to build dome-like structures 100 meters or more below the earth. Several of these ''techno-caverns'' have been baptized ''Alice,'' because they are meant to be wonderlands, free from quakes and maintained at a steady temperature.

What do we see in this deep underground project for the ultimate inverted high-rise? In order to restore commodity and firmness, the Japanese proposal seems to eliminate the visual delight. There is no reason to be concerned over the structural envelope. The environmental envelope is also taken care of. And the need to tart up the aesthetic envelope has entirely disappeared, for the building is invisible as a structure from the outside. All three envelopes have fused together, and have been submerged. Hopefully the China-Syndrome will not come to us in the end, from the inventive Japanese, who never fail to amaze us.

CHAPTER 25

Appearance - Innovation - Synthesis: The Technology of Frank Lloyd Wright's Residential Work

MAX UNDERWOOD
Arizona State University

> "A house we like to believe is the status quo; a noble consort to man and the trees; therefore the house should have response and such texture as will quiet the whole and make it graciously at one with external Nature. Human houses should not be like boxes, blazing in the sun, nor should we outrage the machine by trying to make dwelling places too complementary to Machinery. Any building for humane purposes should be an elemental, sympathetic feature of the ground, complementary to its natural environment, belonging by kinship to the terrain and place" - Frank Lloyd Wright[1]

As we examine the residential work being completed in America today, we are immediately confronted with a dilemma, the apparent lack of concern with Technology, and the inherent relationships of material, construction and structural systems. What we discover upon closer examination is that many of the houses, whose generative ideas and formal vocabularies are exemplary, only superficially deal with technology in the following three basic ways.

First is the "Technology of Applique", where images of current technological systems and methods are simply applied to the forms of the house, with no understanding of their material, construction and structural reality.

Second is the "Technology of Appearance" where current technology is used solely as a means to realize a formal gesture, concealing the reality of the technological systems and methods by a layer of fashion.

Third is the "Technology of Innovation" in which a new cutting edge technological system or method is relentlessly applied, resulting in a functional box of systems.

Yet there are a series of truly great houses being built today which have attained something greater, a "Technology of Synthesis". In these houses the architect has developed a clear technical vocabulary, which reinforces their own developing ideology and formal vocabulary, and is able to synthesize both the formal and technical concerns into a coherent language of architecture. How can residential architects today achieve this "Technology of Synthesis"? By what process? With what results?

To help us answer these questions, this presentation will examine the prolific residential career of Frank Lloyd Wright (1869-1959), and how he was able to formulate a coherent technical vocabulary out of two investigations, one into the "Technology of Appearance" and a second into the "Technology of Innovation", which ultimately led to a "Technology of Synthesis" and the realization of his masterpiece, Fallingwater in 1935.

THE TECHNOLOGY OF APPEARANCE

Frank Lloyd Wright's first investigation, I will identify as "The Technology of Appearance", in which he focused his efforts upon the spatial destruction of the shingle style box house, and the development of a clear formal vocabulary, which simply used the evolving 19th century light timber frame technology, at the expense of clearly defining his own technical vocabulary. The resultant early residential work, for all its exemplary spatial and formal richness, denies the nature of its construction and structural reality. The employed platform frame, balloon frame, and steel composite systems, are used solely as a means to realize Wright's spatial and formal gestures, and became suppressed behind a layer of horizontally banded surfaces which define the house's spatial volumes.

Following his apprenticeship with Louis Sullivan and Joseph Silsbee, Frank Lloyd Wright's residential work began with the adoption of the formal and technical vocabularies of the American Shingle Style[2], which can be seen in the Gale and Parker Houses of 1892. These three houses are straight forward applications of the technical vocabulary of the platform light timber frame, which define the shingle clad volumes and box of enclosed cellar rooms.

In 1893, with the Winslow house Wright began to explore the visual destruction of the shingle style box, by breaking up the surface of the facade, through the use of a large overhanging roof, and a horizontally banded terra cotta and brick wall, which are veneered to a standard platform frame structural system[3]. The result of this technical decision is immediately seen on the interior where Wright attempts to visually destroy the cellar enclosure of the rooms, by enlarging the door openings and introducing continuous horizontal wood stripping, yet he is limited spatially by the physical reality of the platform frame's enclosing structure.

Following his exposure to the half scale Japanese Ho-o-den Pavilion at the World's Columbian Exhibition of 1893[4], Wright's interest begins to shift to the spatial destruction of the house box, which results technically in his use of a balloon frame structural system, as in the Willits House of 1902[5]. What we find formally in the house is a series of partly connected one and two story internal spatial volumes, which exploit their new found vertical freedom independent of the exterior structural walls of the balloon frame. However, a problem remains for Wright how to ultimately destroy the exterior wall balloon frame which is caging in his spatial volumes from the Prairie and Nature, the ultimate symbols of individual freedom and America for Wright.

In 1908 with the Robie House[6], Wright continues his investigations to spatially destroy the box, through the development of a masonry pier and cantilevered beam structural system, whose origins are in the Ho-o-den Pavilion and early American heavy timber frame. What we now find in the house is a series of connected one and two story spatial volumes, which are free both vertically and horizontally, due to their independence of enclosure from the pier and beam structural frame. But where is this structural frame and how is it made? In looking beyond the enclosing surfaces of the house, we discover that the real horizontal structure of the house is a series of concealed steel cantilever beams which support secondary wood framing. This system is a result of the inability of a wood beam system, due to the structural capabilities of wood, to achieve Wright's grand gestures of a large roof cantilever and free span rooms.

It will not be until 1935 in Fallingwater that Wright resolves the dilemma of a spatially destroyed box, both formally and technically.

THE TECHNOLOGY OF INNOVATION

Frank Lloyd Wright's second investigation, I will identify as "The Technology of Innovation", in which he focused upon application of the architect's new tool, the machine and its impact on the house[7]. This was achieved by Wright through the invention of a series of new materials, construction methods and structural systems, which were best suited to machine craftsmanship and modern methods of construction, instead of imitating the costly hand work or skilled handicraft of his earlier custom houses. The resultant residential work, for all its elemental and systematic richness, denies Wright's own spatial and formal aesthetics. The employed repetitive formwork, pre-cut parts, concrete textile blocks, and owner built Usonian systems, are used solely as a means to realize Wright's interest in innovative technology, resulting in boring functional boxes of systems.

In 1906, following Wright's investigations at Unity Temple into the use of cantilevered concrete slabs and repetitive cast-in-place formwork, he executed a project for the *Lady's Home Journal*, a Fireproof house, in which he transferred to his residential work those concrete systems, in an attempt to provide an economical, $5,000 house for the average middle class American. The result of this technical decision was immediately seen by the readers, who were put off by the solidity and tomb like character of this newly defined concrete box.

In 1916 Frank Lloyd Wright was approached by Arthur Richards, a Milwaukee builder, who wanted him to began to apply his architectural ideas to the design of a series of houses for mass production. What Wright developed was the American System Ready-cut Houses[8], which consisted of a system of pre-cut and prefabricated components made in a factory and then shipped to sites to be assembled. The components were two by four inch wood members with attached plaster and stucco finishes, and based on a three foot module, originating from Wright's studies of the components of a Japanese house, such as Tatami mats and Shoji screens. The resultant houses reflect the two major problems of his approach, first, the houses formally are a series of articulated individual components, rather than the unified spatial experience of his early houses, and second, the unclear division of labor among the tradesman on the site, caused many cost increases. These major problems contributed to the closing of Richard's factory within one year.

In 1921 beginning with the Millard house, Wright's application of mass production shifted from wood back to concrete with his development of the Textile block construction system[9], which was a prefabricated system of patterned concrete shell-blocks with steel rod reinforcement that when erected made bearing walls to support cantilevered wood framed roofs. The Textile block houses of the 1920's suffer formally from the structural limitations of the elemental bearing wall construction, which limits the spatial continuity and the unreality of the technical detailing of the block component regarding lateral loading and waterproofing.

In response to the Great Depression, Frank Lloyd Wright began once again to develop an economical pre-fabricated house, which he called Usonian houses[10], employing new industrial products and construction techniques. These new houses consisted of a series of pre-cut and prefabricated modular components, which the owner builder could buy and assemble into a plan of his selection, and add on to as future space needs arise. The Usonian houses evolved as Wright experimented with various technical systems, from the wood board panels in 1935, to the all steel panels of 1937, to the textile blocks of 1950 and finally to the three dimensional timber grid of the Carlson House of 1951. The resultant Usonian houses ended up for the most part to be endless expressions of a triangular, hexagonal or square modules of components, of little spatial richness. But probably most distressing was that in the end many of the owner built houses had to be finally constructed by Harlod Turner and Ben Wiltscheck, Wright's master craftsman contractors.

THE TECHNOLOGY OF SYNTHESIS

These two previous investigations by Frank Lloyd Wright led several times in his residential career to what I will identify as "The Technology of Synthesis", in which he was able to clearly define both his own formal and technical vocabulary, for expressing his general ideas on the American House and his ideas about the specific site. One such point was in 1935 in the Kaufmann House, better known as Fallingwater.[11]

In Fallingwater, Wright finally achieves his desire to spatially destroy the house box, through the development of a unique structural system, of masonry piers and tied cantilever concrete slabs with the railings acting as horizontal edge stiffeners, whose origins are in concrete bridge design and the studio house of 1923 by Theo Van Doesburg. The resultant house is exemplary at every level, what we discover in the house is a series of continuous one and two story spatial volumes extending from inside to outside, which are free both vertically and horizontally, due to their independence from the clearly expressed pier and slab structural frame, and only being defined by a minimal machine made mitered glass curtain wall of horizontal steel mullions.

Fallingwater is a synthesis of both formal and technical innovation, finally achieving what Wright so eloquently described in 1927 in his "In the Cause of Architecture" articles on the materials for *Architectural Record*, that "architecture is the search for an expression of the unique qualities of the materials as definitions of spaces"[12].

NOTES

1. Frank Lloyd Wright, "The Cardboard House" 1931.
2. Vincent Scully Jr., *Frank Lloyd Wright* (New York; Braziller, 1960). pp. 14-16.
3. Grant C. Manson, *Frank Lloyd Wright to 1910* (New York; Reinhold, 1958) pp. 62-68.
4. *Ibid*, pp. 34-39.
5. Frank Lloyd Wright, *His Life, His Work, His Words* (New York; Horizon, 1966) pp. 153-165. on The New Sense of Space.
6. Donald Hoffman, *Frank Lloyd Wright's Robie House* (New York; Dover, 1984).
7. Frank Lloyd Wright, *Truth Against the World* (New York; Wiley, 1987) pp. 87-107. on The Art and Craft of the Machine.
8. *Ibid*, pp. 108-141 on The American System Ready Cut House and The Preassembled House.
9. Egar Tafel, *Apprentice to Genius* (New York: McGraw-hill, 1979). pp. 125-127.
10. John Sargent, *Frank Lloyd Wright's Usonian Houses* (New York: Whitney, 1975). pp. 108-119.
11. Donald Hoffman, *Frank Lloyd Wright's Fallingwater* (New York: Dover, 1986).
12. Frank Lloyd Wright, *In the Cause of Architecture* (New York: Architectural Record Books, 1975).

CHAPTER 26

The Architect and the Housewife

JACQUELINE LEAVITT
University of California, Los Angeles

HOUSES OF TOMORROW: THE HOUSE AS TECHNOLOGY

> The startled housewife watches the iron as it automatically and faultlessly goes over the shirt. The shirt flies through the air folding itself into a package as if never worn and lands perfectly in a laundry basket. Throughout these events, the housewife uses her freed-up time to chat on the phone. The television audience watching this commercial has seen another technological wonder in what must be a house of tomorrow. Yet the house of tomorrow looks quite conventional. As unconventional an architect as Peter Eisenmann confirms that the house of tomorrow "will still look like a house, not a machine or a spaceship."[1]

The list is small of houses of tomorrow that promised great technological innovation:[2] Buckminster Fuller's 1927 4-D (Fourth Dimension) House, later followed by his Dymaxion House, Walter Gropius' and Konrad Wachsmann's 1942 Packaged House, Koch's 1950's Techbuilt House, and the steelbuilt houses of the California 1945 to 1966 case study period. These architects and engineers faced insurmountable problems with unions, bureaucrats enforcing building codes, and material suppliers. The American public saw the "new" houses as temporary, hence inferior, and found them expensive, their costs often as much if not greater than conventional looking houses.

The major exception was Fuller's 1927 4-D Dwelling Unit.[3] Fuller preferred a hexagonal plan, but he followed his attorney's advice and the patent "indicates that the system could also be used to provide a conventional box-like structure."[4] The 12,000 cubic foot house was made with transparent glass, casein walls, and inflated rubber flooring, suspended from a central aluminum mast. The mast contained the service core--two bathrooms, each stamped out of one piece with no cracks for bugs, and a vacuum electric hair clipper, vacuum toothbrush, and chinning bar; a self-activating laundry unit that would wash and dry clothes in three minutes; all-equipped kitchen with automatic refrigeration, and a dish washing machine that would clean, dry, and return dishes to shelves. Pneumatic beds in two bedrooms would not require sheets or blankets because the entire house would be climate controlled. A "get-on-with-life" or "creative" room was equipped with a factory-assembled unit that included the equivalent of today's at-home office/communications/entertainment/education station; in Fuller's scheme, new models would continuously replace a typewriter, calculator, telephone, dictation machine, television, radio, phonograph, and mimeograph machine. There would be built-in globes, maps, drawing boards, and revolving shelves. Doors throughout the house would be open and closed with a wave of the hand across a light beam of a photo-electric cell. Floors and partitions would be soundproofed. Different rooms would be individually controlled so that each could be flooded with lights of any desired color. Beneath the house was a family auto-airplane "transport unit". Attachment to public utilities was unnecessary because the house would be self-sufficient through its own sewage disposal tanks, electric generator, air compressor, and humidifier. Water was provided through a self-cleaning, circulating system. A dirigible would individually site 4-D units or stack them in a ten-deck apartment house.

Brian Horrigan writes that the 4-D house provided a "thematic checklist for subsequent homes of the future," including the relation to art, technology, and creating a liberatory environment.[5] The technology was embedded in society's growing industrialization and fascination with machines. Fuller's work may also have been prompted by first-hand experiences with housework. Lloyd Steven Sieden's biography relates how the teenage Fuller took over household chores following the death of his father and the loss of household income:[6]

> the servants who had supported the Fullers' comfortable lifestyle were dismissed, and Bucky assumed the physically demanding chores such as stoking the furnace through long New England winters, cleaning heavy rugs, and all the yardwork required for a large house. It was while toiling at those arduous, yet necessary, chores

that Fuller began to develop a respect for housework and appreciate the enormous amount of time and energy it demanded.

At that time, even the simplest cleaning chores required strength and endurance. For instance, heavy rugs were carried outside and hung over clotheslines, where they were beaten and brushed by hand. Years later, Fuller would recall his early house-cleaning experiences when developing the ultramodern Dymaxion House and other dwellings, and because of those recollections, he would mindfully design built-in, labor-saving devices, such as suction ducts which automatically removed loose dirt and dust from a home.[7]

Other architect-inventors were influenced by Henry Ford's automobile production techniques and encouraged by wartime induced advancements. Walter Gropius and Konrad Wachsmann, emigres to the United States from Germany, drew from the early 1900's tradition linking architecture and industry in their native country. In 1942, they introduced the Packaged House; it could be delivered by truck and built in a few hours by unskilled labor or the homebuyer. All elements slipped into place and locked; the homebuyer, using standardized parts, was free to rearrange the layout. Gropius, Wachsmann, and different businessmen formed the General Panel firm. The firm failed, its products neither cheaper than housing on the market nor appealing to a widespread public.

Lustron Homes, a steel-paneled house with a traditional exterior, fared somewhat better but also failed in 1950-1951. Its inventor, Carl Strandlund, developed a house built "much like the standard kitchen stove of the era...a steel frame upon which porcelain-enameled steel panels (in any one of six colors) were mounted providing both inner and outer wall surfaces)."[8] The house was fireproof, rustproof, and termite-proof; it withstood chipping and came complete with radiant heating, everything except a stove and refrigerator.

In the fifties, B. F. Goodrich presented a "House of Today" at the National Plastics Exhibition. Vinyl was everywhere: on roofs, as siding, ceilings, walls, floors, and around the kitchen sink. Other companies, such as Armstrong Cork and Monsanto, experimented with cork and plastic. ALCOA, integrating aluminum, offered the "Care Free House" by Charles Goodman. Arthur J. Pulos writes that only Carl Koch's Acorn House and Techbuilt House, in collaboration with John Bemis, "were able to achieve respectability," as houses for manufacture rather than display cases for materials.

Public resistance to changes about the house form and materials did not extend to the use of technology within the house. This may be because the many appliances that appeared were relatively small and easier to accept; even if initially expensive, did not require a lifetime's savings; or affirmative images attached to the traditional look of the house were overarching. Technology in the form of appliances usually has been sold as laborsaving devices, appealing to housewives. Later studies have demonstrated that housework increased instead and remained firmly women's work.

HOUSEWORK: THE IMPACT OF TECHNOLOGY IN THE HOUSE

Christine E. Bose and Philip L. Bereano distinguish between four types of technologies concerning housework: utilities such as running water, electricity, gas, and sewage provided collectively to virtually all households; small and large appliances used in performing housework such as washers and driers; convenience and prepackaged foods that replaced "growing, preserving, preparing, and even many cooking chores;" and private sector market services such as garbage collection, fast food restaurants, and diaper services.[9]

In a separate article, Bose writes: "Over the last 50 years, despite the introduction of 'labour-saving devices', the amount of time which women spend on housework has either remained constant or actually increased."[10]

> Today, not only rising standards, but also the proliferation of small and medium-sized appliances that are task-extending or -- adding rather than task-eliminating have offset many of the original gains made by utilities in decreasing time. It sometimes seems that what technology may give with one hand it can take away with another. New small appliances involve more elaborate cleaning, more storage problems and increased likelihood of maintenance.[11]

Charles Thrall found that technology sometimes transferred tasks from one household member to another rather than eliminating work for the woman. He reported, for example, that when families had garbage disposals, wives took on this responsibility rather than the husband handling his traditional task.[12]

Both younger and older husbands avoid housework. Barbara R. Bergmann reports on a University of Michigan time-use study in the mid-seventies that revealed younger husbands "appear to do even less housework than their older counterparts, although neither group of men averages as much as half an hour per day."[13] There is little difference between husbands of women who work full-time outside the house and those who do not. Bergman writes:

> Husbands of wives with full-time jobs averaged about two minutes more housework per day than did husbands in housewife-maintaining families, hardly enough additional time to prepare a soft-boiled egg. Only four of [the] 290 couples studied had arranged their affairs so that both husband and wife had full-time jobs and shared the housework fairly equally.[14]

Heidi Hartmann, summarizing a number of different studies, writes that when children are present, the disparity is even greater between women and men's contributions to housework.[15]

Since Fuller, promotion of maintenance free houses occasionally resurfaces. But complete models like Frances Gabe's Self-Cleaning House (SCH) have not found very many adherents. Frances Gabe, an artist and inventor, has been building a Self-Cleaning House since the early 1960s, explicitly to relieve women.[16] She says, "I don't see why women have to do their work either on their knees or with their head hanging in a hole."[17] Gabe's central thesis is based on a:

> General Room-Washing Apparatus [is] connected to the feeder pipe. The feeder pipe is used to bring the water to the cleaning apparatuses, to dispense warm air for heating the building in winter and cool air for cooling it in summer, to eject a fine mist of germicide into a room where there has been a communicable disease, and to dispense bug repellent or killer, in case of infestations of termites, carpenter ants, bedbugs, cockroaches, fleas, or stinging or biting insects.[18]

The Self-Cleaning House will wash clothes and closets. Self-sealing tops will protect furniture from moisture. Waterproof mattress covers will ensure that beds are not damaged, and plastic shades over the mattress and bedding--the only items that are covered--will keep them fresh. Any building material that can be waterproofed, such as glass, wood, cement, frame, stone, or brick, can be used. The furniture does not have to be plastic and chrome steel. "The type of windows used throughout, for example, are windows as we know windows."[19]

In a survey in *Ms.* magazine about the readers' opinions of ideal homes and neighborhoods, one respondent--possibly with the Gabe House in mind, writes:

> About 10 years ago, an article appeared in either 'Woman's Day' or 'Family Circle' about a 'self-cleaning' house designed, naturally, by a woman. She went a long way toward this goal by simplification and elimination. As I remember she couldn't interest builders. Was it because women preferred a standard house that would occupy their days? Or were the builders (mostly men, of course) subliminally enraged at the prospect of more free time and therefore liberation for women?[20]

SEPARATING TECHNOLOGY AND HOUSEWORK IN THE HOUSE OF TOMORROW

That technology has not led to a reduction of housework in the past leads to questioning this premise for tomorrow's future house. What may be hailed as improvements in architecture, planning, decorating, and engineering journals may not diminish women's labor in the home, whether designers are male or female. Powerful reasons account for this. Women, in general, do not escape society's identification with housework. Michele Barrett and Mary McIntosh write that the idea of housework is so constructed that women are tied to its association with femininity and family.

> Wielding a needle or a mop, changing a nappy or a bed, not running out of flour or into debt comes easily to women, it seems. We are blamed if we cannot manage them, whereas men are praised if they can. Girls are thought unnatural if they do not want to learn these skills as children; boys are thought unusual, if not unnatural, if they do.[21]

In the mid-sixties, Alison Ravetz questioned whether housework could ever become more communalized because it had become so "emotion-laden."[22]

That housework has not been redistributed and that women's housewifely-type responsibilities are undiminished because she is in the waged labor force, leads to reassessing the role of technology in the house of tomorrow. The house of the future, such as Pierre Sarda's prototype in Belgium, and Motorala's in the United States, intends to be all-inclusive.

> The aim of domotique engineering is to free the home owner of the daily management of the household, to ensure the security of the home in the widest sense, and to provide communication with the exterior. New communication techniques can be grouped into three major fields: the robotization of household chores; the control of audiovisual appliances, security and surveillance systems; connection with public and private communication systems.[23]

Gender roles and how people feel about themselves are socially produced. Historical evidence demonstrates that the old houses of tomorrow became marketing tools for those who could afford the gadgets more than liberatory forces for society.[24] Proponents of today's Smart House are suggesting a proprietary system whereby they purchase the right to use the technology "to allow their products to communicate with one another (so the vacuum cleaner can shut off, for example, when the doorbell rings)."[25] One manufacturer has "developed a method of sending intricate signals over power lines, so not only can appliances be controlled, but a computer can receive data through an ordinary electric outlet." Within electronics, the industry's association is proposing who controls the standards for the automated home. Max, a firm in Portland, Oregon, is developing a system where the computer will set the standards.

> Max can sense where people are in the house, talk with them over the intercom, and actually *learn* from observing living patterns how best to control the alarm system, the thermostat, and the telephone. It can announce

messages to individuals, and even decide that the house is likely to be empty at noon, and adjust heating and security accordingly. Max is the first example of the next evolutionary stage of dwellings--the intelligent home with a life and voice all its own.[26]

The bulk of architects who will be involved in fitting in the new technology are among those unfamiliar with the new inventions. Finding out what is happening in order to create better designs is one step. Using architecture's collective voice to question who saves labor with laborsaving technology should precede this. Improvements in isolated houses at costs that only the better off can afford further polarizes a society that is increasingly divided into haves and have-not's. Raising these questions begins to open discussion about the complicated role of architects in response to women's changing roles inside and outside the house. This may lead to more inventive solutions rather than simply executing a reflexive architectural response to technology, blithely accepting that women will benefit because technology will release them from housework. That might not have happened even in Fuller's wondrous scheme.

NOTES

1. Jerry Adler, "The House of the Future," *Newsweek* special edition, winter/spring 1990, pp. 72-76, p. 72.
2. See Robert Marks, *The Dymaxion World of Buckminster Fuller* (Garden City, New York: Anchor Books, 1973); Gilbert Herbert, *The Dream of the Factory-Made House: Walter Gropius and Konrad Wachsmann* (Cambridge, Massachusetts: MIT Press, 1984); Carl Koch with Andy Lewis, *At Home With Tomorrow* (New York: Rinehart & Company, Inc., 1958); Arthur J. Pulos, *The American Design Adventure: 1940-1975* (Cambridge, Massachusetts: MIT Press, 1988); Esther McCoy, *Case Study Houses: 1945-1962* (Los Angeles: Hennessey & Ingalls, 1977, 2nd ed.); Peter Cook, et al. eds., *Archigram* (New York: Praeger Paperbacks, 1973).
3. Also see Marks; Pulos; Brian Horrigan, "The Home of Tomorrow, 1927-1945," in Joseph J. Corn, ed., *Imagining Tomorrow* (Cambridge, Massachusetts: MIT Press, 1987, 2nd printing), pp. 136-163.
4. Marks, p. 81.
5. Horrigan, p. 142
6. Lloyd Steven Sieden, *Buckminster Fuller's Universe: An Appreciation* (New York: Plenum Press, 1989).
7. Seiden, pp. 14-15.
8. Pulos, p. 51.
9. Christine E. Bose and Philip L. Bereano, "Household Technologies: Burden or Blessing?," In Jan Zimmerman, ed., *The Technological Woman: Interfacing With Tomorrow* (New York: Praeger Publications, 1983), pp. 83 - 93; p. 85.
10. Christine E. Bose, "Technology and Changes in the Division of Labour in the American Home," In Elizabeth Whitelegg et al., eds., *The Changing Experience of Women* (Oxford: Basil Blackwell, 1984 reprinted), pp. 226-238, p. 230.
11. Bose.
12. Bose.
13. Barbara R. Bergmann, *The Economic Emergence of Women* (New York: Basic Books, Inc., 1986), p. 264.
14. Bergmann, p. 263.
15. Heidi I. Hartmann, "The Family as the Locus of Gender, Class, and Political Struggle: The Example of Housework," *SIGNS* 6 (Spring 1981), pp. 366-394.
16. Frances GABe, "The GABe Self-Cleaning House," In Zimmerman, ed., *The Technological Woman*, pp. 75-82. Also see, Frances GABe, "The GABe Self-Cleaning House," In Terri P. Tepper and Nona Dawe Tepper, eds., *The New Entrepreneurs: Women Working From Home* (New York: Universe Books, 1980), pp. 190-197.
17. Zimmerman, p. 73.
18. Gabe, p. 77.
19. Gabe, p. 81.
20. Jacqueline Leavitt and Susan Saegert, "The Ideal American House" questionnaire, *Ms.* 14 (1985), pp. 81-82. Excerpt from Jacqueline Leavitt, *The Double Dream: The Single Family House and Community*, manuscript.
21. Michele Barrett and Mary McIntosh, *The Anti-social Family* (London: Verso, 1982), p. 61.
22. Alison Ravetz, "Modern Technology and an Ancient Occupation: Housework in Present Day Society," *Technology and Culture* 6 (1965), pp. 256-260.
23. Bert MacClure translation of Georges Bichet, "Domotique, Present et Futur," Archi/Cree, 223(1988), pp. 56-152, p. 152.
24. Adrian Forty, *Objects of Desire* (New York: Pantheon Books, 1986).
25. Edward Rothstein, "Control Central," *House and Gardens* (May 1988), p. 238.
26. Rothstein.

CHAPTER 27

The Home as Information Factory: The Changing Role of the Home for Home-Based Workers

PENNY GURSTEIN
University of California, Berkeley

Transportation and communications technologies are integral elements that contributed to the decentralization of urban spaces and altered social and spatial relationships in cities. The organization of urban transportation systems reinforced the trend towards the separation of work from home life, and central office work from production work. Telecommunications technologies, such as the telephone, contributed to urban sprawl and the mass migration to suburbia since it allowed communication without face-to-face contact. It has also been suggested that telephone use created 'psychological neighborhoods' of physically dispersed social relations, sustained the extended family and provided a sense of security and sociability. New telecommunications and information technologies in the home now allow for the relative self-sufficiency of a household's work and leisure activities. While these technologies are providing the opportunity for a reintegration of home and work life they, as well, are reinforcing the trend towards more privatized forms of modern life.

This paper argues that for people working at home using telecommunications and information technologies the home is being transformed into an 'information factory' where work can be created, processed and disseminated, eliminating many of the work-related functions of the city. Work in these settings takes precedence over home activities both spatially and temporally. What the uses of information and telecommunications technologies are capable of creating are 'virtual' workplaces and communities in the privacy of the home. This new use for the home has implications for the planning and design of future residential communities.

The research for this paper is based on 52 interviews with home- and office-based workers who use information and telecommunications technologies to conduct their work. These workers include both male and female full- and part-time homeworkers. Both self-employed and corporate-employed workers were interviewed.

Definitions vary on what constitutes a 'homeworker' but 'professional homeworkers' refer to people who work in their home as paid labor, either on a part-time or full-time basis. One survey estimated that 18% of U.S. households in 1987 were part- or full-time homeworkers. The full-time homeworker population is probably not that large, while the number of part-time homeworkers appears to be quite significant. Electronic homework is gaining in popularity as telecommunications and information technologies are making it easier for many office functions to be done in the home. As office settings become increasingly undesirable places to work - both because they are distracting and because they may involve long commutes - more people are opting to work at home.

There is currently considerable speculation that home-based computer work is having, and will have, a major impact on home and work life, but there is little empirical evidence on what the impact may be. Futurists such as Toffler (1980) and Nilles et al (1976) have hypothesized that through electronic 'homework' the home will re-emerge as a central unit in society with enhanced economic, educational and social functions. Critics of the 'electronic home' such as Castells (1985) and Robins and Hepworth (1988) argue that individuals in these homes will lead increasingly more fragmented and privatized forms of existence which will lead ultimately to the delocalization of community life.

Though pressures in society are making 'homework' necessary or conducive for segments of the population, critics such as Forester (1988) are questioning why the use of electronic home-based activities has not increased as many futurists predicted. They argue that futurists have consistently underestimated the psychological problems of working at home and that consumers have found that new information-based services (such as teleshopping) are not useful, nor do they fulfill their psychological needs. Specific issues that have been raised by these critics regarding electronic 'homework' include financial exploitation, conditions of employment, lack of union representation, problems with local planning laws and management problems encountered by companies trying to run telecommuting programs.

Other concerns cited in previous research include problems of spatial constraints and conflicts for people who live in small houses or apartments that are unsuitable for home working. As well, job performance difficulties which might arise working at home include a lack of motivation and discipline, inability to organize work and manage time effectively, and difficulty in being self-managers. While the possibilities of teleworking from home have been explored by many large corporations, they are concerned about the lack of control that managers will have in this new form of workplace. Homeworkers need to cope with the serious psychological problems that arise in relationships with the family or spouse, as well as feelings of loneliness or isolation from colleagues and concern about social status, especially in the neighborhood.

HOMEWORKER PROFILE

Two profiles of homeworkers emerged during my research: the home-centered individual and the work-centered individual. Home-centered homeworkers chose to work at home because they could not cope with the office environment and prefer the solitude of their home. They have a strong attachment to their home and value the control they have over their home environment. Working at home has allowed them to integrate their work life with their home life. In contrast, the work-centered individuals chose to work at home because working at home allows them flexibility and control over their work. For them, the home environment is a facilitator of their work goals and reflects their professional identity.

The homeworkers I interviewed on the whole regarded working at home as a retreat from the negative social and physical environment of the office. There are marked differences between the use of time and space between homeworkers and office workers. Work appeared to dominate homeworkers' lives and though working at home gave them a lot of flexibility, it also meant that they could never get away from it. In contrast, office workers had much more structured days and more separation between work and home activities. However, because of the long commutes that many had, they did not have any more time for leisure activities and many office workers reported problems in balancing their home and work responsibilities.

The home took on much more meaning for homeworkers. The home had both a special character as a retreat, and a utilitarian character as a work space. Homeworkers were much more conscious of the home as a functioning unit as they were constantly aware of things that had to be done at home. Women with families exhibited more conflict between their work and home responsibilities. Those who were the most successful developed rigid spatial and temporal boundaries in order to cope. There were only appreciable differences between homeworkers and office workers in their use of their neighborhood as neither group had many social contacts in their neighborhood nor did they do many activities in their immediate community.

CONSEQUENCES OF HOME-BASED WORK

There appears to be no easy relationship between home and work life for homeworkers. Work life is taking precedence over home life both spatially and temporally. Work settings dominate the home environment in many incidences and homeworkers' daily schedules are organized around their work. Homeworkers work long, irregular hours which means that they can never leave work responsibilities. In spatial terms home spaces are being usurped for work functions. For example, living rooms are being converted to offices because they are no longer being used for entertainment.

Though homeworkers tend to work long hours, I found that they feel that they are perceived by employers, clients, family, friends, and neighbors as not really working and they have the perception that their work is invisible to these people. Homeworkers are not being recognized as real workers because they don't exhibit the role trappings of a worker. Homeworkers also find that they are limited in the kind of work that they can do as their isolated locations means that they work on segments without ever being able to see the whole product. For many home-based workers their work setting, the home, is isolating and does not provide the needed venue for social support. The most positive benefits that working at home offers are flexibility and control over work. The most satisfied homeworkers appear to be those who only work part-time at home and go to an office the rest of the time.

PLANNING AND DESIGN IMPLICATIONS FOR THE HOME AND NEIGHBORHOOD

What are the implications of the homework phenomenon on the planning and design of future homes and neighborhoods? Conflicts between family and work roles have been identified as a major problem for homeworkers and these conflicts have been observed to be manifested spatially and temporally. The successful integration of home-based work in the home environment will require the planning of homes to incorporate a clear separation between home and work activities within the same structure. Separate entrances to home-based work settings and common work areas in large housing developments are some of the possibilities that need to be investigated for future homes.

Public life is intruding into the home to a greater extent than ever before by means of the information that can be received, and the social connections that are now possible, electronically, without having to go outside the home. New gradations of privacy need to be defined and new kinds of boundaries need to be incorporated.

The real challenge, however, in the planning of home workspaces is to find ways of incorporating opportunities for community and privacy within the same setting. The neighborhood has been perceived by urban designers as a physical locale where permanent residents are in face-to-face contact with each other because of their proximity. My research has found, however, that urban North Americans do not live as envisioned by planners. They have limited contacts with neighbors and their important social contacts are with friends, workmates and family. The traditional belief that the 'authentic' personal community is the local one is now being contrasted with the theory that modern life allows people to create social worlds almost entirely free from the artificial limits of place. Homeworkers are no more prone to interact closely with their neighbors nor perceive their neighborhood as their community than office workers. With the use of computer networks home-based workers are interacting more on the basis of function and interest than propinquity. Homeworkers, nevertheless, have a greater perception of the isolating nature of their home environment. Neighborhood work centers like those experimented with in Sweden within walking distance of residences is a possibility that could be investigated to alleviate the more negative aspects of working at home.

CONCLUSION

Homework as a social phenomenon has implications for child-care services, commuting patterns, the transportation system and a variety of work-related resources. If a significant portion of the population were encouraged to telecommute it could have a major effect on the restructuring of corporations to create less hierarchical organizations. Home-based work could potentially allow opportunities for more employee control and responsibility for aspects of their work, precipitating a breakdown of the traditional manager/employee relationship. Conversely, information technologies could be used for greater surveillance and remote management.

Though 'electronic homework' may not be having the kind of positive social and environmental impact that was originally envisioned for the 'electronic cottage', homework, generally has the potential to alter roles in the home, and change how the home is used. In certain situations, when homework allows greater flexibility in daily life, the impact may be positive. However, in other situations, homework may constrain daily activities. Home-based work could potentially have an impact on the way homes and neighborhoods are structured, precipitating a change from the segregation of single use zoning to a natural integration of housing, workplaces, and services.

REFERENCES

Ahrentzen, Sherry. (1986) "Blurring Boundaries: Socio-Spatial Consequences of Working at Home." Unpublished Manuscript, Department of Architecture, University of Wisconsin-Milwaukee.

Castells, Manuel. (1985) "High Technology, Economic Restructuring, and the Urban-Regional Process in the United States," in Manuel Castells (ed.), *High Technology, Space and Society*. Beverly Hills CA: Sage.

Christensen, Kathleen (ed). (1988a) *The New Era of Home-Based Work: Directions and Policies*. Boulder, CO: Westview Press.

de Sola Pool, Ithiel (ed). (1977) *The Social Impact of the Telephone*. Boston: MIT Press.

Engstrom, M. et al. (1986) "Tomorrow's Work in Today's Society." Stockholm: Swedish Council for Building Research.

Fischer, Claude. (1985) "Studying Technology and Social Life", in Manuel Castells (ed.), *High Technology, Space and Society*. Beverly Hills: Sage, 284-300.

Forester, Tom. (1988) "The Myth of the Electronic Cottage." *Futures*, June: 227-240.

Gottlieb, Nina. (1988) "Women and Men Working at Home: Environmental Experiences", in *EDRA 19 Proceedings*. D. Lawrence et al (eds.) Washington, D.C.: EDRA.

Hayden, Dolores. (1980). "What Would a Non-Sexist City Be Like?" *Signs: A Journal of Women in Culture and Society*.

Mason, Roy with Jennings, Lane and Evans, Robert. (1982) "The ComputerHome: Will Tomorrow's Housing Come Alive?" *The Futurist*, February.

Meyrowitz, Joshua. (1985) *No Sense of Place: The Impact of Electronic Media on Social Behavior*. New York: Oxford University Press.

Miles, Ian. (1988) "The Electronic Cottage: Myth or Near-Myth?" *Futures*, August: 355-366.

Naisbitt, John. (1984) *Megatrends*. New York: Warner Books.

Nilles, Jack et al. (1976) *The Telecommunications-Transportation Tradeoff*. New York: John Wiley.

Robins, K. and Hepworth, M. (1988) "Electronic Spaces: New Technologies and the Future of Cities." *Futures*, April: 155-176.

Saegert, S. (1980) "Masculine Cities and Feminine Suburbs: Polarized Ideas, Contradictory Realities," *Signs*, Vol. 5, No. 3, Suppl.: S96-S111.

Telecommuting Review. (1988) "Analysis of Data from National Survey Shows Surprising Trends, Raises Interesting Questions about Home Work." February, 12-17.

Toffler, Alvin. (1980) *The Third Wave*. New York: William Morrow & Company.

Webber, Melvin M. (1964) "The Urban Place and the Nonplace Urban Realm," in Melvin M. Webber, et al, *Explorations into Urban Structure*. Philadelphia: University of Pennsylvania Press.

Zuboff, Shoshana. (1988) *In the Age of the Smart Machine: The Future of Work and Power*. New York: Basic Books.

CHAPTER 28

Teaching Technology: What *Do* Architects Need to Know About Structures?

JONATHAN OCHSHORN
Cornell University

Architects are required to know something about the technological systems in their buildings, yet the specialized knowledge needed to actually design those systems is usually left to others. Proposals to "integrate" design education with the study of technology seem to be concerned mainly with organizational strategies (e.g., bringing technology "consultants" into the design studio; or suggesting various forms of team teaching) rather than addressing the basic question of content: what *do* architects need to know about technology?

Using the teaching of structures as an example, I propose to examine the conflicting requirements of *competence* (implying a simplification of both numerical methods and scope of material covered); versus *literacy* (implying a broadened understanding of not only the technical issues actually encountered in architectural/engineering practice, but also the social, economic, historic and intellectual context in which these technical issues are framed) in an attempt to reconcile the *content* of these courses with the diverse needs of the practicing professional.

WHY TEACH STRUCTURES?

At the outset, there are three broad explanations I have encountered for why structures should be taught to architects: first, so that architects can solve structural problems; second, so that they can talk more or less intelligently to their engineering consultants; and finally, so that architectural design, informed by a sound grasp of structural theory, becomes more rational and therefore, perhaps, more beautiful. Let us examine each of these arguments in turn.

SOLVING STRUCTURAL PROBLEMS. The first rationale for teaching structures is that architects need to know how to actually solve structural problems -- determine the distribution of stresses, compute beam and column sizes, etc. -- but only for a relatively simple class of buildings. In other words architects, especially in small practices, might find it necessary or convenient to design and even prepare construction documents for small buildings without utilizing the services of an engineering consultant. The case is never made, however, that architectural education in structures should therefore duplicate the more thorough training given to engineering students.

Yet even if architects are taught to design structures for relatively simple buildings, that does not necessarily imply that they need to understand the mathematical underpinning of the results they obtain. Because of the widespread availability and use of tables, charts and "pre-engineered" items of all sorts, many structural elements can be sized without recourse to any computations (or structural theory, for that matter). Additionally, even where mathematical formulas are introduced in the classroom, they are not always derived or explained -- see, for example, Harry Parker's presentation of column formulas for steel structures.[1] Thus, the goal of solving structural problems cannot by itself determine the content and methodology of structures courses.

COMMUNICATING WITH CONSULTANTS. The second rationale for teaching structures is that, given the extent to which the engineering profession has taken over the task of actually designing structures for buildings, architects must at least be able to discuss structural design issues with these engineers. For one thing, the architect is more often than not the leader of the design team; it would be difficult to act in this leadership role,coordinating all the design and engineering specialties, without possessing some knowledge about each area. Equally important, it would not be possible to successfully *collaborate* with engineers on large scale projects.

Specifically, architects would need to know, at a minimum, the essential *vocabulary* of structures: "moment," "shear," "deflection" and so on. Beyond this minimum vocabulary, insight into the behavior of structures would also be necessary unless, as R.E. Shaeffer warns, architects are willing to risk losing control over some basic design decisions.[2]

DESIGNING RATIONAL/BEAUTIFUL BUILDINGS. The third rationale for teaching structures is that architects need a basic *qualitative* understanding of structural theory in order to design rational buildings. "Only then," according to Nervi, "will a structure be born healthy, vital and, possibly beautiful."[3] While this view can easily degenerate into such sterile debates as, for example, whether the "extra" mullions in Sullivan's Guarantee Building are structurally ambiguous and therefore aesthetically (or morally) wrong, there is certainly some merit to the basic argument.

A qualitative grasp of structural behavior can sometimes emerge through the use of formulas in which the relationships among various parameters are expressed mathematically. For example, the bending stress formula, f_b=Mc/I, reveals in a remarkably concise way that bending stress will be reduced precisely to the extent that the cross section's moment of inertia is increased. But are we justified, therefore, in simply presenting formulas, or should architects be required to actually understand their derivation. And if so, do these derivations need to be more or less rigorous; should they be relegated to textbook appendixes; or can they be simplified, for example, by examining only special cases of a general condition, as in the derivation of the bending stress formula without calculus by considering only rectangular cross sections.[4]

The use of physical models or computer graphics provides another means of encouraging a qualitative understanding of structural behavior. If, as Salvadori suggests, "purely structural messages originate in our *intuitive* understanding of structural behavior, which stems both from our daily experience with structural actions and from our perception of structural forms in nature,"[5] then it would certainly be useful to harness this latent knowledge. Physical models or interactive computer graphics offer the possibility of extending this intuitive response, ordinarily limited by the kinds of structural behavior that can presumably be grasped through our daily experiences, to a broader class of more complex structural types.[6]

LITERACY VS. COMPETENCE

We are still left with the task of translating these various rationale for the teaching of structures into specific curricular guidelines. Leon Trilling makes a distinction between *literacy* and *competence* which is relevant to this discussion. He says: "We are literate in a discipline when we understand its presuppositions, its research techniques and some of its more important results. We are competent in it when we are able to use it for our own purposes."[7] But what exactly are our purposes?

Given the "division of labor" within the profession of architecture (and therefore within the schools) in which practitioners with various levels and types of technical competence find useful employment, it is improbable that a single unified purpose will emerge, or that a single strategy for teaching structures to architects will be found or should be sought. What is important is not that a particular selection of structural topics and methods be canonized, but rather that course objectives be articulated within each school, and course content be made to correspond to those objectives in a more systematic way.

Principal Stresses. As an example in which objectives tend to become somewhat obscure, consider the typical treatment of principal stresses in structures textbooks written specifically for architects. Where the topic is not omitted altogether, considerable effort is expended to derive the rather complicated relationships between principal stresses and the more familiar bending, axial and shear stresses; yet it is unusual for a specific procedure or numerical method to be suggested that would actually allow one to solve the types of problems for which the topic was presumably introduced in the first place.[8] The question of whether or how such a topic should be integrated into an architectural curriculum becomes clearer when we assess its importance according to the dual criteria of literacy and competence.

From the point of view of structural *competence*, it would be necessary not only to master the technique, in this case of determining the magnitude and direction of principal stresses resulting from all possible combinations of axial, bending and shear-type stresses, but more importantly to be able to use the technique in a purposeful way. Given the tendency of structural codes to propound design and analysis methods for typical elements in which these principal stresses are *not* explicitly acknowledged -- in other words, where a purposeful application of those techniques is made largely irrelevant by the standardized procedures suggested by design manuals -- it is doubtful whether competence, defined in this way, is a reasonable goal in an architectural curriculum.

From the point of view of structural *literacy*, on the other hand, what becomes crucial is not so much the technique itself, but that connections be made between the derivation or presentation of rather abstract sets of relationships -- the formula for the maximum principal stress has no obvious intuitive meaning, except perhaps in the graphic form invented by Mohr -- and the whole range of *results* to which they contribute. In this example, these results might well include the failure mechanism of beams; the crowding of isostatic lines at points of stress concentration; and the complex combinations of stress in thin shell structures. Where the results are found to be either inconsequential, obscure, or in some way beyond the scope of the architectural curriculum, then the topic itself might well be omitted. Where the results are deemed important, then the derivation or manipulation of mathematical formulas ought to be considered, not as an end in itself, but rather judged by the extent to which it contributes to a deeper appreciation of those results.

STRUCTURAL DUALITIES

This conflict between literacy and competence in the teaching of structures to architects could be framed as a series of *dualities* in which the second term is typically suppressed. In the previous example, the treatment of axial, bending and shear stress as a collection of discrete entities, each with its own method of analysis and its own criteria for design, was contrasted with the more unified notion of an elemental "state of stress."

In a similar way, a whole series of such pairs -- statics vs. dynamics; member vs. system; strength vs. stiffness; elastic vs. inelastic; even abstraction (load, shear, moment diagrams) vs. reality (actual structure/building behavior) -- all can be seen as expressing a certain tension between the desire for competence and the search for structural literacy. This tension comes about because, by essentially circumscribing the areas of inquiry to those topics represented by the first terms and thereby providing a semblance of structural competence, the kind of structural literacy that would be engendered by an appreciation of *both* terms of the pairs tends to suffer. Consider the following example.

DETERMINATE VS. INDETERMINATE. Since the early part of this century, it has been hard to make the case that architects ought to be able to do the engineering design for large or complex buildings, which are often statically indeterminate. At the same time, it is hard to imagine how an architect can design and execute such buildings without some insight into their structural behavior and without some method of evaluating different structural options. Yet even if the architecture student possesses some reasonable means of analyzing indeterminate structures, the following pedagogical dilemma remains: how does one impart a sense of structural literacy when the behavior of complex structures and the choices among structural systems often hinge upon the subtle interaction of many variables, some of which, like the costs of material and labor or the availability of particular technologies, are in a constant state of motion and, strictly speaking, are not even structural parameters.

Eduardo Torroja says that the "achievement of the final solution is largely a matter of habit, intuition, imagination, common sense, and personal attitude. Only the accumulation of experience," he continues, "can shorten the necessary labor or trial and error involved in the selection of one among the different possible alternatives."[9] But given the relatively small amount of time allocated to structures within typical professional programs in architecture, coupled with a general insecurity in the use of mathematical tools, how can the architect accumulate such experience?

PEDAGOGICAL GOALS

In fact, there are several reasons why the quest for structural literacy is not hopelessly compromised by the architect's lack of quantitative technical competence. As I have suggested elsewhere, architects are able to obtain particular kinds of knowledge about appropriate structural systems either because they have designed similar projects in the past, or because they have studied similar projects designed by others.[10] Knowing the typical spans and depths of beams, the approximate sizes of columns, and the usual options for the provision of lateral bracing becomes more or less routine in architectural offices that deal repeatedly with conventional structures. Yet this type of "competence" should not be confused with that of the engineer: an architect's "rule of thumb" methodology implies neither insight into structural behavior nor the facility for quantitative analysis. This is not meant as a criticism. Architects, after all, are in the habit of "controlling the spaces to be used by people," and do not primarily think of form "as the means of controlling the forces of nature."[11]

And what about unconventional structures -- "the emergence each year, "according to Nervi, "of new structures of increasing size, such as railway and air terminals, industrial buildings, stadia, large theatres and very tall buildings."[12] For these types of structures, conventional wisdom and rules of thumb may well be inadequate. A more substantial understanding of structural behavior -- a more educated intuition -- is required. But designing structures of the sort represented in the works of Nervi, Torroja or Frei Otto cannot be the goal of architectural courses in structures. For one thing, few engineers, let alone architects, possess the combination of mathematical competence and artistic intuition which the design of such structures presuppose. As Felix Candela has said, this type of creative act is the "result of long and painstaking work, the fruit of many years of constant effort and steadfast mental occupation with the problem concerned. This is, " he says, "...the only way to get the sort of inspiration that all ambitious young architects so ardently wish for."[13]

Additionally, this quest to "cover increasingly large spans with ever diminishing quantities of materials,"[14] that is alleged to have animated the history of building construction, has a far more limited role within the great majority of architectural practices. Architecture is no longer defined primarily by the sorts of temples and churches amply represented in history of architecture texts in which the expression and continual refinement of structure contributed to the sense of architectural accomplishment. While structures of that type continue to be built, the heirs to that tradition have generally separated themselves from the profession of architecture, becoming engineering specialists with enormous skill acquired from years of study and practical experience. Architects, on the other hand, have increasingly come to view technical systems as *preexisting* products of an "optimized technology," to use Frampton's phrase, that can be assembled and manipulated according to rules embodied in codes, specifications and so forth.

The appreciation of structures that can be attained through both qualitative and quantitative study within the limited framework normally provided by architectural curricula should not be confused with the type of creative act outlined by Candela. Even the most rigorous presentation of structural concepts will not promote real structural competence if the material is not internalized -- taken apart and re-synthesized -- by each student over a period of many years of careful study. And where sufficient information about the structural systems used in the overwhelming majority of building types can be assimilated by the typical architect without such a lifelong commitment to the pursuit of structural knowledge, it is unrealistic to expect such an effort to be made. What should be expected is a certain degree of structural literacy, in which mathematical relationships are studied and employed, not to engender a false sense of competence, but so that the vocabulary of structures, intrinsic to any definition of literacy, becomes more tangible and intelligible.

NOTES

1. Parker, Harry *Simplified Design of Structural Steel*, 5th Ed. John Wiley & Sons (New York, NY) 1983, pp.197-198
2. Shaeffer, R.E. *Building Structures: Elementary Analysis and Design* Prentice-Hall (Englewood Cliffs, NJ) 1980, p.4
3. Nervi, Pier Luigi, "Foreword" in Salvadori, Mario with Heller, Robert *Structure in Architecture: The Building of Buildings* Prentice-Hall (Englewood Cliffs, NJ) 1986
4. This approach is adopted in Salvadori, Mario *Statics and Strength of Structures* Prentice-Hall, Inc. (Englewood Cliffs, NJ) 1971, pp.153-157
5. Salvadori, Mario *Why Buildings Stand Up: The Strength of Architecture* W.W. Norton & Co. (New York, NY) 1980, pp.292-293
6. The construction and use of physical models to illustrate structural concepts is discussed in Cowan, Henry J. *Architectural Structures* Elsevier (New York, NY) 1976, pp.289-300; for a discussion of interactive computer graphics as well as "interactive-adaptive methods," see Abel, John F.,"Interactive Computer Graphics for Applied Mechanics," *Proceedings of the Ninth U.S. National Congress of Applied Mechanics* American Society of Mechanical Engineers (New York, NY) 1982, pp.3-27
7. Trilling, Leon, "Technology as Part of a Liberal Education," *Technology and Science: Important Distinctions for Liberal Arts Colleges* Davidson-Sloan New Liberal Arts Program (Davidson, North Carolina) 1984, p.70
8. Several texts omit the topic altogether: for example, Lauer, Kenneth *Structural Engineering for Architects* McGraw-Hill (New York, NY) 1981; and Benjamin, B.S. *Structures for Architects* Van Nostrand Reinhold Co. (New York, NY) 1984. Where it is discussed, the stated objectives -- that is, the reasons given as to why an understanding of the topic might be important -- vary strikingly from book to book. According to Giuseppe de Campoli, referring to concrete and steel beams in *Strength of Structural Materials* John Wiley & Sons (New York, NY) 1984, p.67, the topic is included because of the "importance of diagonal stresses as triggers of the failure of the structural materials..." Salvadori and Levy, on the other hand, in *Structural Design in Architecture* Prentice-Hall (Englewood Cliffs, NJ) 1981, p.285, emphasize its importance in terms of visualizing stress concentrations. Finally, according to Shaeffer, *op. cit.*, p.170, the "combinations [of internal stresses] must be considered... in the more form-resistant structures which use thin shell or membrane action to carry loads."
9. Torroja, Eduardo *Philosophy of Structures* University of California Press (Berkeley, CA) 1958, p.313
10. Ochshorn, Jonathan, "Separating Science from Architecture: Why Technology is Taught Outside the Design Studio," *Proceedings* of the 1990 ACSA Annual Meeting (San Francisco, CA), to appear.
11. Billington, David P. *The Tower and the Bridge* Basic Books, Inc. (New York, NY) 1983, p.14
12. Nervi, Pier Luigi *Buildings, Projects, Structures 1953-1963* Frederick A. Praeger (New York, NY) 1963
13. Candela, Felix, "Foreword," in Roland, Conrad *Frei Otto: Tension Structures* Praeger Publishers (New York) 1970
14. Candela, *ibid.*

CHAPTER 29

Beyond the Bauhaus: Integrating Technology and Design in the Studio

DR. MARK GELERNTER
University of Colorado at Boulder

INTRODUCTION

One of most perplexing problems facing architectural education is how to integrate technology into the design studio. Many student design projects in modern schools of architecture show little evidence of coherent structural or HVAC systems, nor do they fully explore the constructional or aesthetic qualities of building materials, nor do they display much understanding of energy conservation or natural climate control. These technological shortcomings often surface in the studio even after the students have taken courses on structure, construction, building materials and HVAC.

According to modernist mythology, design education inherited this problem from the Ecole des BeauxArts. In the Ecole, it is usually assumed, students learned a limited repertoire of Classical forms which was no longer appropriate for 20th century life or for 20th century technology. They conceived of form as something separate from its means of construction, and so did not learn to generate new architectural forms in terms of the new technological means available. According to the same modernist mythology, Walter Gropius and the Bauhaus repaired this Academic split between form and technology by teaching art and craft as one. The Bauhaus, it is usually assumed, taught students how to find good form in the properties of materials. The reason we still have some difficulty integrating design and technology in our modern studios, it is sometimes suggested, is that we have not yet fully implemented the Bauhaus educational vision.

But this interpretation does not stand up to the facts. The student projects created at the height of the BeauxArts tradition display an astonishing command of structure and construction, and a sympathetic understanding of the quality of building materials. The shapes of spaces in plan integrally relate to their shapes in section and plan, and are significantly determined by the logic of the structural system. The students' drawings demonstrate in considerable detail how various building materials are put together, and how a sensitive use of different building materials can enhance the aesthetic quality of the building. Student projects in the Bauhaus tradition, in contrast, usually employed an amorphous cardboardlike material indiscriminately applied to walls, ceilings, and columns. The large glazed walls and flat roofs of the Bauhaus projects arguably make less sense in terms of climate control than the thick masonry walls of the BeauxArts tradition.

The Bauhaus, this paper will argue, did not develop a magical synthesis of art and craft, design and technology. Indeed, the underlying curricular structure of the Bauhaus actively worked against such a synthesis. If we have problems today integrating design and technology in our studios, it is because we continue to employ several problematical Bauhaus educational concepts. In particular, this paper will identify two troublesome notions: first, the Bauhaus' curricular distinction between "form teaching" and "craft teaching"; and secondly, the Bauhaus' use of an abstract language of form for teaching principles of design. This paper will conclude by discussing how we might teach more effectively without these two Bauhaus traditions, and how we might consequently bring design and technology into closer union.

THE BAUHAUS SPLIT BETWEEN DESIGN AND TECHNOLOGY

Walter Gropius founded the Bauhaus in 1919 explicitly to reunite art and craft. His founding manifesto proclaimed:

> Architects, sculptors, painters, we all must return to the crafts! For art is not a 'profession'. There is no essential difference between the artist and the craftsman. The artist is an exalted craftsman. In rare moments of inspiration, transcending the consciousness of his will, the grace of heaven may cause his work to blossom into art. But proficiency in a craft is essential to every artist. Therein lies the prime source of creative imagination.[1]

To reunite art and craft, Gropius proposed as a model for the Bauhaus the medieval German *Bauhutten*, or craft guilds.

Workers in the *Bauhutten* were not divided into those who conceptualized and those who built, he pointed out, but rather were trained to design and execute in one continuous process. The medieval artist/craftsmen found their forms in the nature of their materials, in their constructional systems, and in the functional requirements to which the objects would be put. Gropius proposed to recapture this organic relationship between design and craft by reestablishing the the craft guild's educational structure, which was of course the master/apprenticeship system based in the master's workshop. Bauhaus students would learn about both design and craft entirely within the workshop, as they collaborated in the practical work of the teachers.[2]

Within the first year, unfortunately, Gropius discovered that the students were unable to learn design in the shops. They were acquiring craft skills, but they did not know to what forms these skills should be applied. Gropius felt compelled to give the students some additional training in conceptual design. To do this, he split both the faculty and the curriculum in the *Werklehre*, or instruction in craft, and the *Formlehre*, or instruction in conceptualization and the principles of design. In doing so he split asunder the intimate medieval relationship between form and craft, but he felt he had no recourse. In modern times, he regretfully explained, art has been divorced from everyday life for so long that few teachers combine both skills.

Now with this curricular split, Gropius essentially returned to precisely the same educational structure which had dominated in the old art and architecture academies for several centuries.[3] The Academies also distinguished between the lecture courses, where students learned principles of history, structures, and construction, and the ateliers, where the students applied those principles to design problems. In the former, the students concentrated on aspects of technology, and in the latter they created the forms which might incorporate this technology.[4]

Gropius had been right to reject this dual curricular structure in his original founding manifesto, and his return to it after the first year of the Bauhaus unfortunately neutralized any opportunity he might have had to heal the split between form and technology. Although it seems logical that one ought to learn the principles of a field before attempting to apply them to practical problems, I have argued in "Reconciling Lectures and Studios" that this notion flies in the face of how we actually learn.[5] Principles do not make much sense to usand are therefore not retainedunless we are faced with a practical problem which those principles will help us solve. The education process is cyclical and interactive, because we need principles to help us solve problems, but we have to face problems in order to learn the principles effectively.[6] By teaching these in two separate parts of the course, we are actively discouraging the students from making the essential connection between the two.

This fundamental flaw of the dual curricular structure was disguised in the Academies, because they taught their principles mostly in concrete terms of existing building forms and materials. For example, the students learned about structure by studying and drawing the structural systems and materials which accompany the Classical repertoire of forms. At the same time they learned how to make floor plans with a hierarchy of circular and rectangular rooms, they also learned how to put trusses over rectangles and and domes over circles. Also, the language of Classicism already had built into it traditional and functional solutions to rainwater control, ventilation, solar control, and so on. The Beauxarts students learned technological principles in terms of the forms they would most likely be designing and, once they turned their attentions to designing in the studios, the forms they manipulated were already imbued with technological realities.

Unfortunately, this fusion of technology with traditional forms which saved the Academies from their own dualistic structure was the very characteristic which Gropius most detested in the academic tradition. Gropius insisted that the problems facing designers in the 20th century were entirely unprecedented, and so they demanded unprecedented solutions. He refused to teach the students any existing repertoires of forms for fear of hindering original solutions.

So Gropius needed some instruction in principles of design, but instruction which would not give the students preconceptions about particular forms. For this he turned to the contemporary avantgarde painters. By 1920, when the need for some preliminary instruction in the Bauhaus was painfully obvious, the abstract painters had already explored what they considered to be the essential, underlying characteristics of form in the abstract, divorced from any particular phenomena. To teach the Bauhaus students these abstract characteristics of form seemed like the ideal solution to Gropius, because the students could learn about visual form without compromising his abhorrence of preconceived ideas.

The principles of abstract visual design which Josef Albers and Laszlo MoholyNagy subsequently taught in the *Formlehre* are now so firmly established in most modern schools of architecture that they are a commonplace. Students are asked to manipulate abstract shapes, forms and patterns in order to discover principles of visual design like balance, rhythm, symmetry, and proportion; and to learn about the inherent characteristics of the materials they employ for these exercises, like string, cardboard, and wood. Once the students have learned about proportion in the abstract, divorced from any particular architectural manifestation of proportion, then they will be able to generate unprecedented architectural forms which nonetheless display characteristics of good proportion.

Now this conception of teaching principles before practical application can be objected to on the grounds that this is not how we actually learn; and this objection is borne out, I would suggest, by the reality that many students who tackle their first real architectural problem after a year of abstract basic design do so without much evidence of understanding how balance, proportion, and rhythm relate to their architectural forms. But equally worrying, for the purposes of this paper, is that the typical abstract basic design course abandons any discussion of building technology as it relates to form. Realistically, artfully stretching a piece of string in an abstract composition does not go very far in teaching the complexities of tensile building structures and connections; carving a piece of plywood does not explain stressed skins; piling up a collage of boxlike shapes does not teach anything about waterproof junctions between verticals and horizontals; and no abstract exercise I have ever heard of teaches anything about climate control, ventilation, or energy conservation.

Although the Academy had gone some way to splitting design from technology with its dualistic curricular structure of lectures and studios, Gropius severed the connection altogether when he made his principles of design so abstract and general that they no longer referred to building construction at all. From the Bauhaus on, one set of teachers would discuss technology in the lecture room, divorced from the students' efforts to create building forms, and another set of teachers would discuss form in the studio as an entity with no technological implications. It is not surprising that students in modern schools of architecture fail to see the relationship between these two. No amount of inspired teaching in independent technology courses, nor any amount of haranguing in the studios to think about technology, can heal this mistaken educational rift.

REINTEGRATING TECHNOLOGY INTO THE STUDIO

If we still hold the integration of design and technology as a desirable end, then we must rethink some of our pedagogical methods. I would suggest we have at least two possible routes open to us. First of all, we can return to the Academy solution, and teach a specific repertoire of architectural forms and their accompanying technology. This is a common approach in numerous architectural engineering programs, where students study and draw traditional steel, wood, and concrete building structures. Clearly, students learn more about real building technology in these courses than they currently do in most schools of architecture. The disadvantage, of course, is that the students learn only a limited repertoire of technology, mostly restricted to the particular examples which the teacher asks them to study. This approach cannot answer Gropius' original concern about restricting creative solutions to new problems.

A better approach, I suggest, is to return to Gropius' original idea for the Bauhaus, derived from the old craft guilds. That is, teach design and technology integrally in the same studio. Give the students architectural problems which equally require technological solutions, and then teach them appropriate technological and aesthetic concepts as they work on the problem.

We have begun to experiment with a course like this in the first year studio in the College of Environmental Design, University of Colorado at Boulder. In place of the usual abstract basic design course, the first year students begin directly with real architectural and planning problems. Throughout each project, they are given specific and applied information about structure, construction, human behavior, and visual form which helps shape their ideas integrally as they attempt to create architectural forms. Form is taught in terms of how it is made, technology is taught in terms of its practical consequences for formmaking.

For example, the very first day of the studio the students are asked to design a simple shelter to adjoin a popular pedestrian path along a creek in Boulder. They are required to design this structure with a wooden post and beam frame with no plywood, and to build an accurate 1/2" scale model showing every structural member. We ask them to propose an initial solution within the first two days, at which time it becomes painfully obvious that they know little about how their forms might be constructed. Since they know they will eventually have to build a model of their heretofore unbuildable forms, they are intellectually and emotionally quite open to the simple concepts of structure and construction which we then offer in the studio. We run a simple seminar on the principles of beams and columns, lateral stability, layering of structural members, and so on. At this point the students' architectural forms usually change dramatically, and always for the better. What often started out as stodgy octagonal Victorian gazebos quickly turn into dramatic cantilevered structures, umbrella structures, braced triangular structures, tree houses built on columns cantilevered out of the ground.

Far from constraining formal creativity, this immediate infusion of technology enhances the students' compositional abilities.[7] And instead of learning about the principle of a cantilever solely in terms of an abstract stress diagram because the teacher tells them it is important, the students have learned the principle because they know they need it in order to solve an engaging problem. In subsequent studio projects, they begin to conceive of form in terms of the constructional principles they have learned. And in later technical lecture courses, the principles of structures the students learn are more memorable because they have already consciously employed them in a real design project.

This studio is still experimental, and there are many projects still to explore. We have not, for example, specifically addressed the relationships between form and climate control, or form and weather proofing. But these early efforts convince us that we are more likely to reconcile design and technology in this integrated studio, than in a dual curricular structure which isolates principle from practice.

NOTES

1. Walter Gropius, 'Programme of the Staatliche Bauhaus in Weimar', April 1919, in Hans Wingler (ed.), *The Bauhaus* (MIT Press, Cambridge, Mass. and London, 1978), p. 31.

2. Gropius' interest in the medieval craft guilds was largely inspired by the Romanticism then dominant in German art and architectural circles. See Marcel Franciscono, *Walter Gropius and the Creation of the Bauhaus in Weimar: the Ideals and Artistic Theories of Its Founding Years* (Urbana, University of Illinois Press, 1971); and Wolfgang Pehnt, *Expressionist Architecture* (London,Thames and Hudson, 1973).
3. Rayner Banham notes how many of the Bauhaus ideas ''resemble those of French academic origin''. Banham, *Theory and Design in the First Machine Age* (London, The Architectural Press, 1960), p. 15.
4. A useful discussion of BeauxArts teaching methods can be found in Arthur Drexler, *The Architecture of the Ecole des BeauxArts* (New York, The Museum of Modern Art, 1977). For a discussion of the Academic tradition generally, see Nikolaus Pevsner, *Academies of Art Past and Present*, (Cambridge, Cambridge University Press, 1940).
5. Mark Gelernter, ''Reconciling Lectures and Studios'', *Journal of Architectural Education*, Vol. 41, No. 2, Winter 1988, pp. 46-52.
6. The theoretical justification for this is developed at length in the works of Jean Piaget, including *Biology and Knowledge*, trans. Beatrix Walsh (Edinburgh, Edinburgh University Press, 1971); Piaget, *Structuralism*, trans. Chaninah Maschler (London, Routledge & Kegan Paul, 1971); and Piaget, *The Principles of Genetic Epistemology*, trans. Wolfe Mays (London, Routledge & Kegan Paul, 1972).
7. The theoretical justification for this is discussed in Mark Gelernter, ''Teaching Design Innovation Through Design Tradition'', in the proceedings of the Association of Collegiate Schools of Architecture 76th national conference, Miami, March 1988, pp.441-445.

CHAPTER 30

Representation and Function: Teaching the Art of Detailing

GIL SNYDER
University of Wisconsin-Milwaukee

> *''Too much attention can not be given to produce a distinct Character in every building, not only in great features, but in minor detail likewise; even a moulding, however diminutive, contributes to increase or lessen the Character of the assemblage of which it forms a part''* - John Soane[1]

Instruction about construction materials and construction technology is a difficult and elusive task. In current practice and pedagogy, the thrust of interest appears to revolve primarily around discussion of materials and performance based on a need to provide educated cannon fodder for the construction documents wars, with only peripheral discussion about its relation to the art of building and design. Yet the development of the detail in architecture is critical to the production of meaningful building.[2] In fact, the development of generative details for a project not only solve a large number of technical problems but also establish the visual order and coherence of the architecture.

To better establish this connection between technology and design, we have developed a seminar course at the University of Wisconsin-Milwaukee which focuses on exterior detailing strategies related to buildings of civic, institutional and commercial character. It is the detailing of their facades that is concentrated on, because enclosure systems, by their very definition, necessarily deal with most of the critical problems found in architectural technics: moisture migration, fireproofing, building movement, thermal efficiency, freeze-thaw and similar problems. But construction of a building's skin also confronts issues of design directly and makes imperative an understanding of the immediate relationship between literal technical solutions and the symbolic, phenomenal expression of enclosure. To approach the making of a connection between construction and construing, the ''art of detailing'' course proposes an in-depth study of seven ''generic conditions'' which it is posited comprise the elements in all buildings and constitute the design vocabulary in which the building's concept is expressed. A principal thesis of the course is that an understanding of construction detailing not only transforms building design, but also the way architects approach the design process.

DEFINING THE BUILDING ELEMENTS

The approach to discussion about the ''art of detailing'' is organized into two major divisions of class time. The first half of the course is allotted to establish a basis for making the connection between design and construction. This is accomplished by putting forward seven generic conditions[3] in the design and construction of a building which purportedly encompass all the significant aspects of detailing and provide a framework against which constructive debate can take place. The seven generic conditions which are put forth are: ''grade conditions'', ''spandrel conditions'', ''eave/parapet conditions'', ''corner/end conditions'', ''window/glazing assemblies'', ''main entrance conditions'', and ''special features''. To substantiate discussion around each of these generic conditions, three different and reinforcing pedagogical techniques are employed: a lecture introducing the ''condition'', a class seminar/discussion around the ''condition'' and a series of student exercises testing the ''conditions''.

LECTURES: MAKING THE CASE. *''The present has not time to come to terms with the profusion of things forced upon it. The situation resembles the Chinese being forced to eat with knife and fork.''* - Gottfried Semper.[4] The lecture is used to provide an initial introduction to the concepts inherent in each of the ''conditions''. For example, the lecture addressing grade conditions is entitled ''Meeting the Ground'' and deals as comprehensively as possible with the technical and design requirements for developing details for this element of the building. The formatting of the lecture into discussion based on both technical and design concepts is an important aspect of the investigation, especially later when the students undertake their own exercises. The lecture strives to provide examples from modern and pre-modern sources which establish the initial visual arguments about the conditions under discussion.

A primary mission of the lecture is to examine the construction logic which informs the development and subsequently the design of any detail condition. In this case, issues surrounding the selection of materials and their connection to each other form the basis of the analysis. Much attention is paid in the lecture to design opportunities provided by the need to satisfy performance criteria. Again using the lecture on "grade conditions" as an example, a great deal is made of the intersection between the ground plane and the vertical enclosure plane. As one design option, it is pointed out that expression of the joint between the ground and the wall, by a materials change for example, is an effective way to control ground staining of the wall, to hide flashing and vent the vertical enclosure system, to allow differential movement to occur, as well as satisfying cultural and visual requirements for good design. An operating theme in the lectures is that careful evaluation of tectonic requirements can positively inform building design.

To insure a holistic analysis of enclosure systems, joining of materials to each other is further evaluated against their joining to the primary structure. As most modern construction employs some sort of frame as the primary structure, the lectures evaluate enclosure systems by focusing on the frame as the primary means of structural support. From this vantage point, it is possible to venture a definition of both vertical and horizontal "enclosure types". With respect to enclosure types and their relationship to structure, the lectures differentiate between "by-passing membranes", a non-bearing system, itself separate from, but attached to the structure, and "infilled frames", an enclosure type defined as a non-bearing system used to fill in between the openings of a structural frame. In establishing this somewhat simplified view of structural options, detailing considerations can concentrate on expression as well as fitness.

SEMINAR/DISCUSSION: MAKING THE DIALOGUE. "*The science of building, the rationalization of construction and assembly, however vital in themselves, remain in the world of literal action. It is only when the architect, seizing this world, organizes it according to the logic of symbolic forms that architecture results.*" - Alan Colquhoun.[5] Once the topic has been introduced in the lecture format, the ideas and categories presented are followed with a discussion in seminar format. To supplement the specific and technical arguments implied by the establishment of the seven "generic conditions", short excerpts of writings by architectural construction theorist are employed. For example, in the discussion about differentiating between the "infilled frame" and the "by-passing membrane", readings from Adolf Loos and Gottfried Semper are assigned.[6] Other selections include writings from both modern and pre-modern sources. These readings provide substantiating and alternative points of view which enrich the discussion and raise the general level of literacy surrounding the debate. They also help in understanding that issues of construction, design and meaning are ones that have confronted the act of building since building began.

EXERCISES: MAKING THE CONNECTION. "*When I get close to an old construction I feel the need to have a tactile rapport with it, to verify its solidity, its constitution, its surface. It is part of man's primitive need to know and distinguish the various elements of his own space. This is why I try to express every construction and every kind of material for what it really is. There's no such thing as good or bad material; materials are either well used or ill used.*" - Mario Botta.[7] The final testing of the proposed "generic conditions" and their framework for evaluation occurs when the students are asked to develop their own solutions to specific tectonic conditions. Through a series of carefully structured and formatted exercises, the ideas introduced in lecture and discussed in seminar are tested. These exercises build on each other to include all the categories put forth in the lectures and discussions.

The exercises are based on an overall analysis of the building elements already discussed and structured around a macro level tripartite division of the building into base, shaft and top. This approach may even be employed at the micro level of the detail itself. It may just as easily be rejected out of hand by the students, but always within the framework established by previous discussion. Continuing with the example of the "grade condition", in the first exercise each student is assigned a specific material from a list of enclosure materials, in this case brick masonry, stone masonry, precast concrete, glass curtainwall and metal curtainwall. They are also assigned a specific primary structure of either steel or concrete where the enclosure system solution is predicated on the assumption that the enclosure system type to be detailed is a non-bearing "by-passing membrane". In the exercises following investigation of the building meeting the ground, elements of a building which address the articulation of the "shaft" are pursued. These exercises deal with the "spandrel", "end/corner", and "opening" generic conditions. In this case, investigation of two different enclosure types, either "by-passing membrane" or "infilled frame" are added to the problem to allow exploration of different means of tectonic expression and their detailing consequences. The concept of building modularity and its importance in ordering the building is also introduced. All solutions are required to conform to an assigned module both vertically and horizontally.

For the final series of exercises dealing with the vertical termination of the building as it "meets the sky", the concept of differentiating between the vertical and horizontal enclosure systems is addressed. In this case the horizontal enclosure is seen as consisting of two "types". They are the condition where the vertical enclosure overrides the horizontal enclosure and creates a parapet condition. When the horizontal enclosure system overhangs the vertical enclosure system, then an eave condition exists. Again the students are assigned an enclosure material, a primary structure, a vertical enclosure type and a horizontal enclosure type for which they must engage a design following the same principles of modularity proposed in the initial problems.

CRAFT: REPRESENTING THE MAKING. "*The degree of dexterity, together with understanding of properties of materials used, are essential ingredients to craft. The studio work serves as a beginning analogue for craft in architecture, striving toward craft, quality, and intensity of meaning before quantity.*" - Steven Holl.[8] A critical element for discussion and description of detailing is the attention to craft. Studies produced to develop design and detail are indicative of the building process and must be undertaken with great care and thought. Therefore a distinction is drawn between the "representation" of detail and the "notation" of detail in this class, where the former strives to convey the visual, tactile experience of the detail, and the latter becomes a tool for communicating the precise methods and materials of construction.

This distinction is an important aspect of the student exercises and informs their format requirements. To allow for comparative discussion, each student solution is put in a mandated form which is easily comparable to any other student solutions. Towards that end each student is required to submit their design solution to any given problem on two eleven inch by seventeen inch mylar sheets with the long axis horizontal. They are required to present their solutions in drafted ink. The first sheet, or "notational exercise", is required to contain a typical bay of the "condition" under discussion. That is to be accomplished by showing a wall section to the right of the sheet, a plan section at the bottom of the sheet and an elevation of the design to the left of the sheet, all at half inch scale. The argument for this arrangement is that all detail studies should be undertaken with no less than these drawings all developed to the same level of resolution. The second sheet, or "representational" exercise, contains a section axonometric of the detail centered in the sheet showing critical elements of the construction. This is a three dimensional test of the ideas presented in the first sheet. The students are also required to prepare two written paragraphs about their solution on this page. To the left of the axonometric, they are to present a written statement about their "technical concepts" for the resolution of the design. To the right of the axonometric, they present a statement about their "design concepts". Both statements are expected to give a terse synopsis of all the ideas informing the decisions they made about their details.

Each student is rotated through the combinations of enclosure materials, enclosure types, primary structure types, and in the final problem, horizontal enclosure types, which are assigned to them by the instructor. This means that each student must address each "condition" using different materials and relationships of skin and structure. It also means that no student will work with any combination of elements twice. This forces students to work with all materials, and to develop solutions to the "conditions" which do not always accord with their preconceived notions of form and style. With the current stylistic interest in stone and masonry as materials of choice, for example, exposure to the design and use of other materials is generally lacking in the typical student repertoire.

Finally, and most importantly, every solution is reviewed in group discussion led by students. The author of a particular exercise presents the work, and another student is selected to specifically critique it. This is followed by general student discussion and debate which draws together lectures, readings and previously developed insights to create a solid foundation from which to proceed to the detailed design of a complete enclosure system.

TESTING THE BUILDING ELEMENTS

Once the initial premise based on a method of analysis using the seven "generic" conditions and definitions of primary structure and enclosure types is discussed and debated in the first half of the course, the second half concentrates on applying them to a singular building design. In this case an institutional building type is investigated in student teams, much the way it would be handled in professional practice. Here the concepts developed earlier are tested and employed to form, for the first time, not only strategies for exterior detailing but also approaches to the building of the interior architecture of the major public spaces.

In a recent "art of detailing" class, this pursuit was devoted to the design of an addition to an Engineering School - in this case a student design competition sponsored by the Engineering School at the University of Wisconsin-Madison. The problem statement called for the insertion of a new 60,000 square foot building terminating an important campus axis. The program consisted of classrooms, research labs and combinable auditoria with a particular emphasis on creating an identifiable entry and image for the Engineering campus.

The time for development of a building "parti" was purposely held to a minimum in order to allow time for comprehensive examination of detailing strategies. This led to simplified, almost diagrammatic, solutions to the problem. This conscious effort to work with very simple initial design solutions served as a test of the reliability of thorough and thoughtful detailing in the making of architecture. Can God really be found in the details? The intent of the second problem is to test the ability of thorough and thoughtful detailing to create the visual order and coherence of the building. Another goal of this problem is to address the detailing of exterior enclosure systems and its relationship to the detailing of hierarchically important interior public rooms. For the Engineering School competition, the significant interior spaces developed were the main entrance lobby and the auditoria. Here again similar strategies of the tripartite division of and analysis of detailing requirements were used to develop these rooms. Technical requirements to suit the advanced communications systems planned for these auditoria were analysed for their potential contribution to the design of the rooms.

Revealing the process and craft of building through descriptive drawings is a particularly troublesome problem and one which is key to relating design and instrumentality. In this final design, students are asked to investigate the potential of the drawing to study and reveal the act of construction, as a method for conveying meaning and information to both the user and the builder.

CONCLUSION

Establishing a methodology for dealing with the tectonic requirements of building is elusive and generally exclusive where design is considered. Bringing design and instrumentality together through analysis of the parts which in their turn make up the whole is an approach to architecture with a long tradition of theoretical and practical support. The intent of the pedagogical approach to instruction about detailing outlined above is to reestablish the ''art'' of building based not just on the literal technical requirements of construction but also the symbolic, cultural aspects of construing. Perhaps in this way we can bridge the current gap between the art of building and the art of design to create the congruity, or *concinnatis*, that Alberti sought: ''*a Harmony of all the parts, in whatsoever subject it appears, fitted together with such proportion and connection that nothing could be added, diminished, or altered but for the worse*''.[9]

NOTES

1. John Soane, *Lectures on Architecture*, as quoted in Marco Frascari, ''The Tell-The-Tale Detail'', in *VIA 7: The Building of Architecture*, eds. Paula Behrens and Anthony Fisher (Cambridge: MIT Press, 1984).
2. See for example Marco Frascari, op. cit.
3. For the early definition of these categories, I am deeply indebted to my colleague, Professor David Evan Glasser, from whose ideas and syllabi I have mercilessly borrowed; for their refinement, to Professor Michael Utzinger, with whom I have taught this course.
4. Gottfried Semper, as quoted in Wolfgang Hermann, *Gottfried Semper* (Cambridge: MIT Press, 1986), p. 167.
5. Alan Colquhoun. *Essays in Architectural Criticism: Modern Architecture and Historical Change.* Cambridge, MA : MIT Press, 1981, p. 26.
6. See Adolf Loos. *Spoken Into the Void.* Cambridge, MA: MIT Press, 1988, pp. 36-39, and Wolfgang Hermann, op.cit., pp. 139-152.
7. Mario Botta, as quoted in Vernon Mays, ''PA Technics: The Many Faces of Brick'', *Progressive Architecture*, July 1988, p. 104.
8. Steven Holl, ''First Year M Arch Design Studio'', *Abstract 87-88: Columbia University Graduate School of Architecture Planning and Preservation*, 1988, p. 6.
9. Alberti. *De re aedificatoria*, book 9, chapter 5.

CHAPTER 31
Boston's Central Artery

YIM LIM
Massachusetts Institute of Technology

In Baudelaire's description, modernity cannot be compared to anything in the past. He thinks that what has survived (aesthetically) from the past is nothing but the expression of a variety of successive modernities, each one of them being unique and, as such, having its unique artistic expression. There is no link between these individual entities and therefore, no comparison is actually possible. "That is why an artist cannot learn from the past." The masterpieces of the past can only hinder the imaginative search for modernity. Because of this discovered but deep hostility to the past, modernity can no longer be used as a periodizing label. With characteristic logical rigor, Beaudelaire means by modernity the present is in its 'presentness,' in its purely instantaneous quality.

In this framework, the proposal presented is a critique of the Central Artery Project of Boston, *the technology of civil engineering and transportation,* and the virtual and real impact to the urbanity and landscape of the city. The link to the land formation and the technological trace is reciprocal, and the history of the city reveals this to be true even in future endeavors.

The proposition of the central Artery as an epic task in the framework of modernity is pursued further in a studio project whose chosen site embodies a technological trace of the past, the railroad (which a part leads to North Station), and whose program is a cemetery, an agenda supported by a group who wants to see the urban landscape continue.

BOSTON'S CENTRAL ARTERY

The Boston's Central Artery was constructed in the early 1950's to serve as a collection-distributor roadway whose design reflected the requirements of local service, with many closely spaced on- and off-ramps. Given the design standards and service requirements of its day, the road was considered adequate for its local service function, providing access to and from the Central Business District. Over the past 30 years, the Central Artery has become part of a regional expressway system - Interstate Route 93 - serving users both north and south of Boston. The artery serves a distinctly regional function in the transportation system, while accommodating multiple traffic movements within a short distance, which is considered inconsistent with modern interstate design standards.

1. Motorway Construction, Leonardo Benevolo, *The History of the City*, Cambridge: MIT Press, 1980, p. 840.

The need for the proposed depression of the artery stems from the inability of the existing Central Artery and cross-harbor tunnels to accommodate both current and future traffic demands imposed on these regional facilities. These facilities, all constructed more than 25 years ago, were designed to handle projected traffic volumes that were approximately one-half the current level. Three major improvements are addressed by the project: increased north-south highway capacity; increased cross-harbor highway capacity; and improved access to the developing South Boston seaport area. The result of this Central Artery depression will be the opening-up of a large 22-block swath of Boston's downtown for use as surface streets and open spaces, or as new building sites.

The artery begins at North Station, where the future ramps

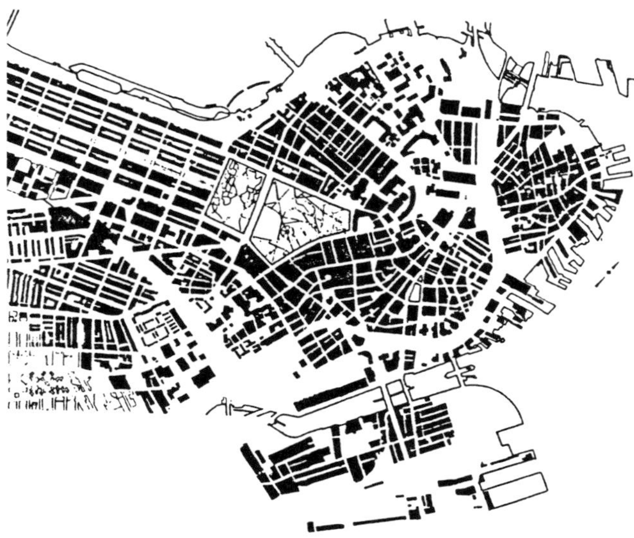

2. Figure ground of Boston indicating swath of Central Artery Project, *Boston Society of Architects, BSA Central Artery Task Force.*

to a reconstructed Tobin Bridge will drive below Causeway Street. It then proceeds generally south past the North End and the Kallman, McKinnell and Knowles-designed Government Center parking garage. Passing Government Center (Federal Buildings and Boston City Hall), the Central Artery alignment bends along the edge of the historic Blackstone Block bounded by Congress, North, and Hanover Streets as well. The Blackstone Block is a mixture of 18th-, 19th-, and 20th-century buildings and an 18th-century street pattern. It is a remnant of the traditional texture of this area of Boston before the massive urban renewal initiative which created Government Center in the early 1960's. Along the Blackstone edge street border of this area is a small remnant of the traditional "Haymarket" open-air public market area.

The artery nears the waterfront as it passes by the Faneuil Hall Market. This popular retail and restaurant center occupies the restored market buildings, two- and three-story structures built in the Greek Revival style between 1824 and 1826. Adjacent to the Faneuil Hall Market area is the historic Customs House district. Composed of distinctive mercantile buildings of brick and granite, the district is dominated by the campanile of the Customs House tower. Boston's waterfront edge sweeps along the eastern border of the artery alignment. The waterfront contains a mixture of hotel, office, and residential uses, including the new mixed-use Rowes Wharf.

Another significant area bordering the artery is the Financial District. The heart of Boston's banking and financial industry, this densely developed area contains a mixture of historic low-rise buildings and modern skyscrapers. In the last decade, the Financial District has supported an enormous amount of growth. As a result, many negative impacts of overcrowding such as shadows on streets and open spaces, street-level winds, and overall traffic congestion exists. Consequently, the Boston Redevelopment Authority is gradually directing future large-scale development to other areas of the city. The Central Artery area ends in Dewey Square, where Summer Street crosses the alignment. The odd-shaped open space created by the surrounding building walls defines an important open space, filled today with street and highway surfaces and a major bus terminal. This terminal will eventually be relocated within the South Station transportation center and the artery structure depressed and capped.

ISSUES

The future character of the Central Artery alignment is a subject of the intense debate in the Boston community. Specific challenges include:

1. Should the redevelopment of the alignment be used to reconnect the fabric of the city, and how?
2. How should the surface street pattern be restored? How can the surface pattern reinforce adjacent street patterns?
3. Should the Central Artery cap be used as a transportation corridor between North and South Station areas particularly for mass transit? Would a trolley-car connection (light-rail vehicle system) be appropriate and how should it be integrated with other open space or building development?
4. Should the artery be used for new building construction? Where should new construction occur? What should be its character? How should it relate to the diverse character of adjacent districts?
5. Should the artery alignment be used for new public open space? Where should this space be located? How should it relate to adjacent districts and open spaces?
6. What view-corridors should be reinforced or protected?
7. How can downtown Boston be reconnected to the harbor edge?

In addition, there is a series of practical constraints on the redevelopment of the Central Artery focus area that should be noted:

-The "cap" structure is being designed to accommodate a maximum of four to six stories of new construction.

-Building proposals of a greater scale would require substantial construction and up-front investment to provide adequate foundations; although not ruled out, such development is highly unlikely.

Current propositions and aspirations to mend the tear of the urban fabric caused by the spaghetti network of highway has created an opportunity for the City of Boston to reintegrate and redesign sections of the city. Ideas generated by the BRA, the BSA Boston Visions National Design Competition in 1988 and consultants such as Alex Krieger of Chan Krieger, Levi, Architects, Cambridge, and Ricardo Bofill of Taller Architecture, Barcelona include:

-Generously landscaped Park Boulevards.
-Reintegration of the historic block pattern and buildings to scale.
-Landscaped open spaces and Public Buildings such as museums and markets.
-Two avenues of a city scale which frames a fabric of streets and square.
-Retaining fragments of the elevated highway and adopting these parts to new uses such as housing, mixed use public buildings.

The vision is varied and many more ideas will surface during this epoch effort to re-design Boston's Central Artery Corridor.

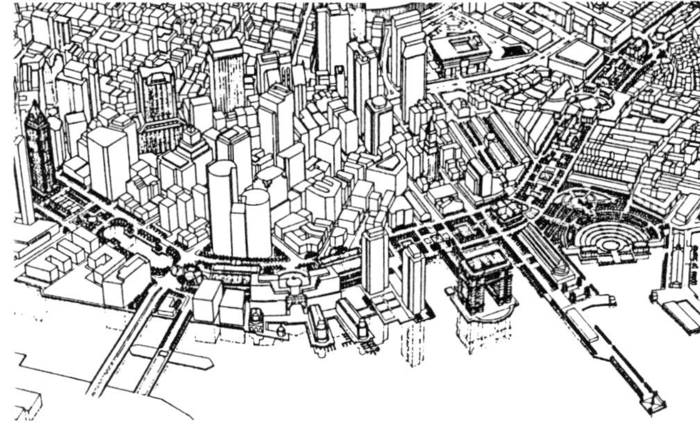

3. A Promenade of Public Grounds and Buildings.
Artery as a Vertebra Spine Boulevard, Ricardo Bofill, Principal, Taller Architecture, Barcelona.

CHAPTER 32

Landfills: The Confluence of Technology and Landscape

RICHARD W. MAYER
Troller Mayer & Stein and California State Polytechnic University

THE CRISIS OF WASTE DISPOSAL

Our latest crisis has been where to dump all of the garbage created by a consumer society. Historically, landfills have been places on the fringe of our urban settlements -- ''way out there.'' This is no longer the case; landfills are everywhere as the growth of our cities has leapfrogged further and further out. Potential new sites for landfills are hard to come by as most communities and neighborhoods, although recognizing the need, do not want a landfill nearby.[1]

In an effort to control growth, the newly incorporated city of Santa Clarita, California, has proposed a sphere of influence beyond its boundaries. Located within this area, are four existing and/or proposed landfill sites. A unique landscape environment of valleys and oaks, characteristic of California's heritage, is perceived by residents to be threatened by growth and development. ''City officials already are drafting plans that envision a valley where parks are plentiful, schools uncrowded, and oaks and hillsides preserved for posterity. Many residents, disillusioned with explosive growth allowed by county government, fear those goals will remain just dreams unless the city extends its grasp over the surrounding valley.''[2] Santa Clarita is an example of a city attempting to preserve the quality of its environment while allocating sufficient space for competing land use priorities.

ENVIRONMENTAL HAZARDS

The competition for remaining open space and the conflicts between dissimilar land uses have aggravated landfill problems. Residential and industrial park developments have been built up against existing landfills, focusing greater attention on the landfills' potentially harmful effect on environmental health.

Landfill planners must guard against ground water pollution, oozing fluids, methane gas, and soil erosion. This has made the process of landfill planning an important and politically sensitive issue in our time.

PLANNING CONSIDERATIONS AND PROBLEMS

The landfill process requires careful planning partially due to anaerobic decomposition below the landfill's surface. This causes tremendous subsidence by as much as 35% of the original volume, thus preventing large structures from being built and focusing reuse planning efforts on open space and recreation facilities.

The process of decomposition causes another major consideration: the natural production of heat and gas in the form of methane and carbon dioxide. This heat can create hot spots on the surface that affect plants and animals. In addition, if left unchecked, these areas create strong odors that preclude the landfill's use for many years. A gas migration and odor control system can be installed to withdraw and collect these gases.

Leachate formation is the third major consideration and potential problem. Leachate is any liquid that has contact with the waste material. Often leachates form at the bottom of landfills and require special drainage solutions to be constructed. Subsurface barriers have to be constructed to prevent leachates from migrating offsite or from polluting ground water.

RECYCLING LANDFILLS

All too often, landfills have become useless areas of derelict land once they have been ''closed''. Engineering considerations for efficiency and economy have left large areas virtually unusable for a second generation of use. The landfill takes on the appearance of a series of steep slopes and benches and has severe limitations for other functions.

This is the case in Burbank, California with the Burbank Landfills 1 and 2. These old landfills were closed many years ago. Today they have only limited potential for new uses. At the time they were planned and engineered, the Los Angeles metropolitan area was not as crowded as it is now and land costs were a fraction of today's prices. The idea of ''recycling the land'' for a second generation of use was not a priority with city officials and local planning authorities.

Severe slopes and benches of Burbank Landfill

Burbank officials have now undertaken an enlightened program of slope revegetation with predominately native and drought tolerant plants. This project, conducted by the office of Troller Mayer & Stein, will help restore the visual aesthetics of the mountains as a sweeping backdrop for the city. It will also prevent erosion, enhance wildlife habitat and "green" the city with semi-arid plan communities suitable for the Southern California basin. The reclamation of these derelict lands is an important contribution to a more livable city.

The Spadra Landfill Resource Conservation Project, known as LandLab, is studying regenerative technologies which will sustain our natural resource base. This project is being planned jointly by the California State Polytechnic University, Pomona, the Sanitation Districts of Los Angeles County, and the County of Los Angeles. Research will be conducted by interdisciplinary teams of scientists and planners on a wide range of issues including:

Urban recreation
Energy recovery processes
Landfill processes
Uses of sewage sludge
Water and refuse recycling
Native pastures
Botanical experiments
Tree crops
Urban agriculture
Integrated agriculture/aquaculture systems
Wildlife habitat enhancement
Plant communities for semi-arid zones

By focusing on resource issues, LandLab will bring together many viewpoints and technologies for in-depth study and research in the use of sustainable resources. The Spadra Landfill Project is an exciting opportunity to turn adversity -- man's abuse of land -- into ecological diversity and productive land use.[3,4,5]

SUMMARY

The crisis of waste disposal is a significant problem in the environmental chain. The landscape environment in urban metropolitan areas has suffered from technological advances, continued population growth and urban sprawl. Land use and reuse have become prominent issues on the nation's political and social agenda. The use of regenerative technology in landfill planning and reclamation of derelict lands will enhance the landscape environment of our cities.

NOTES

1. Bob Drogin, "Paradise Lost: Now It's a Dump," *Los Angeles Times*, Jan. 11, 1990.
2. Steve Padilla, "Lines Drawn in Santa Clarita Bid for Control of Growth," *Los Angeles Times*, Nov. 13, 1989.
3. *LandLab: A Laboratory for Education and Research in the Sustainable Use of Land Resources*, California State Polytechnic University, Pomona, May, 1987.
4. *LandLab: Institute for Regenerative Studies*, California State Polytechnic University, Pomona, Nov., 1987.
5. Ashley Dunn, "Trash Dump Will Become a Living Lab for Scientists," *Los Angeles Times*, Jan. 22, 1989.

CHAPTER 33

The Urban Landscape and Technology

ACHVA BENZINBERG STEIN
University of Southern California

INTRODUCTION

There are two separately definable systems in the landscape of the city: man-made or cultural and natural. The man-made is obvious to most of us, consisting of buildings, transportation facilities, water provision, disposal systems, and so on. The natural system includes the land and its geomorphology, the soil, the air, water, plant materials and wild life. These are the elements which occupy the open spaces between buildings. The natural system in the city has been under such heavy human control and manipulation that it has begun to resemble real life only in the manner that processed food resembles the materials from which it is made, as processed cheese resembles milk, bread and pasta resemble wheat and wine resembles grapes. We have limited and controlled the varieties and the growth of plants and wild life, and we interfere with their reproductive processes. We have reduced the number of species, we change the morphology of streams and rivers, the quality of water, air and even the climate.

Although plants, wild-life, air, land and water are certainly as important to us individually and collectively as bread, cheese and wine, and their psychological importance is at least as neccessary as that of art objects, we have not yet learned to deal with them using the same sophisticated levels of technology that we employ with food stuffs, or to apply the same imagination and care that we expend on our cultural art objects.

Technology over the last ten thousand years has been based primarily on the concepts of power and control. These in turn have led to our attitudes toward resource utilization and progress as motivating forces. Today we have reached a stage in our physical development where we may have to shift our ideas about technological innovation from concepts of change to those of maintenance, based not on growth and expansion but on efficient processes. Deteriorating natural environments, many of them on the verge of total destruction, point to the need for maintaining natural cycles, for respect for the laws of nature, and for the redirection and integration of human technology into harmony with the processes of nature. This need grows daily in urgency and importance. This change in attitude and in the resulting technologies will have its greatest impact in our cities, where, by the year 2000 half of the world's human population will be living, and our cities will be growing at an ever increasing pace as technologies continue to accellerate the depopulation of the countryside.

THE TWO SYSTEMS IN THE LANDSCAPE OF THE CITY

The technology used at present in our cultural system presumes an inefficient use of energy. It takes for granted immense quantities of waste with very little consideration to either disposal or reduction. It is based on obsolescence and replacement, and on ever increasing technical complexity.

Natural systems on the other hand, are characterized by equilibrium. They are based on the efficiency of energy conversion in which no energy is ever lost. Natural systems exhibit cyclical changes and metamorphosis: passing through death and decay, renewal and regeneration.

As we begin to recognize that the natural environment in the city is a necessity for continuation of human life as we understand it, and for human survival, it becomes necessary to treat the landscape of the city as a cultural system parallel to and in many aspects resembling a natural system. We have to look at both the man-made and natural simultaneously as part of two interacting systems. While certain aspects of the natural cycle cannot be reproduced, some principles, such as the conservation of energy and matter can surely be applied.

PRESERVATION OF NATURE IN THE CITY

The designer who works with natural systems is put in the position of being the ''guardian of nature''. His role is to protect and defend exisiting natural elements with the technology available to him or to bring nature into the city. Instead of exposing the flaw in this thinking, he perpetuates the illusion that nature is still *autonomous*, that it is *everlast-*

ing and that it *can be maintained in its natural state* despite the city, urban technology and its imperative to control. This is a very dangerous illusion, especially for those who view themselves as being the stewards of the land.

''Natural'' urban gardens are theatrical set pieces which cover rather than expose these issues which were so brilliantly described in Bill McKibben's article, *The Death of Nature.* No meaningful energy conservation measures are practiced. Grass, ponds, fountains, and waterfalls are still the main design elements used to define spaces. Tree species are further and further reduced in number to create ever more standardized and limited images. All our cities begin to look alike regardless of their specific location and natural condition, let alone the concepts of variety and multilayered systems. ''Evergreen'' and ''maintenance free'' conditions are the order of the day to such an extent that the cyclical aspect of the nature, the decay and regeneration are believed only to be the results of neglect or oversigntedness. Long-term economic efficiency and sustainability, which is one of the defining characteristics of natural systems is never incorporated in the design program. To the contrary, nature in the city manifested in the gardens, parks and beaches is treated as a luxury requiring large investments and expensive maintenance, beyond the means of the average citizen. Ironically, care of the ''natural elements'' in the city is typically delegated to those who are least skilled or qualified, who often use the most outdated technology (some of it six millenia old!), while ownership resides with those who control the means of production to enjoy on part time basis only.

THE ABOLITION OF NATURE IN THE CITY

The second approach views design with natural elements in the city as engineered solutions using ''man and his machine as the measure of all things''. Recognizing the falsehood of the concept of bringing ''nature to the city'', designers rebel by totally disregarding characteristics of natural elements and their requirements for maintenance of natural processes. They seek and present objects of the cultural system only, devoid of life and rooted in contemporary culture. In such cases, designers not only lack the knowledge of nature, they deny the meaning of human psychological and physiological make-up which has evolved in relation to the surroundings and which still obtains basic emotional nourishment from the natural environment. This attitude also fails to acknowledge the latest developments in the use of natural materials, and neglects to incorporate the technology of the natural sciences into the design.

Honesty in architectural design includes, among other attributes, reflection on the state of technolgy and innovation. For instance, steeped in knowledge of cultivation and irrigation, the Moors built their gardens in Spain. The engineers of the quanats of Iran were also the designers of towns, villages and gardens in the Persian plateau. The great French gardens of the Baroque incorporated advanced knowledge of optics and hydrological engineering. The success of land reclamation in northern Holland was due to the accumulated knowledge of dike construction and the introduction of the windmill for pumping water. The rolling hills and grasslands of the English landscape came into being with the introduction of the lawn mower, which, when it became self-powered and was combined with hydrological engineering, allowed the suburban landscape of the Southwest to become the dominant style, spreading all all over the world. This attitude which treats open space in the city merely as outdoor exhibit for man made- made nonliving things while may be ''honest'', limits the artist in the designer from opening himself to new forms and from seeking new solutions to problems which nature has devised over million of years. Innovation in aviation is based on improving knowledge of the behavior of airodynamic bodies in air. The invention of ''velcro'' was based on an understanding of the mechanical organization and structure of a particular plant. When we reinterpret cultural forms , on the other hand, we are only further digesting ideas already chewed on rather than exploring more imaginative and original concepts. With better knowledge of the natural forms exhibit found in our urban environment, a more meaningful approach to landscape design, conservation and resource utilization can be developed. Architectural thinking will have the opportunity to become more profound, incorporating more than mere surface manipulation or stylized fashionable artifacts into design. We have the option of viewing the landscape of the city and in particular the open spaces as decorative, whimsical, and capricious, or we can incorporate relevant and appropriate technologies to create meaningful designs.

'PROCESSED' NATURE IN THE CITY

When we look at 21st century technology in the city, we should be looking at integrated systems based on both the man-made and on natural laws. We will have to look at a ''package of technology''. Rasmussen describes this approach in relation to the ''mechanical tomato''. Such a system includes the machines for the total process: the seed-often hybrid, the breeding stock, careful tillage, fertilizer, productive use of water through irrigation anf drainage, and the application of chemicals to control weeds, fungi and insects. Rasmussen goes on to describe the team which came up with the mechanical tomato made up of engineers, horticultural groups, agronomists, irrigation specialists, etc. It is a description of the way we learn to process food. The only difference is the accelerated time period involved and the naming of the specialized advisers. Surely the numbers of people, and the varieties of machines, tools and production processes involved in the creation of wine from grapes over the centuries have been as diverse and interwoven as the processed tomato.

There is a still largely untapped opportunity to incorporate many of the latest advances brought about by agricultural and hydrological technology, knowledge which has been gained about the efficient supply of water, transplanting, hybridization and reintroduction of indiginous plant materials, the control of plant diseases through plant companions and organic agricultural techniques. The tapping of both wind and solar energy and more. The technology of maintenance and sustainability developed by space technology could be used by the urban landscape designer in order to further understand issues of human adaptation to space and efficient resource utilization and recycling. Obviously none of the products of such a process are going to be 'natural''. Nor is that the intention. Very few of us enjoy nature it its raw form. What we do enjoy are our assumptions and the illusion of nature, an idealization and romantization of life which rarely actually exists. We abhore decay and react with fear to signs of the termination of life. We are interested in observing but not in participating, and as such, ''processed nature'' suits the urban population more.

Together with the utilization of new technologies, we must also accept the idea that these technologies which aim at the maintanance of natural processes and sustainability will need to develop a very wide base of educated and aware technicians. We must raise the level of technical competence and awareness for the leaders of the next generation who will be responsible for planning and design in the coming decades. In building museums of science and technology one might say that we have already started this education. The open spaces in the city are wonderful laboratories for additional educational experiences.

The appropriate level of technology for open space is what is often termed ''intermediate'' technology. Open space which is exposed, like structure in a building, can communicate a clearer understanding of the functions and forms of the natural elements which are integrated into the urban fabric. Water systems, for example, can be designed in such a way as to utilize the entire water cycle - the strorage of rain water, tapping from other sources, and the techniques of distribution. The force of the wind and the effects of glare, heat, and sun are subjects worth exploring. Designs incorporating these elements not only invite the public to notice them, but also help to change our aesthetic sensibilities. Certain sites should be maintained to provide controlled demonstrations of large scale transitions from one state to another, in which trees and other live things are sometimes permitted to complete their natural cycle of growth, maturity and decay. Finally we should provide urban spaces not only as recreational spaces trying to emulate the styles of a bygone aristocracy, but as places where we can learn to understand the aesthetics of production while helping to grow and produce materials to help maintain and sustain urban life. Such an approach would not only involve hobby vegetable gardens. It could also include growing fruit, raising fowl, planting trees for building materials, and growing materials for making cloth. Although the technology of production and harvesting of these materials in a poison-free manner has been available for some time, the ideological base is not yet firm.

WHERE WILL NATURE BE?

Sometime ago, with the development of cities, we divided our world into zones. These zones radiate from and surround our cities, with diminishing levels of technological application as the distance from the city increases. Today, there is a commonly felt fear that if we continue to process nature, even in the most sensitive way, we will destroy our world. While this scenario is certainly possible, the solution of going back or creating the illusion that nature is still there in a state we were once used to is clearly erroneous. We have to scale down our ambition to control. As a result, we will be forced to reshape our technology.

We will have to set aside larger and larger tracts of land where control by natural elements outweighs that of cultural technology, where other creatures are allowed to have their world within the limited resources available. We have to establish hierarchies of use on our planet, and not turn every domain of nature into a recreational shelter in our flight from our technological settlements. We should come to terms with the fact that the nature we are seeking in our cities is not the real system. We should build our illusionary image of nature in our cities to make them livable and productive, composed of both living and non-living matter. Let the wild wheat and rice grow happily in their place, let the cultivated wheat come to live with us in the blurred zone of our productive city, and let us enjoy bread and wine obtained from organic processes in our own den without destroying and manipulating every piece of the environment.

BIBLIOGRAPHY

Adas, Michael, *Machines as the Measure of Men: Science, Technology, and Ideologies of Western Dominance.* Ithaca and London: Cornell University Press, 1989

Douglas, Ian, *The Urban Environment.* London and Baltimore: Edward Arnold, 1983

Dunn, P.D., *Appropriate Technology.* New York: Schocken Books, 1979

Ellul, Jacques, *The Technological Society.* New York: Vintage Books, 1964

McKibben, Bill, ''The End of Nature'', *New Yorker Magazine.* Sept 11, 1989, pp 47-105

Mumford, Lewis, *The City in History.* New York: Harcourt, Brace & World, Inc., 1961

Mumford, Lewis, *The Myth of the Machine: Technics and Human Development.* New York: Harcourt, Brace and Jovanovich, 1967

Mumford, Lewis, *The Myth of the Machine: The Pentagon of Power.* New York: Harcourt, Brace and Jovanovich, 1970

Rasmussen, Wayne D., ''Advances in American Agriculture: The Mechanical Tomato Harvester As a Case Study'' in Melvin Kranzberg and William H. Davenport, eds., *Technology and Culture.* New York: Schocken Books, 1972

Rybczynski, Witold, *Taming the Tiger: The Struggle to Control Technology.* New York: The Viking Press, 1983

Watson, Richard A. and Patty Jo Watson, *Man and Nature: An Anthropological Essay in Human Ecology.* New York: Harcourt, Brace and World, Inc. 1969

Appendix

Additional papers were presented at the 1990 ACSA Technology Conference by the following people:

BARTUSKA, TOM J. AND MICHAEL S. OWEN
Washington State University
"Bio-Technology and the City: Analysis, Theory and Design"

BASSLER, BRUCE AND JAMES PATTERSON
Iowa State University
"Innovative Tall Building Design:
New Technologies from Other Design Disciplines"

BODDY, TREVOR
Carleton University
"From Physics Envy to Philosophy Abuse:
Architects Look for Meta-Theory"

BRYAN, HARVEY J., Ph.D.
Harvard University
"Le Corbusier and the Mur Neutralisant:
An Experiment in Environmental Controls"

CHEN, HUI-MIN
State University of New York at Buffalo
"From the Water-trough to the Theodolite"

CHIUINI, MICHELE
Ball State University
"Teaching Technology to Architecture Students:
Towards a Change of Attitudes and Objectives"

CHUSID, JEFF
University of Southern California
"Frank Lloyd Wright: The Textile Block System"

CLINE, ANN
Miami University
"Technology, Poetics and the Urban Significance of the Hut:
Some Thoughts on AT&T, Humana and Eisenman's Idea of the Little-House"

COOK, JEFFREY
Arizona State University
"Bioclimatic Order in Palladio's Villas"

DAY, GARY E.
State University of New York at Buffalo
"The Green Structures of Our Cities"

DIMITROPOULOS, HARRIS
Georgia Institute of Technology
"The Sublime Considered in Terms of the Connections Between Modernity, Technology, Building in the City"

DROWST, UWE
University of Maryland
"A Place for Meeting: The Herbert-Keller House"

EBELTOFT, RICHARD A.
University of Arizona
"How Can We and Should We Be Using Computers to Teach Structural Technology to Architecture Students?"

EL-KHOLY, SUZAN
University of Pennsylvania
"Temporal Influences on Architectural Design:
Tendencies in the Fast-Track Design Process"

FINDLAY, ROBERT A.
Iowa State University
"The Need to Elaborate Interstitial Infrastructures
in Urban Centers: Des Moines as an Example"

FINROW, JERRY V.
University of Oregon
"Composite Industrialized Energy Efficient
Construction for Housing: Case Studies of
Recent Danish and Swedish Housing Projects"

FRIEDMAN, JONATHAN BLOCK
New York Institute of Technology
"Exoterrestrial Dwelling"

GALLEGOS, PHILLIP AND SOONTORN BOONYATIKARN
University of Colorado at Denver
"The Kimbell Art Museum:
A Case Study Approach to Architectural Technology"

GAMI, BHARAT M.
New Jersey Institute of Technology
"Towards Medium Size Cities: Global Prospects"

GILLEARD, JOHN D., Ph.D.
Georgia Institute of Technology
"The Technology of Expedient Buildings"

GOLDMAN, GLENN AND M. STEPHEN ZDEPSKI
New Jersey Institute of Architecture
"What Am I Looking At?"

GRULKE, BRUCE
Mississippi State University
"Famous Baseball Trades and Life on the Street"

GUISE, DAVID
City College of New York
"Frank Lloyd Wright's Price Tower:
A Case-Study of Form Ignoring Function"

HAGLUND, BRUCE, BRIAN SUMPTION AND ALEX ZABRODSKY
University of Idaho
"Facts, Slides, and Videotapes...
Technologies for Daylighting Case Studies"

HARTMAN, THOMAS
University of Michigan
"Detailing: A Seminar Course Exploring the Integration of
Technical and Design Aspects of theArchitectural Curriculum"

HATHEWAY, ROGER AND JOHN CHASE
"Irving Gill: Tilt-Slab, Poured Concrete"

JOHNSTON, GEORGE BARNETT
Georgia Institute of Technology
"C.D.'s"

KENZARI, BECHIR
Georgia Institute of Technology
"Plotting and Disaster:
Error Detection in a Simulated Architecture"

KILPER, DENNIS J., D.Arch.
Virginia Polytechnic Institute and State University
"Deploying the House"
"Technology, Terror, and Teaching"

LaFON, ALAN B.
Auburn University
"Strip Joints from Top to Bottom"

LANGENBACH, RANDOLPH
University of California, Berkeley
"Technology, Public Policy and the Earthquake"

LeJEUNE, JEAN-FRANCOIS
University of Miami
"The Death of the Engineer "

MacLEOD, ROBERT M.
University of Florida
"Orlando and Detroit: Machine Cities in the
Age of Information and Entertainment"

MacLEOD, ROBERT M. AND WILLIAM L. TILSON
University of Florida
"Spatial Cartography: Mapping the Post-Industrial City"

McAULIFFE, MARY
Tulane University
"In Pursuit of the Ineffable: A Visit to the Wexner Arts Center"
"Three Streets, Two Cities:
Alternating Configurations in New Orleans"

McCULLOUGH, MALCOLM
Harvard University
"Modernity and Design Representation"

MELARAGNO, MICHELE, Dr.
University of North Carolina at Charlotte
"Sheltered Sidewalks"

MOHSINI, R.A., Ph.D.
State University of New York at Buffalo
"Of Conflicts and Temporary Organizations:
Some Issues of Integrating Technologies in Design"

MOORE, JAMES A., Ph.D.
University of South Florida
"Form Follows Fantasy: Why No One Lives in Disney World"

MOSTAFAVI, MOHSEN
Harvard University
"The Standardization of Standards"

NOVAK, MARCOS
University of Texas at Austin and UCLA
"Technology and Poetics: A Question of Priority"

OWEN, MICHAEL S.
Washington State University
"Technology and the Role of Winter City Infrastructure"

POLYZOIDES, STEPHANOS
University of Southern California
"Rudolph Schindler: Lift Form and Tilt-Slab"

PROWLER, DON
Princeton University and University of Pennsylvania
"Pedestrian Pockets"

RENO, JUDITH
University of Tennessee
"Economic & Social Circumstances with
Innovation in L.A. Architecture"

SAUDA, ERIC
University of North Carolina at Charlotte
"The Machine as Creaky Paradigm"

SCHIPPOREIT, GEORGE
Illinois Institute of Technology
"The Teaching of Technology as Design"

SHANE, GRAHAME
New York University
"The Aldwych-Kingsway, London 1905"

SPITZGLAS, MARK
Texas Tech University
"Design for Solar Radiant Management
through Daylight 'Pumping'"

STREUBER, JAMES V., DONNA C. NELSON, Ph.D.
AND JORGE A. VANEGAS, Ph.D.
Purdue University
"Integration of Video, Computer-Based Graphics,
and Hypercard for Technical Courses"

TILSON, WILLIAM
University of Florida
"The Parking Garage as Technological Pharmakon"

WACHS, MARTIN
University of California, Los Angeles
"Taming the Automobile in the Modern Metropolis:
A Realistic View"

WU, HOFU, Arch.D.
Arizona State University
"Technological Issues in Cooling Strategies for Homes
in Hot, Arid Climates"

ZAMBONINI, GIUSEPPE
Georgia Institute of Technology
"Construction Drawings as Conception of Design"